BROWNELL LANDRUM

The Art

and

Science

of

Wishing

The Art & Science of Wishing

Foreword

This book started as a wish, and ends with a wish.

But then don't all books?

I want to be transparent from the beginning: I am not a scientist. I'm a storyteller. In fact, the tagline for my novels is:

Lose yourself in the fiction... Find yourself in the truth.

Said another way, there's truth in fiction, and sometimes fiction opens the path to truth.

I describe myself as an 'explorer of metaphysical mysteries' who's also fascinated by science. This book isn't intended to be the definitive or final source to explain the science of wishing, but instead a stimulus to encourage more research on this universal, relatable, and fascinating topic.

My mission as a storyteller is to get you to think – and feel. To propose ideas and ask questions, whether in the form of fiction or nonfiction. I agree with scientists like Neil deGrasse Tyson who said, "No one is dumb who is curious. The people who don't ask questions remain clueless throughout their lives" and Albert Einstein's words, "The important thing is not to stop questioning. Curiosity has its own reason for existence."

All science begins with theory, and those theories can come from philosophers, children, or even imaginative fiction writers.

Remember when the *Simpsons* showed Homer writing an equation on a chalkboard that, when solved, gives the mass of a Higgs Boson that's only a bit larger than the nano-mass of a Higgs Boson actually is - 14 years before it was discovered? Or universal translators from Star Trek? And then there's HAL 9000 in Arthur C. Clarke's *2001: A Space Odyssey* (1968) which showed many people's first glimpse of artificial general intelligence - a machine that could think, feel, and make decisions.

> *Science is, at least in part, informed worship.*
> *Carl Sagan*

But wait, you might say. Most of my books are "out there" in the metaphysical realm. And you're right! This book was inspired by a semi-autobiographical novel I wrote called *A Love Story to the Universe* where I talk about such crazy things as "Wish Fairies" in a realm "Upstairs" dedicated to the processing of wishes.

> *Religion and science go together.*
> *As I've said before, science without religion is lame and religion without science is blind.*
> *They are interdependent and have a common goal—the search for truth...*
> *The soul given to each of us is moved by the same living spirit that moves the universe.*
> *Albert Einstein*

Metaphysics is "derived from the Greek meta ta physika ("after the things of nature"); referring to an idea, doctrine, or posited reality outside of human sense perception. In modern philosophical terminology, metaphysics refers to the studies of what cannot be reached through objective studies of material reality.[i]"

Yet.

This book starts with a group of assertions and assumptions I take full credit (and blame) for. Feel free to disagree! I was recently interviewed on a podcast and when the interviewer mentioned my book, *Five Reasons Why Bad Things Happen*, she confessed, "I don't believe everything happens for a reason," to which I replied, "Great!"

I say the same thing to you, too, dear reader. Feel free to disagree and debate, though I have to admit that if you're a hard-core scientist reading this I won't be much of an adversary. I want to learn from YOU!

I would like you to keep an open mind and at least consider what I'm suggesting in this book. You may see things differently...

...and you may end up seeing things differently.

> *Absence of evidence is not evidence of absence.*
> *Carl Sagan*

To that end, it's my hope that this book is, instead, much like science itself: evolving and improving when new data comes forth, and I invite you to join me in that adventure.

Another confession: If I was a traditional scientist in an academic environment, I'd have a team of researchers mining sources and references. Thankfully, a "regular person" has a shortcut these days.

As a writer, I have a strict standard in dealing with AI, and that is that I never – ever – want it to write for me. I won't even take a sentence written by AI. I have programmed my AI apps to never even suggest a sentence. I won't use it for artwork either. However, I will use it for research, insights, and grammar.

What you're about to read is a significant exception. A complete departure. This book is a collaboration with AI, primarily Claude.

Why the seismic shift? Because AI has access to massive amounts of information. Besides, it's nearly impossible to conduct any research these days without accessing AI in one way or another, even if it's a simple Google search. Not only that, I felt a compelling need to get this message out into the world – now – even if others challenge my (or AI's) assertions and attributions.[1]

1

[1] If this is you, please feel free to do your own research! That's the thing about science: it's evolving every day, thanks to diligent, brilliant men and women dedicated to the TRUTH.

If I have seen further it is by standing on the shoulders of giants.
Isaac Newton

Why this project? Several reasons.

First, my own curiosity. As I was writing *A Love Story to the Universe,* I got curious about wishes and wishing a whole world of science emerged, like watching one of those videos a where a seed expands into a full plant before your eyes. Following through on that analogy, I didn't have either the patience nor the expertise to till the earth, source the seeds, and wait. Besides, even if I did, how many PhDs would I need? More than I could get in one lifetime. And even with multiple lifetimes, it couldn't be achieved!

So I turned to Claude and a few others with a splash of Google. All that being said, it wasn't just a snap of my fingers to make this book appear. The tone, framework, purpose, and scope are all from (and on) me. It's not "point and shoot" – it's a LOT of work to do it correctly and much more difficult than I ever imagined. Still, I was relentless and persevered. This is the result.

My wish for this book?

That all your peaceful, positive, and purposeful wishes come true.

Chapter 1: What is Wishing? A Personal Perspective

Imagine you're blowing out candles on a birthday cake. Or you see a shooting star. Maybe you're writing on an Ema board or throwing a coin into a fountain.

What do you wish for?

When you made your wish, did you realize you just engaged at least a dozen scientific disciplines, including neuroscience, cognitive and social psychology, anthropology, evolutionary biology, sociology, behavioral science, consciousness research, physics, and even the frontiers of information theory and complexity science—proving that wishing is far more than a simple superstition. It's a uniquely human, richly scientific act.

Before we get into that, let's start with ART and the question that started everything.

The Art of Wishing and The Question That Started Everything

I started wondering about the science of wishing while writing my semi-autobiographical novel entitled *A Love Story to the Universe*. In it, I conjured a magical realm called Astraea. Named after a star, Astraea was the Greek goddess of truth and justice, which felt fitting to describe a world populated by Wish Fairies processing the hopes and dreams of humans everywhere. It was meant to be pure fiction—a whimsical exploration of what might happen behind the scenes when we make our deepest wishes.

As I was crafting the world of Astraea, I had to distinguish what a wish is—and isn't—how wishes are collected, sorted, and granted (or not), and the other factors that determine the outcome. As a novelist, I'm not held to any strict standards of reality, but as a human being I wanted to bring the worlds together as much as I could.

Fiction met fact as I integrated the theories from two of my nonfiction books, *Five Reasons Why Bad Things Happen* and *The Hero's Playbook* into the worldbuilding for Astraea. *Reasons Why* helped me understand the "why" dynamics of wishing and *The Hero's Playbook* showed how wishing is universal, mythical, and timeless.

This learning led me to create the Cosmic Wish Experiment, including a *Cosmic Wish Playbook* with activities following the scientifically sound process in this book to help readers hone their wishing skills and *Cosmic Wish Tracker* to help you collect, track, and measure the outcomes of your wishes. (More information is in Chapter 15).

I'm also releasing a book about Cosmic Wishing for children.

The Science of Wishing

While developing this imaginary world, the "truth" part of my brain activated even further after listening to a YouTube lecture on neuroplasticity.[ii] The questions kept popping up like a game of Whack-a-Mole:

1. What is a wish?
2. How are wishes different from prayers or goals?
3. Why do people wish?
4. What do people wish for?
5. Do all cultures wish? What wishing rituals exist around the world? How long has humanity embraced wishes?
6. Are all wishes answered? If so, what are the responses?
7. What sciences are involved in the practice of wishing?
8. What happens to your brain when you wish?
9. How do wishes interact with the quantum world?
10. Who – or what – determines whether a wish comes true?
11. Are there things we can do to improve our effectiveness when making a wish?
12. How might a book on the science of wishing interest and benefit others?

Let's get started.

What is a Wish?

Before we can study wishes scientifically, we need to define them and distinguish them from related phenomena.

Characteristics:

First: A wish has three characteristics: They are clear, prompted, and instinctive.

- Clear, in that they are generally not much longer than a single sentence.
- Prompted, meaning that they're usually connected to a ritual of some kind, whether blowing out birthday candles, catching a stray eyelash, or seeing the first star of the night.
- And they're instinctive, in that they're usually "in the moment," the first thing you think about when the prompt arises.

So, what's the difference between a wish, a prayer, and a goal?

The Difference Between Wishes, Prayers, and Goals

Goals: The Territory of Personal Control

When you set a goal to:

- Lose 20 pounds
- Get a promotion
- Learn to play piano
- Save money for vacation

You're operating from the assumption that the outcome is within your sphere of influence. You can create a plan, take action, measure progress, and adjust your approach.

Goals are about what you can control.

Prayers: The Territory of Divine Partnership

Prayers are the opposite. They are asking for help from a force or energy outside your control, whether called God, the Divine, Infinite Intelligence, the Upstairs, angels, or Guides.

Prayer often includes:

- Reverence and humility
- Recognition of limitations
- Request for guidance, strength, or intervention
- Surrender to wisdom or force greater than your own

Prayers are about surrendering to higher wisdom or force outside your control.

Wishes: A Unique Blend

Wishes occupy a unique middle ground. They feel both personal and transpersonal, both within your influence and beyond your complete control. When you wish for:

- A callback on that job interview
- Your uncle's medical checkup to show a clean bill of health
- A job opportunity that aligns with your purpose
- Your family to be happy and healthy

You're acknowledging that while you can prepare yourself and take aligned action on some aspects of the wish, the full manifestation requires a connection to an energy or force outside yourself.

But what is that energy or force, and how to you engage with it? In this book, we'll introduce the concept of Cosmic Wishes and Cosmic Collaboration.

Cosmic Wishes lie in the realm of Cosmic Collaboration

What is cosmic collaboration?

Cosmic

First, let's look at the definition of cosmic is defined by Merriam Webster as:

a) of or relating to the cosmos, the extraterrestrial vastness, or the universe in contrast to the earth alone; cosmic radiation
b) of, relating to, or concerned with abstract spiritual or metaphysical ideas; cosmic wisdom
c) characterized by greatness especially in extent, intensity, or comprehensiveness

Wow, right? Cosmic can be defined as the universe, metaphysics, or greatness!

What Makes a Wish a Cosmic Wish

Not all wishes leverage the universe, metaphysics, and that greatness and comprehensiveness. Most wishes are just vague hoping—wishing on a ladybug and crossing your fingers.

A cosmic wish is different. It's bigger. More powerful. And it's made with understanding.

Understanding of the science: the neuroscience of how your brain creates and processes wishes, the psychology of hope and motivation, the quantum mechanics of consciousness and intention, the sociology of collective wishing across cultures, and the cutting-edge research into how consciousness might interact with reality itself.

Understanding of the art: storytelling, meaning-making, and the role of intention in shaping outcomes.

When you understand both the art AND the science, you're no longer hoping blindly. You're engaging consciously with the entire collaborative process—maximizing what you can control, and working skillfully with what you can't.

That's what makes it cosmic. And that's what this book will teach you.

So what is Cosmic Collaboration?

Cosmic Collaboration is what happens in that sweet spot—where your intentions, actions, and energy meet opportunities, synchronicities, and responses from the wider universe. It's the collaborative space where what you CAN control works together with what you CAN'T control.

This isn't woo-woo. And it transcends religion, spirituality, and even metaphysics. Because here's the truth: The more you understand the SCIENCE of wishing, the more control you'll have over the parts that

ARE controllable. And the more you understand the ART of wishing, the better you'll collaborate with the parts that aren't.

And when combined with others?
Cosmic Wishes Light the Sky!

What Are We Wishing For?

Wishes can take countless forms, but most fall into several broad "wheel of life" categories: recreational, social, physical, financial, professional, mental, emotional, and spiritual. While these categories are familiar, research reveals that their expression and significance vary profoundly across cultures, developmental stages, and individual values. As we'll see, the most meaningful wishes are not defined by their content alone, but by the purpose and consciousness with which they are made.

Who is Wishing?

If wishes lie in the realm of Cosmic Collaboration, who is collaborating with whom?

Here's something most people never consider: when you make a wish, you're not one unified voice. You're actually a team of three distinct aspects, each with different perspectives, needs, and ways of knowing.

Have you ever wanted something with your logical mind, but your gut said "no"? Or felt a deeper wisdom whispering that what you think you want isn't what you actually need? That's because you have three selves doing the wishing:

Your Outer Self - the logical, planning part that sets goals and analyzes options.

Your Inner Self - the emotional, instinctive part that feels, senses, and knows things your mind hasn't figured out yet.

Your Higher Self - the wisdom that connects you to something beyond your individual consciousness, whether you call that intuition, divine guidance, or universal intelligence.

When all three selves align around a wish - when your mind, body, and spirit all say "yes" - that's when cosmic wishing becomes truly powerful.

But when they're in conflict? That's when wishes feel stuck, confusing, or impossible.

Most people make wishes from only one self, wondering why they never manifest. In Chapter 6, you'll discover how to recognize each self's voice, understand what each one needs, and create the alignment that transforms ordinary hoping into cosmic collaboration.

How Does This Relate To Science?

Certainly, these three selves align with Freud and Jung (though perhaps my interpretation might be unique). Additionally, the connection to energy/physics has been expressed by well-known scientists:

Albert Einstein: "Everyone who is seriously involved in the pursuit of science becomes convinced that a spirit is manifest in the laws of the Universe."

Max Planck (The Father of Quantum Theory): "Science cannot solve the ultimate mystery of nature. And that is because, in the last analysis, we ourselves are a part of the mystery that we are trying to solve." And another by Planck: "In all my research I have never come across matter. To me the term matter implies a bundle of energy which is given form by an intelligent spirit."

This is why wishes feel different from goals or prayers—they require internal integration AND external – or "cosmic" – collaboration.

How Are Wishes Answered? The Four Responses

Here's something I discovered while creating the magical realm of Astraea for my novel *A Love Story to the Universe*: every wish receives one of four responses. Not just "yes" or "no" - there are actually four distinct ways reality responds to your intentions.

When you understand these four responses, everything changes. You stop seeing "no" as rejection and start reading it as information. You stop experiencing delays as punishment and start recognizing them as preparation. You stop missing the gifts that arrive in unexpected packaging.

Each response contains intelligence. Each one is designed to serve you, even when it doesn't feel that way in the moment. And here's what most people never realize: the response you get has as much to do with your internal state when you make the wish as it does with external circumstances.

In Chapter 10, you'll learn to read these responses like a cosmic conversation - understanding what each one means, how to work with it skillfully, and why even a "no" might be the universe's greatest gift to you.

For now, just consider: What if the wishes you thought "didn't come true" actually DID receive a response - you just didn't know how to read it?

What Makes a Wish Work?

As I considered the question of whether there are things we can do to improve our effectiveness when making a wish, several ideas materialized that are worth evaluating from a scientific perspective. What is the role of energy and intention? How might our conscious, subconscious, and superconscious play a role? And going even deeper, how might getting clearer on our wants vs. needs and our individual fears, desires, and misbeliefs help our wishing achievement?

The 3 P's and The Energy of Effective Wishing

Here's something most people get wrong about wishing: they focus entirely on *what* they're wishing for, without paying any attention to the state they're in *when* they make the wish.

Your internal state when you wish might be just as important as the wish itself.

Think about it: have you ever made a desperate wish - lying awake at 3am, stressed about money, pleading with the universe for help? How did that feel? Now compare that to a moment when you felt genuinely peaceful, grateful for what you have, and simply opened yourself to even more goodness flowing your way.

Can you feel the difference in those two energies?

Research across neuroscience, psychology, and consciousness studies reveals that your emotional and mental state doesn't just affect how you *feel* about your wishes - it actually influences how your brain processes information, what opportunities you notice, and potentially how reality itself responds to your intentions.

The most effective cosmic wishes are made from what I call **the Three P's** - a specific internal state that amplifies your wishing power exponentially.

In Chapter 9, you'll discover exactly what the Three P's are, the science behind why they work, and how to cultivate this state before making any wish. You'll learn practical techniques for shifting from desperation to alignment, from grasping to flow, from forcing to allowing.

At the end of this chapter, I'll guide you through making your wish again using the Three P's, so you can feel the difference immediately.

The Art Part and The Power of Storytelling

This book was inspired by art – a novel I'd just written (*A Love Story to the Universe*), my love for art/writing, and the principles I've learned as a storyteller. Using the framework outlined in Joseph Campbell's Hero's Journey, aka The Hero with A Thousand Faces, a model often used by screenwriters and novelists to craft a compelling story of what it takes to be a hero, I created a book/workbook called *The Hero's Playbook*[3] *"for the hero in all of us."* The book offers a variety of activities covering other techniques storytellers use that are relevant to wishes and wish-making, including motivation, wants vs. needs, and the role of fears, desires, and misbeliefs.

Motivation: The Engine Behind Your Wishes

Are you wishing toward something – or away from something else? Here's something most people never consider: understanding why you want what you want might be just as important as the wish itself.

Are you moving toward something you genuinely desire, or running away from something you fear? Do you actually want the thing you're wishing for, or do you want what you think it will give you? Is your motivation coming from authentic need or from conditioned beliefs about what you "should" want?

In Chapter 7, we'll explore the psychology and neuroscience of motivation - including frameworks that help you distinguish between surface wants and deeper needs, approach versus avoidance motivation, and the profound difference between wishing from attachment versus wishing from authentic desire.

Because here's the truth: you can make all the wishes you want, but if you don't understand what's truly motivating them, you might be wishing for things that won't actually fulfill you even if they manifest.

The Role of Fear, Desire, and Misbelief

As a writer, I'm a fan of using a character's fears, desires, and misbeliefs to understand their motivations and obstacles to overcome. In *A Love Story to the Universe*, the protagonist (a loosely based version of myself) struggled with a misbelief that she would never be loved unless she became successful and learned that the opposite was true.

In wishing, getting clarity on your wants and needs as well as your fears, desires, and misbeliefs will help provide the necessary clarity to improve your results, and in this book, we'll endeavor to explain not just why, but how.

Bridge to Fiction

Throughout this book you'll find references we call a "Bridge to Fiction," where I provide relevant fictional examples to add context to the lessons in that chapter.

Mysteries of Manifesting

We'll also be exploring Metaphysical Mysteries in the context of science and wishing, including what I call "The Blue Balloon Phenomenon" and more.

The Science We'll Explore

Our journey through the science of wishing will take us across multiple disciplines, from well-established neuroscience to cutting-edge consciousness research. For a complete list of the several dozen sciences, go to Appendix A. For now, just know that since this book bridges established research with speculative frameworks, it serves as a guideline for further exploration. Throughout our journey, I'll do my best to distinguish between peer-reviewed evidence and exploratory possibilities that need further validation. My role is to map the territory of what's possible, not to claim scientific certainties.

I will also offer opportunities to "Meet the Scientists" to acknowledge the incredible work of the dedicated scientists to which this book owes a debt of gratitude.

Goals and Roles

My goal is to set up the framework and map the territory of relevant scientific research to get you to think.

Your role is to remain open-minded yet beautifully skeptical. Test everything. Trust your own experience. Feel free to check the citations and read the original research. Track your own results objectively as we explore evidence-based approaches to conscious wishing. And most importantly, share and discuss!

Your Invitation to Scientific Wonder

This book is simultaneously an intellectual exploration and a practical experiment. You're not just learning about the Science of Wishing, you're participating in it. In each section, we'll return to the wish you made at the beginning of this chapter. Throughout our journey together, pay attention to what happens with that wish. Notice synchronicities. Track circumstances. Observe your own internal changes. Document what unfolds. You might just discover that the universe appears to be far more responsive to consciousness, far more collaborative with our intentions, and far more mysterious in its wisdom than current scientific paradigms suggest.

Ready? Let's begin exploring why the capacity for conscious, purposeful wishing might be one of the most important skills you can develop for creating a life of meaning, contribution, and authentic fulfillment.

Remember that wish you made in the beginning? Make it again, but this time using the Three P's.

1. Get Peaceful: Take three deep breaths, relax your shoulders, and settle into present-moment awareness. Feel your body becoming calm and centered.
2. Generate Positive: Think of three things you're genuinely grateful for right now. Let that gratitude fill your chest with warmth and appreciation.
3. Clarify Purpose: Ask yourself: "How would this wish manifesting serve not just me, but others as well? How does it align with my deepest purpose and growth?"

Can you feel the difference?

Next: What Wishing? A Scientific Perspective

Next, we'll look into how different branches of science define a wish in order to set the framework for the rest of the book.

Chapter 2: What Is Wishing? A Scientific Perspective

Remember that wish you made at the beginning of this journey? Hold it in your awareness as we transition from the personal to the scientific. What you're about to discover may fundamentally change how you think about that wish—and about the remarkable capacity of human consciousness to interact with reality in ways we're only beginning to understand.

From Intuition to Evidence

In Chapter 1, we explored wishing through personal experience. We recognized that wishes feel different from prayers, goals, or simple daydreams. We identified frameworks like the Three P's and the Four Responses. We acknowledged that wishing involves "something bigger than ourselves."

That was intuition. Art pointing toward truth.

Now here's what fascinated me: When I started digging into the research, scientists were discovering remarkably similar patterns. Different language, rigorous methodology, peer-reviewed evidence—but pointing toward the same truths about how wishes work.

The Scientific Definition: Three Essential Elements

From a scientific perspective, research across multiple disciplines reveals that all wishes—whether you're blowing out birthday candles or throwing coins in a fountain—share three core elements:

1. Desire — You want something specific to happen.
2. Uncertainty — You don't know if it will happen.
3. Agency — You believe your intention might influence the outcome, even if you're not sure how.

This is why wishes feel different from other mental activities:

- **Unlike goals**, wishes embrace uncertainty rather than demanding clear pathways
- **Unlike fantasies**, wishes involve a sense that our intention might influence reality
- **Unlike prayers**, wishes may or may not involve divine intervention

Understanding these three elements scientifically is the first step in transforming a regular wish into a cosmic wish.

The Scientific Territory We'll Explore

The science of wishing spans an extraordinary range of disciplines. This book references the work of 78 different scientists across dozens of varied scientific realms—everything from evolutionary psychology to quantum mechanics, from neuroscience to sociology, from consciousness research to motivation science.

But don't worry—we'll break it down for you!

Our journey follows a logical path through the fundamental questions about wishing:

PART 1: The Foundation (Chapters 2-5)

- **What is a wish?** (this chapter) — The scientific definition and framework
- **Why do we wish?** (Chapter 3) — The evolutionary, psychological roots (Evolutionary Psychology, Positive Psychology, Neuroscience)
- **How do we wish?** (Chapter 4) — Universal rituals and cultural practices (Anthropology, Sociology, Ritual Studies)
- **What do people wish for?** (Chapter 5) — Patterns across humanity (Cross-Cultural Psychology, Motivation Science, Values Research)

These chapters establish that wishing is universal, timeless, and deeply embedded in human nature. But understanding WHAT wishing is and WHY we do it is just the beginning.

PART 2: The Science of Cosmic Wishing (Chapters 6-10)

This is where we get to the heart of the matter—the science that transforms regular wishes into cosmic wishes:

- **Who is wishing?** (Chapter 6) — **The Three Selves** and why alignment matters (Psychology of Consciousness, Psychodynamic Theory, Internal Family Systems)

- **What drives wishes forward?** (Chapter 7) — **Motivation science** and the forces behind desire (Behavioral Psychology, Self-Determination Theory, Neuroscience of Reward)

- **What happens in the brain?** (Chapter 8) — **Neuroscience** of conscious intention (Cognitive Neuroscience, Neuroplasticity, Psychoneuroimmunology)

- **How do we optimize wishing?** (Chapter 9) — **The Three P's**: Peaceful, Positive, Purposeful (Positive Psychology, Affective Neuroscience, Consciousness Studies)

- **How does reality respond?** (Chapter 10) — **The Four Responses** and what they mean (Systems Theory, Complexity Science, Emerging Research in Consciousness)

Each of these chapters reveals another scientifically-validated piece of how wishing actually works—and how to work WITH it consciously.

PART 3: Beyond Individual Wishes (Chapters 11-14)

Finally, we'll explore:

- The shadow side of wishing (what can go wrong) (Clinical Psychology, Ethics, Shadow Work)

- Collective wishing and emergent change (Social Psychology, Field Theory, Collective Consciousness Research)

- The power of storytelling in manifesting wishes (Narrative Psychology, Neuroscience of Stories, Social Contagion)

- Frontier questions at the edge of current science (Quantum Mechanics, Consciousness Studies, Information Theory)

What Makes a Wish "Cosmic"

Here's the difference between a regular wish and a cosmic wish:

A regular wish: "I hope I get that job." (Vague, fingers crossed, hoping blindly)

A cosmic wish: Applying the Art and Science of Wishing when you wish, including the motivation driving your desire, which of your Three Selves wants this and why, how to align with the Three P's, and how to recognize and work with the Four Responses.

When you understand the SCIENCE of wishing, you're no longer hoping blindly. You're engaging consciously with the entire process—maximizing what you can control, and working skillfully with what you can't.

That's what makes it cosmic.

Pay attention to what happens with that wish you made at the beginning of this book. Notice synchronicities. Track circumstances. Observe your internal changes. Document what unfolds.

You're not just learning about the science of wishing. You're participating in it.

Ready? Let's start by exploring why humans developed the instinct to wish in the first place.

Next: Why Do We Wish?

Understanding what wishing is from a scientific perspective naturally leads us to our next question: Why do we wish? What evolutionary, psychological, and social factors led to the development of this remarkable human capacity?

In Chapter 3, we'll explore how wishing may have emerged as an adaptive trait that enhanced our species' survival and continues to serve crucial functions in human psychology and social organization. We'll discover that the ability to envision better futures and maintain hope through uncertainty may be one of the most significant features that makes us human.

The journey from personal experience to scientific understanding opens doorways to even deeper questions about human nature and our relationship with the cosmos itself.

Chapter 3: Why Do We Wish? The Evolutionary, Psychological, and Social Roots

Think about that wish you made at the beginning of this book. Hold it for a moment. Now here's a fascinating question: Why do you—why do *any* of us—have this capacity to wish at all?

The answer takes us way back. Not just to your childhood birthday parties, but thousands of years into human history. Because wishing isn't just something cute we do when we blow out candles or see a shooting star. It's something our brains evolved to do. Something that helped our ancestors survive. Something that might be one of the most distinctly human capacities we possess.

Here's what fascinates me: Scientists now believe that having the ability to hope for things—not just react to what's right in front of us, but imagine better futures—gave our ancestors a survival advantage. The humans who could envision "what if" and maintain hope through uncertainty? They lived longer. Built stronger communities. Solved bigger problems.

In this chapter, we'll explore why wishing matters from the perspective of evolutionary biology, psychology, and social science. And as we do, keep that wish of yours in mind. Because understanding *why* humans wish might change how you think about your own agency in shaping your future.

Evolutionary Psychology: Why Wishing Helped Us Survive

Here's a question that puzzled me when I first started researching this book: Why would evolution favor creatures who spend time imagining uncertain futures? Wouldn't it be more efficient to just focus on the here and now?

Turns out, scientists have a powerful answer: hope helps us survive.

Why Hope Matters for Survival

Studies show that people with hope are more likely to persist through difficulties, find creative solutions to problems, and bounce back from setbacks.[4]

For early humans facing food scarcity, harsh weather, and constant dangers, this wasn't just a nice personality trait—it could mean the difference between life and death.

Think about it: If your tribe's usual hunting ground dried up, who had the advantage? The person who gave up and despaired? Or the person who could imagine that *maybe* there was better hunting over the next ridge, who could maintain hope long enough to keep searching?

The Power of "What If"

This is where it gets really interesting for your wish. That "what if" question—which is essentially what every wish is—wasn't just simple storytelling for our ancestors. Research shows that imagining different scenarios and possibilities helped early humans learn, prepare, and make better decisions.[5]

The humans who asked "what if we tried hunting somewhere new?" or "what if we stored food for winter?" had a major survival advantage over those who only reacted to immediate circumstances. Your power to wish—to imagine something different from what currently exists—comes from this evolutionary gift.

Love, Leadership, and Finding Your Tribe

But wishing didn't just help individuals survive tough times. It helped them find partners and build communities too. Research shows that people who can envision and work toward better futures are seen as more desirable partners and more valuable community members.[6]

The ability to inspire others—through storytelling, vision-casting, and shared wishing rituals—made individuals more likely to become leaders. More likely to reproduce successfully. The optimist who could paint a picture of a better tomorrow? That person attracted followers, built alliances, and left more descendants.

The Group Advantage: Wishing Together

Here's where it gets even more fascinating. Wishing and hoping together made entire groups stronger. After all, it can be argued that goals start out as wishes.

Studies on collective rituals show that when people participate in shared ceremonies and activities, trust increases, cooperation improves, and group bonds tighten.[7] It also helps them get clarity on where they align – and not – so they can adjust and unite.

Tribes that could wish for and work toward common goals—finding new territory, winning battles, surviving winters—were far more likely to thrive than groups without this capacity for shared hope. Your wish right now, even if it's personal, connects you to this ancient human capacity for collective dreaming.

The Science of Hope: Foundations and Modern Understanding

So we know that hope and wishing helped our ancestors survive. But what exactly *is* hope from a scientific perspective? And how does understanding this help with your wish?

Psychologist C.R. Snyder's Hope Theory has shaped our understanding for decades, and modern neuroscience is backing it up in fascinating ways.[8]

How Hope Actually Works in Your Brain

Snyder identified hope as having two key components: **agency** (your belief that you can take action toward your goals) and **pathways** (your ability to find different routes to get there. When both are strong, you stay motivated—and you adapt rather than give up when faced with obstacles.

People with high hope scores consistently perform better academically, maintain better physical health, and experience greater emotional well-being. Some research even suggests that our ancestors who were better at "hope-based thinking" had a genuine survival edge.[9]

Think about your wish right now. Do you have both pieces? The belief that you can influence the outcome (agency) *and* the ability to imagine multiple ways it might manifest (pathways)? Both matter.

Hope Actually Lights Up Your Brain

Here's something that blew my mind when I learned it: Hopeful anticipation—not the actual reward, but just *hoping* for something good—triggers activity in your brain's dopamine system.[10]

When you imagine a positive future, areas of your brain related to planning and motivation light up. The act of hoping isn't just a feeling— it's a brain-based boost that encourages creative thinking, persistence, and resilience. *Before anything good has even happened.*

Your wish? It's already doing something real in your brain right now. We'll explore exactly how this works in Chapter 8, but for now, just know: wishing is a neurologically active process, not passive daydreaming.

Wishing Through Crisis: More Than Wishful Thinking

When life gets hard—really hard—wishing becomes even more important. Studies show that during times of crisis and uncertainty, we naturally turn to making wishes. Not to deny reality, but to envision better outcomes and maintain hope.[11]

During the COVID-19 pandemic, researchers found that people who wished for brighter days reported more positive attitudes and greater resilience. Their wishes became small guiding lights through darkness.

Instead of ignoring hardship, wishing helps us imagine heading toward something better. It reframes difficult times as temporary and surmountable, letting us keep faith in the possibility of improvement— even when current circumstances look bleak.

If your wish emerged from a difficult situation, that's not weakness. That's your brain doing exactly what evolution designed it to do: maintaining hope through uncertainty.

Rituals, Emotions, and Social Bonding

Here's something that fascinates me: Anthropologists have found wishing rituals and hope-based traditions in virtually every culture on Earth.[12]

That's not random. That's human nature expressing itself across time and geography.

Why Every Culture Has Wishing Rituals

Studies of global wishing practices reveal common elements that appear everywhere: designated times and places for wishing, symbolic objects that represent hopes, community gatherings centered on collective wishes, and ceremonies that mark transitions from current reality to hoped-for futures.[13]

These ritualistic elements serve multiple purposes: focusing intention, building community bonds, and creating psychological states conducive to positive change. When you made that wish at the beginning of this book, you were participating in a practice that humans have refined over millennia.

Wishing Together Makes Groups Stronger

Research on collective rituals shows something powerful: When people participate in shared ceremonial activities, trust increases, cooperation improves, and group identity strengthens.[14]

Why does this matter for survival? When groups can coordinate around shared hopes and work together toward common goals, they become more effective at everything—from gathering resources to defending against threats to building civilizations.

Wishing rituals served as social technologies that strengthened the bonds necessary for human groups to thrive. Your individual wish connects to this larger pattern of humans dreaming together.

The Psychology of Transcendence and Meaning-Making

But wishing serves purposes beyond immediate survival. There are deeper psychological functions that explain why this capacity became so central to being human.

Meaning, Purpose, and Living Longer

Here's something remarkable: Research shows that people who maintain hopes and wishes for meaningful futures demonstrate greater psychological resilience, improved immune function, and even increased longevity.[15]

The ability to wish for purposes greater than immediate survival needs gave our ancestors motivation to create art, develop complex social structures, and engage in the long-term thinking that built human civilization.

Your wish—especially if it connects to something larger than just personal comfort—taps into this profound human capacity for meaning-making.

Thinking Bigger Than Ourselves

Studies show that wishing often involves what researchers call "self-transcendent" thinking—the ability to envision outcomes that benefit others or serve purposes beyond personal gain.[16] And here's the fascinating part: This kind of thinking is associated with increased well-being, enhanced creativity, and greater life satisfaction.

Thinking bigger than ourselves helped humans care about each other and work together, which made it possible to build stronger communities and larger societies. This capacity for transcendent wishing was essential for the development of altruism, cooperation, and the kind of visionary thinking that changes the world.

Does your wish have an element of this? Does it serve not just you, but others as well? If so, you're tapping into something evolutionarily powerful.

Coping with Not Knowing

Research on stress and coping reveals something important: Hope-based thinking helps us manage uncertainty and maintain psychological stability during unpredictable circumstances.17 People who can maintain hopes and wishes during difficult periods demonstrate better mental health outcomes and more effective problem-solving abilities.

For early humans living in highly uncertain environments—and let's be honest, for modern humans too—this capacity for hoping through uncertainty is essential for psychological survival.

Your wish exists in uncertainty. That's not a bug, it's a feature. The not-knowing is part of what makes it a wish rather than a plan.

The Role of Storytelling and Narrative in Wish Evolution

Now let's get into something I'm particularly passionate about as a writer: the connection between stories and wishes.

Research in narrative psychology reveals that storytelling and shared myths likely evolved alongside wishing rituals, giving people powerful tools to coordinate, find meaning, and inspire collective action.[18] Stories work as engines for hope—they help groups imagine better futures, create shared identity, and inspire collaborative action.

Whether through legends, folktales, or everyday anecdotes, stories don't just help us remember the past and envision the future. They give voice to our wishes and show us how to act on them together.

Joseph Campbell and the Universal Hero's Journey

Here's where mythology meets science in the most beautiful way.

In 1949, mythologist Joseph Campbell published *The Hero with a Thousand Faces*, identifying a universal narrative pattern—the "monomyth" or Hero's Journey—that appears across virtually every culture and time period. Campbell's research, influenced by Carl Jung's concept of the collective unconscious, revealed that hero myths worldwide share a common structure: A protagonist ventures from the ordinary world into a realm of supernatural wonder, faces challenges, achieves transformation, and returns home with wisdom to benefit the community.

Why does this matter for understanding wishing? Because the Hero's Journey is fundamentally a story about hope in the face of impossible odds. Campbell recognized these narratives weren't just entertainment—they were teaching tools transmitting crucial survival wisdom across generations.

Every hero story teaches the same lesson: Obstacles can be overcome. Transformation is possible. Maintaining hope through uncertainty leads to triumph.

Science Validates Ancient Wisdom

For decades, Campbell's insights remained in the realm of literary analysis. But recently, something remarkable happened: Scientists actually tested whether the Hero's Journey has measurable psychological effects. And Campbell was right.

Research published in 2023 found that people who view their lives through the lens of the Hero's Journey report significantly greater meaning in life, enhanced well-being, increased resilience, and reduced depression.[19] The effect was consistent across diverse demographics and cultures—the Hero's Journey really does represent a universal psychological pattern.[20]

This is why I created *The Hero's Playbook*—a collection of activities to "bring out the hero in all of us" based on Campbell's framework. Understanding the Hero's Journey doesn't just make you a better storyteller. It makes you better at maintaining hope through challenges.

Your Wish as a Hero's Journey

Think about your wish right now through this lens. What "call to adventure" does it represent? What challenges might you face? What transformation might it create?

Recognizing your wish as part of your own Hero's Journey—with its inevitable obstacles, necessary allies, and ultimate transformation—changes everything. Obstacles aren't signs that your wish won't come true. They're part of the story structure that leads to transformation.

We'll explore exactly how to use the Hero's Journey to tell and share your cosmic wishing story in Chapter 13, where we dive into the science of storytelling and how narratives spread wishes through human populations.

Stories Keep Wishes Alive Across Generations

Every culture has wish-granting stories—from Aladdin's lamp to fairy godmothers, from shooting stars to wishing wells. These narratives encode wisdom: Hope matters. Envisioning better futures serves a purpose. Maintaining positive expectations even in uncertain circumstances can lead to positive outcomes.

Stories don't just reflect our capacity to hope. They strengthen it. They show us the pattern. They remind us that transformation is possible.

Movements and Social Change

Research on social movements shows that big changes often start with shared stories and collective wishing.[21] When people come together and talk about the future they hope to see, these narratives give rise to powerful movements for transformation.

Every major social transformation—from civil rights movements to environmental activism—started with groups visioning new possibilities and wishing for something better. It's not just strategy or planning that makes movements succeed. It's the energy of shared stories and hopes that help people believe change is possible—and then work together to make it real.

Your wish, even if it's personal, connects to this larger human capacity for envisioning and creating change.

Meet the Scientists

The researchers whose work illuminates why we wish:

Viktor Frankl — Logotherapy and the search for meaning in suffering

Martin Seligman — Founded positive psychology and research on optimism, hope, and resilience

Roy Baumeister — Belongingness, meaning-making, and social bonds

Robin Dunbar — Evolutionary roots of social bonding and group rituals (Dunbar's number)

Jonathan Haidt — Moral Foundations Theory and cultural rituals

C.R. Snyder — Hope Theory (agency and pathways to goals)

Joseph Campbell — Universal Hero's Journey pattern and narrative wisdom

(Full biographies in Appendix B)

Questions to Ponder

As you hold your wish in your awareness, consider these questions:

- **What survival or thriving functions might your wish serve?** Think about how your desire connects to fundamental human needs—safety, connection, meaning, or growth.
- **How does your wishing connect you to others?** Is your wish purely personal, or does it involve hopes for family, community, or humanity?
- **What role does uncertainty play in your wish?** Notice how the element of not-knowing might actually enhance rather than diminish its value and meaning.
- **How does your wish reflect your relationship with transcendence?** Does your hope connect you to purposes, values, or possibilities that extend beyond your immediate circumstances?
- **Where does your wish fall within your own Hero's Journey?** What "call to adventure" does it represent? What challenges might it involve? What transformation might it create?

Next: How Do We Wish?

Understanding *why* humans developed the capacity to wish leads us naturally to explore *how* we express this ability. In Chapter 4, we'll examine the rituals, practices, and cultural expressions that humans have created to focus and amplify their wishes—from ancient traditions to modern adaptations, from individual practices to collective ceremonies that bind communities together in shared hope.

The journey continues. Your wish continues. And as we'll discover, the ways humans have learned to wish across cultures and throughout history reveal profound insights about consciousness, intention, and our relationship with the cosmos itself.

Chapter 4: How Do We Wish? Rituals, Practices, and Cultural Expressions

Remember that wish you made at the beginning of this book? Now think about a wish you made before opening this book. What sparked it? Think about *how* you made it. Did you close your eyes? Take a deep breath? Maybe you felt a little spark of something—hope, possibility, intention?

You participated in a ritual. Even if it felt spontaneous, even if you didn't think of it as ceremonial, you followed a pattern that humans have been following for thousands of years.

Having explored *why* humans evolved the capacity for wishing, we now turn to one of the most fascinating questions: *How* do different cultures around the world actually do this wishing thing? And here's what's remarkable—from the moment you blew out birthday candles as a child to watching shooting stars streak across the night sky, you've been part of ancient traditions that span millennia and continents.

These aren't just quaint customs or primitive superstitions. They're sophisticated technologies for focusing intention, building community, and potentially interacting with forces we're only beginning to understand scientifically.

The Universal Elements: What Shows Up Everywhere

Here's something that fascinated me when I started researching this book: Despite vast differences in culture, geography, and historical period, humans structure wishing practices in remarkably similar ways.[22]

Think about your own wish. Did you make it at a special time? Use any particular objects? Tell anyone about it? These aren't random choices—they connect you to patterns that appear in every culture on Earth.

Sacred Timing: When We Wish

Across cultures, wishing happens at transitional moments—birthdays, new years, seasonal changes, celestial events like meteor showers or eclipses, and life passages like coming of age or marriage. There's a universal human intuition that certain moments offer special opportunities for wishes to be "heard" or to manifest.[23]

Why? Research suggests these timing patterns create heightened states of awareness and openness to possibility.[24] There's something psychologically powerful about threshold moments—times when we're between one state and another. Our brains actually become more receptive to new possibilities during transitions.

When did you make your wish? Was it during a moment of change or transition in your life? That timing wasn't accidental.

Symbolic Objects and Sacred Locations: Where We Wish

Here's another pattern that shows up everywhere: specific objects and places for wishing. Candles and flames. Bodies of water like wells and fountains. Elevated locations like mountains and temples. Natural phenomena like stars and rainbows.

Why these particular symbols? Studies show these elements create psychological states conducive to hope and expanded awareness.[25] The cross-cultural consistency suggests they tap into something fundamental about human consciousness and its relationship with natural forces.

Think about where you were—physically and mentally—when you made your wish. Did the setting matter? Even if you were just sitting in your living room, I bet you created some kind of internal "sacred space" in your mind.

Community and Witnesses: Who Knows About Your Wish

Most traditional wishing practices involve others—family members singing "Happy Birthday," crowds gathering for New Year celebrations, pilgrims visiting sacred sites together. Research shows that shared ritualistic activities increase emotional contagion, group bonding, and collective sense of possibility.[26] The presence of witnesses appears to amplify both the psychological impact and the perceived effectiveness of wishing.

Here's an interesting question about your wish: Did you tell anyone? Or keep it secret? Both approaches have power, and we'll explore why in later chapters. But notice that even the question of whether to share a wish is part of the ritual structure humans have developed.

The Sequence: How We Structure Wishing

Cross-cultural analysis reveals that effective wishing traditions typically follow a specific sequence: preparation (creating sacred space or gathering materials), invocation (focusing intention or calling upon higher powers), expression (articulating the wish), and release (letting go of attachment to outcome).[27]

These structured sequences help create optimal psychological states for both hope cultivation and actual behavioral change. They're not arbitrary—they're refined over millennia to work with how our brains actually function.

Did your wish-making follow any kind of sequence? Even if you weren't conscious of it, you probably prepared in some way (took a breath, focused your mind), invoked something (connected to hope or possibility), expressed it (internally or aloud), and then... let it go.

How Different Cultures Wish: Beautiful Variations on Universal Themes

While these universal patterns exist, the specific ways cultures express wishing are wonderfully diverse. Let me share some of my favorites—and you can find a far more extensive catalog in Appendix C: Wishing Rituals in 50 Countries.

Eastern Traditions: Movement and Beauty

Asian cultures have developed particularly sophisticated wishing practices. Tibetan prayer wheels incorporate written wishes into spinning mechanisms—the rotation sends intentions into the cosmic realm. Chinese lantern festivals involve releasing paper lanterns carrying written wishes into the night sky. Japanese Ema boards at Shinto shrines allow visitors to write wishes on wooden plaques that carry prayers to the kami (spirits).

What I love about these practices is how they integrate movement, visual beauty, and community participation in ways that enhance both psychological impact and social bonding.[28] They're not just functional— they're gorgeous.

Western Practices: Transformation and Transition

European and American traditions often center on moments of transition or celebration. Birthday candle wishes require making a secret desire before extinguishing flames with breath—combining personal intention with the symbolic transformation of fire to smoke. Throwing coins into fountains traces back to ancient Roman traditions of offering something valuable to water spirits in exchange for granted wishes. Wishbone breaking, derived from Etruscan practices, involves two people pulling a dried bone until it breaks, with the holder of the larger piece receiving their wish.

Notice the common theme? Transformation. Fire to smoke. Coin to offering. Bone breaking to create two from one. These rituals encode the understanding that wishing involves change.

Indigenous Traditions: Altered States and Sacred Connection

Native cultures worldwide have developed vision quest practices—ceremonial rituals involving isolation, fasting, and meditation to receive guidance and fulfill spiritual desires. Australian Aboriginal dreamtime practices integrate wishing with cosmological understanding of how individual desires connect to universal patterns.

What's remarkable here is the sophisticated understanding of how altered states of consciousness, natural settings, and ceremonial structure can facilitate both personal transformation and community healing.[29] These traditions recognize that sometimes you need to shift your consciousness to access deeper wisdom about what you truly need.

Modern Digital Adaptations: Ancient Impulses, New Platforms

Here's something interesting—we haven't stopped creating wishing rituals. We've just adapted them. Social media birthday wishes, online intention-setting groups, and digital vision boards represent technological evolution of traditional practices.

And you know what? Research suggests these modern adaptations maintain many psychological benefits of traditional rituals while reaching global communities and creating new forms of social support for hope-based thinking.[30] Your Instagram post about your goals for the year? That's a modern wishing ritual, connecting you to millions of others doing the same thing.

Why Rituals Actually Work: The Science Behind the Magic

So why do these rituals persist across cultures? Why do we keep doing them? Because they serve multiple psychological and social functions that go way beyond just "requesting desired outcomes."

Rituals Focus Your Brain

Studies show that rituals sharpen attention, quiet the mind, and create special states of awareness that make creativity and motivation easier.[31] The structured, repetitive actions found in wishing rituals actually activate brain circuits related to focus and emotional balance. The ceremonial aspects shift consciousness into states more conducive to both hope cultivation and behavioral change.

Think about your wish again. When you made it, did you feel different somehow? More focused? More centered? That wasn't your imagination—that was your brain responding to the ritual structure you created, even unconsciously.

Rituals Bond Us Together

When people participate together in meaningful rituals, they experience increased empathy, enhanced cooperation, and stronger social bonds.[32] This isn't just warm fuzzy feelings—it's measurable changes in how we relate to each other and coordinate action.

Even if you made your wish alone, you're connected to everyone else who's ever wished. That's part of why rituals feel powerful—they link us to something larger than ourselves.

Belief Creates Real Change

Here's something fascinating: Studies on placebo effects and expectancy show that simply believing a ritual will work can spark real changes—both in mind and body.[33] When people trust that their ritual will influence what happens, they tend to feel more hopeful, motivated, and in control—boosts that shape their thoughts *and* their actions.

This isn't just "positive thinking." Scientists have found these factors can lead to better outcomes through real psychological and behavioral shifts. The ritual primes your brain to notice opportunities, take action, and maintain hope through uncertainty.

Sacred or Secular? Both Work

Here's something that surprised me: Wishing practices maintain effectiveness even when stripped of explicit religious content. Studies indicate that secular rituals—like making birthday wishes or New Year resolutions—activate similar psychological processes to religious ceremonies.[34]

This suggests that the structural elements of ritual may be more important than specific belief systems in creating beneficial effects. Whether you're praying to a deity or just focusing your intention into the universe or quantum realm, the ritual structure itself does something real in your brain.

The Symbolic Elements: Why Certain Things Keep Showing Up

Certain symbols appear consistently in wishing practices worldwide, suggesting they tap into fundamental aspects of human psychology and our relationship with natural forces.

Fire and Light: Transformation

Candles, lanterns, stars, and flames appear everywhere in wishing traditions. Fire symbolism activates associations with transformation, purification, and connection between earthly and cosmic realms. And here's the cool part—studies show that candlelight and firelight create specific brainwave patterns associated with relaxation and enhanced creativity.[35]

The universal human fascination with fire in ritual contexts reflects both our evolutionary programming (fire meant safety, warmth, community for our ancestors) and genuine psychological benefits.

Water Elements: Cleansing and Flow

Wells, fountains, rivers, and oceans feature prominently in global wishing practices. Water symbolism connects to themes of cleansing, renewal, and flow toward desired destinations. Research on blue spaces shows that proximity to water reduces stress and increases positive mood.[36]

The psychological benefits of water environments may actually enhance the effectiveness of wishes made in such settings. There's a reason we throw coins in fountains and make wishes by the ocean.

Air and Wind: Freedom and Movement

Dandelion seeds, prayer flags, released balloons, and smoke all represent wishes carried by air currents. Studies of breathing practices show that attention to breath and air movement can create altered states of consciousness conducive to both relaxation and enhanced creativity.[37]

Here's one of my favorite examples from my own storytelling:

Bridge to Fiction: In *A Love Story to the Universe*, I envisioned a scene during the Black Plague where people had lost confidence in their ability to make wishes. It "was a dark time in heaven and on Earth" where "even the Wish Fairies had given up hope and were ready to close down Astraea for good."

The solution? Dandelions. Blowing on a dandelion. "As people all over puffed on the blowball, they made a wish and imagined their loved ones' souls ascending into heaven with love."

I didn't know the science behind breath and air symbolism when I wrote that—I just felt it was right. Turns out, my writer's intuition was backed by research!

Earth and Nature: Grounding and Growth

Trees, stones, mountains, and sacred natural sites serve as focal points for wishing practices worldwide. Research reveals that natural settings activate what scientists call "soft fascination"—a gentle, restorative form of attention that reduces mental fatigue and enhances psychological well-being.[38]

The preference for natural settings in wishing practices reflects both aesthetic preferences and genuine psychological benefits of nature connection. We instinctively know that getting out in nature makes us feel more open to possibility.

Modern Evolution: Ancient Wisdom Meets New Technology

Contemporary culture demonstrates remarkable creativity in adapting ancient wishing practices to modern contexts while maintaining their essential psychological and social functions.

Digital Platforms: Global Wishing Communities

Online communities dedicated to intention-setting, wish-sharing, and manifestation practices represent technological evolution of traditional group rituals. These digital adaptations provide social support, accountability, and sense of global community while maintaining many benefits of traditional practices.[39]

The ability to connect with others worldwide around shared hopes and intentions creates new possibilities for collective wishing that our ancestors couldn't have imagined. (We'll explore how to activate this in Chapter 15.)

Scientific Integration: Evidence Meets Intuition

Modern practitioners increasingly integrate scientific understanding with traditional practices, creating evidence-based approaches to ritual and intention-setting. Research on gratitude practices, visualization techniques, and goal-setting strategies provides scientific validation for many elements of traditional wishing practices while suggesting refinements based on psychological research.[40]

This is exactly what this book aims to do—honor ancient wisdom while understanding the mechanisms that make it work.

Commercial and Therapeutic Applications

Contemporary culture has seen the emergence of wish-focused businesses, therapeutic approaches, and educational programs that adapt traditional practices for modern needs. When conducted with appropriate balance of hope and realism, such practices provide genuine benefits for mental health, motivation, and life satisfaction.[41]

The Future of Wishing

Emerging research on consciousness, quantum mechanics, and collective intention suggests that our understanding of wishing practices may continue evolving as science catches up with ancient intuitions about consciousness and reality interaction. We'll explore these frontier questions in later in this book.

Bridge to Fiction: The Seven Waves

In another story-within-a-story in *A Love Story to the Universe*, a young Brazilian girl participates in a ritual called Pular 7 Ondas—the ritual of jumping over seven consecutive waves on New Year's Eve, making a new wish every time. Seven waves, seven wishes, seven opportunities to reset and reimagine what's possible for the coming year. Beautiful, right?

Meet the Scientists

The researchers whose work illuminates how we wish:

Bronisław Malinowski — Ritual as response to uncertainty

Victor Turner — Liminality and ritual transformation

Émile Durkheim — Collective effervescence in rituals

Mary Douglas — Symbolic anthropology and ritual meaning

Alan Dundes — Folklore and wishing ritual analysis

(Full biographies in Appendix B)

Questions to Ponder

As you reflect on your wish and your own relationship with wishing rituals:

- **What wishing rituals or traditions have been meaningful in your life?** Think about both formal traditions (birthday wishes, New Year resolutions) and personal practices you may have developed without even realizing they were rituals.
- **How do different settings affect your wishing?** Notice whether you wish differently in natural settings, sacred spaces, or during special times. Does your wish feel more powerful in certain places or moments?
- **What symbolic elements resonate most with you?** Are you drawn to fire, water, air, earth, or other natural elements when expressing your deepest hopes? What does that tell you about your wish?
- **Did you create any kind of ritual when you made your wish at the beginning of this book?** Even small things—closing your eyes, taking a breath, holding a particular intention—count as ritual. What did you do?
- **How might you adapt traditional practices to fit your life?** Consider ways to honor the psychological wisdom of ancient practices while integrating them authentically into your modern circumstances.

Next: What Do People Wish For?

Our exploration of *how* cultures express wishing leads naturally to our next question: What do people actually wish for?

In Chapter 5, we'll examine the universal patterns in human desires, from the most basic needs for survival and connection to the highest aspirations for meaning and transcendence. Understanding what humans typically wish for reveals profound insights about our deepest needs and values— and offers clues about what kinds of wishes are most likely to enhance well-being and contribute to both personal and collective thriving.

You'll discover that while the surface content of wishes varies dramatically across cultures and individuals, deeper patterns emerge that reflect fundamental aspects of human nature. These patterns might help you understand your own wish more deeply—and perhaps even refine it as we continue this journey together.

Chapter 5: What Do We Wish For? Universal Patterns in Human Desires

Take a moment to reflect on the wish you made at the beginning of our journey. What does it reveal about what matters most to you right now? Is it focused on survival and security? On relationships and belonging? On achievement and recognition? Or perhaps on meaning and transcendence?

Your wish isn't random. Research reveals that while the surface content of human wishes varies dramatically—from a child's hope for a puppy to an adult's vision of world peace—most wishes cluster around foundational needs and aspirations that transcend culture, geography, and historical period. Studies confirm that universal themes such as health, security, relationships, achievement, and meaning consistently emerge across populations.[42]

Understanding these patterns offers profound insights into which types of wishes are most likely to enhance well-being and contribute to both personal and collective flourishing.

The Hierarchy of Human Wishes

Human wishes generally follow patterns that align with fundamental psychological needs. Abraham Maslow's groundbreaking 1943 work in *Psychological Review* revealed that people tend to wish for basic things first—like being safe and healthy—then for bigger things, like love or making a difference in the world.[43] This hierarchical framework has been supported by decades of additional research on motivation and human needs.[44]

Survival and Security: At the most basic level, humans wish for safety, health, shelter, and financial security. Large-scale research confirms these fundamental concerns appear consistently across cultures.[45] Studies of individuals facing economic hardship, illness, or danger reveal that wishes for basic stability dominate during crisis periods.

Love and Belonging: Once basic needs feel secure, wishes typically focus on relationships, family, friendship, and community connection. Cross-cultural research reveals that while specific forms of desired relationships vary, the fundamental human need for connection appears universal.

Achievement and Recognition: Wishing for career success, creative accomplishment, skill development, and social recognition reflects fundamental human needs for competence, mastery, and community contribution. Research from Harvard Medical School shows that wishes focused on achievement tend to be most fulfilling when also motivated by benefiting others, aligning with studies on purpose-driven life satisfaction.[46]

Meaning and Transcendence: At the highest levels, wishes for spiritual growth, service to others, leaving a legacy, and connection to greater purpose are universal and linked to higher well-being. Studies consistently show that individuals who include transcendent aspects in their wishes report greater life satisfaction and psychological well-being.[47]

Universal Categories and Cultural Variations

While wish content varies across cultures, certain universal categories appear consistently worldwide. [48] Cross-cultural psychologist Shalom Schwartz's research identified ten universal value types—including self-direction, achievement, security, benevolence, and universalism—that appear across all societies and serve as the underlying motivational drivers behind these wish categories.[49] These deep motivational values help explain why certain types of wishes appear universally while their specific expressions vary by culture.

Health and Healing: Health-related wishes—for personal healing, family member recovery, or protection from illness—appear in virtually every culture. These wishes often expand beyond personal concerns to include community health and planetary well-being.

Prosperity and Abundance: Wishes for material prosperity appear universally, though cultural definitions of "abundance" vary dramatically. Research shows these wishes tend to be most fulfilling when they balance personal security with generosity toward others.

Peace and Justice: Cross-cultural studies reveal consistent patterns of wishing for conflict resolution, social justice, and peaceful coexistence. Individuals who include social justice elements in their personal wishes report greater sense of purpose and life meaning.

Cultural Specific Expressions: Eastern cultures tend to emphasize wishes for family harmony and ancestral honor, while Western cultures often prioritize individual achievement. Indigenous cultures frequently include wishes for environmental healing and connection to natural cycles.

Age and Life Stage Patterns

Research reveals predictable patterns in wish content that correlate with developmental stages.[50]

Childhood: Children's wishes focus on immediate desires, fantasy fulfillment, and family harmony, reflecting both developmental needs for play and sensitivity to family stress.

Adolescence and Young Adulthood: Wishes shift toward identity formation, romantic relationships, career direction, and independence, reflecting the tension between autonomy and connection.

Midlife: Wishes focus on legacy creation, family well-being, career fulfillment, and health maintenance, with increased concern for future generations.

Later Life: Older adults emphasize family relationships, health maintenance, spiritual growth, and peaceful transitions, often reflecting desire to share wisdom with younger generations.

The Self-Other Balance in Wishing

One of the most significant patterns involves how we balance personal desires with concern for others. Studies consistently show that wishes including concern for others' well-being are more strongly associated with personal happiness, life satisfaction, and psychological resilience than wishes focused solely on personal gain.[51]

The most psychologically beneficial wishes integrate personal well-being with concern for others. Research from the American Psychological Association shows that wishes framed as "both/and"—such as "may I find fulfilling work that also serves others"—create optimal conditions for flourishing.[52] Simply put, people are happiest when they wish for things that are good for themselves and others simultaneously.

Psychologically healthy individuals tend to develop wishes that expand over time from self to family to community to humanity to planetary well-being. This expanding concern correlates with increased life satisfaction, reduced anxiety, and enhanced sense of meaning. Research on group intention and collective consciousness supports these findings.[53]

Gender Patterns in Wishing

Research reveals interesting gender differences in wish content, though these patterns show considerable individual variation and cultural influence.

Individuals socialized as women often show higher rates of wishes focused on relationships, family harmony, and community well-being. Those socialized as men often emphasize wishes related to career achievement, financial success, and personal recognition. However, contemporary research reveals that traditional gender differences are becoming less pronounced as social roles evolve.[54] Younger generations demonstrate more integrated wishing patterns regardless of gender identity.

Wishes That Enhance Well-Being

Research provides guidance about which types of wishes most enhance well-being.[55]

Process vs. Outcome Focus: Wishes focused on personal growth, skill development, and character enhancement are more fulfilling than wishes focused solely on external outcomes. "Becoming" wishes create lasting satisfaction while "having" wishes provide only temporary pleasure.

Realistic vs. Fantastical Balance: The most beneficial wishes balance inspiring vision with realistic possibility. Wishes that stretch our capacity while remaining believable create optimal motivation and hope.[56]

Present-Moment Integration: Wishes most strongly associated with well-being include elements of gratitude for current circumstances while hoping for positive change.[57]

Service and Contribution: Wishes including service to others or contribution to causes greater than personal gain are most strongly associated with life satisfaction, psychological resilience, and sense of meaning. Studies on creativity and hope support these findings.[58]

Elevation and Intention: What We've Learned

Having explored universal categories—from basic survival wishes to transcendent aspirations for meaning—a compelling insight emerges: a wish's elevation depends less on its category and more on the consciousness from which it originates. (For more about this, see Chapter 9, "The 3 P's."

A wish for financial abundance motivated by fear and scarcity produces different outcomes than the same wish motivated by vision of creating security while contributing generously to community needs. The surface content may be identical, but the underlying quality transforms everything. Research on well-being consistently shows that prosperity wishes focused on sharing produce greater life satisfaction than those focused purely on personal accumulation.

This pattern holds across every category. A wish for knowledge might stem from ego's need to prove superiority, or from genuine curiosity combined with desire to solve problems. A wish for health might focus purely on personal comfort, or extend outward to include healing for community and planet.

As we'll explore in subsequent chapters, the human psyche contains multiple layers—different aspects of consciousness that each bring their own motivations, fears, and aspirations to the wishing process. A wish originating from fear operates differently than one arising from love.

This hidden dimension—the elevation, source, and underlying quality of wishes—may be as important as their content. Remarkably, research suggests that any wish can be elevated through specific practices and qualities of consciousness. As we'll discover in Chapter 8: Wishing and the Brain, three particular elements appear capable of transforming wishes from lower to higher frequencies, from fear-based to love-based, from scarcity-oriented to abundance-focused.

Meet the Scientists

The researchers whose work illuminates what we wish for:

Abraham Maslow — Hierarchy of Needs model

Shalom Schwartz — Universal values theory

Carol Ryff — Six-factor model of psychological well-being

Richard Ryan — Self-Determination Theory co-creator

Edward Deci — Self-Determination Theory co-founder

(Full biographies in Appendix B)

Questions to Ponder

Reflect on your own wish in light of these universal patterns:

- **Where does your wish fit within the hierarchy of human needs?** Consider whether it focuses on security, relationships, achievement, or transcendence, and what this reveals about your current life circumstances and priorities.

- **How does your wish balance self-focus with concern for others?** Reflect on whether your desire primarily serves personal goals or includes benefits for family, community, or humanity.

- **What does your wish reveal about your deepest values and aspirations?** Consider what your desire says about what you consider most important in life and how you define fulfillment.

- **How might you frame your wish to enhance its potential for creating well-being?** Reflect on whether focusing more on personal growth, gratitude, or service might enhance both the meaning and effectiveness of your hoping.

- **How has the content of your wishes changed over time?** Consider how your desires have evolved with age, experience, and changing life circumstances.

Next: The Three Selves: Who Within You is Doing the Wishing?

Understanding what people wish for leads naturally to our next exploration: Who is doing the wishing? In Chapter 6, we'll delve into the fascinating concept of the "Three Selves"---the different aspects of human identity that can each have distinct desires, motivations, and ways of engaging with the wishing process.

This deeper psychological exploration will reveal how our conscious ego-self, our subconscious shadow-self, and our transcendent higher-self each contribute different elements to our hopes and dreams. Understanding these multiple layers of identity helps explain why some wishes feel conflicted, why certain desires persist despite conscious rejection, and how we can align our various internal aspects toward more coherent and fulfilling wishing practices.

The journey from understanding what people wish for to exploring who within us is doing the wishing opens doorways to profound questions about human psychology, spiritual development, and the nature of consciousness itself.

Chapter 6: The Three Selves - Who Within You Is Doing the Wishing?

Have you ever made a wish and felt your stomach tighten with anxiety? Or felt excited in your mind but somehow your body felt heavy and resistant? Maybe you've wished for something you know would be good for you, but some invisible force keeps hitting the brakes?

You're not broken. You're not self-sabotaging.

What's actually happening is that different parts of you are trying to communicate—and they're not always speaking the same language.

Let's return to that wish you made at the beginning of our journey. Which part of you created that desire? Your logical mind that sees what needs to change? Your emotional heart that longs for something more? Or that deeper wisdom that knows what your soul really needs?

More importantly: are all parts of you aligned with that wish, or are some parts working against it?

Here's what scientists have discovered: many wishes fail not because they're impossible or the universe isn't responsive, but because different parts of ourselves are working at cross-purposes. It's like having one foot on the gas and one on the brake—you're burning a lot of energy but not going anywhere.

Modern psychology confirms what ancient wisdom traditions have long understood: humans aren't unified, single-minded beings. We're complex systems with multiple aspects, each with distinct perspectives, needs, and agendas.[59] Understanding and integrating these different aspects is essential for both psychological health and effective wishing.

The Framework: Why You're Not One Voice—You're a Whole Team

Think about your own experience for a moment. Haven't there been times when you felt torn between what you wanted to do and what you felt you should do? Or when your logical mind said one thing but your gut feeling said something completely different?

Across psychology, spirituality, and modern therapy, there's a growing recognition that our minds aren't just one unified voice—they're more like a team with different players, each wanting different things.

Freud was one of the first to officially map this out. He described our minds as having a reactive, body-driven side (the Id), a rational side (the Ego), and a moral side (the Superego), all pulling in different directions. Jung built on this by showing that the key to happiness is letting these different sides work together—integrating our conscious self, our hidden feelings, and even the deeper patterns we all share as humans (what he called the collective unconscious) to create a sense of real wholeness.[60]

In my book, *Five Reasons Why Bad Things Happen: How to Turn Tragedies Into Triumph*, I use the term Inner Self for the Body/Subconscious, Outer Self for the Mind/Conscious, and Higher Self for the Soul/Superconscious. For consistency with my earlier work, I will use these terms through this book. Whichever term you prefer, the Three Selves approach in this book draws on these ideas, helping those inner voices cooperate so wishes can become reality.

Brain science backs this up. Studies show that different parts of your brain can literally be in conflict with each other—one part saying "go for it!" while another screams "danger!"[61] This explains experiences most people recognize: feeling torn between different desires, experiencing internal resistance to things you consciously want, or sensing wisdom that seems to come from somewhere beyond your everyday thinking.

The Three Selves Framework: Based on extensive cross-cultural analysis, we can understand human consciousness as having three primary aspects:

The Inner Self (Subconscious/Body/Emotional Self)
The Outer Self (Conscious/Mind/Thinking Self)
The Higher Self (Superconscious/Spirit/Wisdom Self)

Each aspect has distinct characteristics, needs, fears, and ways of creating or responding to wishes. Understanding their unique perspectives is crucial for creating internal alignment and avoiding the self-sabotage that derails many well-intentioned desires.

The Inner Self: Your Subconscious Emotional Body[62]

Your Inner Self is the part of you that feels, reacts, remembers, and keeps you alive through automatic functions. This is your emotional, physical, "body" self—and it has enormous power to either support or sabotage your conscious wishes.

In Freudian terms, the Inner Self is like the Id—that reservoir of instinctual drives and unprocessed emotion. Freud recognized that wishes often emerge first from subconscious desire, not rational intention, and that unacknowledged drives can shape or distort those wishes in surprising ways.

Here's an example of your Inner Self in action: Imagine you wish for a big promotion at work. Your Outer Self (conscious mind) is excited about the opportunity and the salary increase. But every time you think about applying, you get a headache. Or you "forget" to submit your application. Or you suddenly feel exhausted.

What's happening? Your Inner Self remembers the last time you took on more responsibility—you barely slept for months, your back hurt constantly, you snapped at your kids. So your body is trying to protect you by creating resistance. Your Inner Self isn't being difficult—it's trying to keep you safe based on past experience.

Spoiler alert: One of the *Five Reasons Why Bad Things Happen* is Subconscious Sabotage, which is why understanding this crucial aspect of ourselves is so important!

Key Characteristics:

Emotions Come First: Your Inner Self operates through feelings and physical sensations rather than logic. Scientists studying emotional decision-making have discovered that feelings often drive our choices before our rational mind even gets involved.[63] When you wish for something, your Inner Self immediately responds with emotional associations based on what happened before.

It Doesn't Understand Time: Here's something fascinating: your subconscious mind has trouble distinguishing between past, present, and future. Your Inner Self often responds to potential futures as if they were immediate present threats or opportunities. This explains why wishes can trigger anxiety about outcomes that haven't even happened yet. You're essentially time-traveling emotionally—and your body is reacting to imagined futures as if they're happening now.

It Never Forgets: Your Inner Self stores emotional memories and learned patterns from past experiences. Research on implicit memory shows that subconscious emotional responses can be triggered by situations that remind your Inner Self of previous experiences—even when your conscious mind doesn't make the connection.[64] This is why you might feel inexplicably anxious or resistant to something that seems perfectly reasonable on the surface.

It Speaks Through Your Body: Research increasingly demonstrates the connection between emotional states and physical health.[65] Your Inner Self expresses its responses to your wishes through bodily sensations, energy levels, sleep patterns, and even immune function. When aligned with your wishes, you may feel energized and healthy. When resistant, you may experience fatigue, tension, or illness. Your body is always telling you something—the question is whether you're listening.

It Picks Up What Others Feel: Studies suggest that emotional contagion and interpersonal sensitivity operate largely through subconscious channels.[66] Your Inner Self can pick up on the emotional states and intentions of others, influencing your responses to social situations in ways your conscious mind doesn't understand. Ever walked into a room and immediately felt the tension, even though no one said anything? That's your Inner Self at work.

It Craves Joy and Play: Your Inner Self isn't just trying to avoid pain— it's actively seeking pleasure, fun, and enjoyment. Research on motivation shows that the brain's reward system releases dopamine not just when we achieve goals, but when we're engaged in playful, enjoyable activities.[67]
This is why wishes that feel heavy and serious often fizzle out, while wishes that incorporate elements of fun, creativity, and play gain momentum. Your Inner Self gives you energy for things that feel good, and withdraws energy from things that feel like drudgery—even if your Outer Self thinks they're "good for you."

The Outer Self: Your Conscious Thinking Mind

Your Outer Self is the part that plans, analyzes, makes decisions, and typically initiates the wishing process. This is your rational, conscious, strategic self—the "you" that's reading these words right now and thinking about what they mean.

Here's your Outer Self in action:

You make a pro/con list about moving to a new city. You research neighborhoods, calculate budgets, compare job opportunities. You set goals and create timelines. You tell friends, "I've decided to move by summer." This is your Outer Self doing what it does best—being logical, practical, and planning-focused.

However, sometimes your Outer Self can get stuck in analysis paralysis, overthinking every detail until the wish loses its magic and momentum. Or it can become a "bully" to the subconscious Inner Self, leading to tricky sabotage.

Key Characteristics:

Logic Is Its Superpower: Your Outer Self excels at rational thinking, problem-solving, and strategic planning. Research on executive function shows that this aspect can evaluate options, consider consequences, and make decisions based on available information.[68] When you wish for something, your Outer Self typically starts the process by recognizing the gap between where you are and where you want to be.

It's Goal-Obsessed: Studies of conscious intention show that your Outer Self naturally organizes experience around goals and outcomes.[69] This aspect excels at breaking down large wishes into smaller steps, creating timelines, and maintaining focus on desired results. It's the part of you that loves checking boxes and tracking progress.

It Can Only Focus on So Much: Unlike your Inner Self's broad awareness, your Outer Self has limited bandwidth. Conscious awareness operates like a spotlight—it can only illuminate a few things at once while everything else fades into the background. This is why you can become so focused on one wish that you completely miss other important things happening around you.

It Cares What People Think: Your Outer Self maintains your sense of social identity and manages how you present yourself to the world. This aspect considers how wishes might affect your reputation, relationships, and social standing. It's the part that asks, "What will people think if I do this?"

Willpower Is Limited: Studies of self-regulation show that your Outer Self manages impulse control and maintains commitment to long-term goals.[70] However—and this is important—research also reveals that willpower operates like a muscle that can become fatigued. This explains why maintaining focus on wishes can be challenging over extended periods. You literally run out of mental energy.

The Higher Self: Your Superconscious Wisdom

Before dismissing the Higher Self as purely metaphysical, consider this: Some researchers in consciousness studies, quantum neuroscience, and theoretical physics describe what we're calling the Higher Self as nonlocal consciousness—the hypothesis that awareness is not produced by the brain alone but may be part of an interconnected field that operates beyond space and time.[71] Neuroscientists point to the default mode network, a system associated with self-awareness, imagination, and internal reflection that becomes active during states of insight and creative flow. While science frames this as interaction within a wider informational field, many people experience it as guidance—a sense of insight, coincidence, or timing that feels mysteriously supportive, as though intelligence beyond conscious awareness were helping direct the path. Such moments need not be considered supernatural; they can also be understood as the subtle ways consciousness communicates across its deeper, interconnected layers. (We'll explore these quantum and consciousness theories in much greater depth in Chapter 14: Wishing on the Frontier.) Whether you understand your Higher Self as quantum field interactions, collective consciousness, spiritual connection, or simply untapped dimensions of your own awareness, this aspect of your being operates beyond the boundaries of everyday thinking.

Your Higher Self is the transpersonal, intuitive, wisdom aspect of your being. This is the part that connects you to inspiration, spiritual guidance, and perspectives beyond ordinary thinking. It's that quiet voice that whispers "there's something more here" when you're about to settle for less than you deserve.

Jung saw the Self (with a capital S) as the part of us that brings together everything we are—both what we know about ourselves and what's hidden below the surface. This Self helps us move toward feeling whole and finding meaning in our lives. In this book, what we call the Higher Self is very similar to Jung's idea: it's the deep, wise center that guides us to connect our thoughts, feelings, and intuition.

Jung also explained that becoming our best selves—what he called individuation—means facing all parts of who we are. This includes our everyday personality, our hidden feelings (the shadow), and even the deeper patterns shared by all humanity (the collective unconscious). When these sides work together, our wishes become more powerful and alive.[72]

Here's your Higher Self in action:

You're about to accept a job offer that looks perfect on paper—great salary, impressive title, all the benefits. But something feels off. You can't explain it logically. Your Outer Self says "This is exactly what you said you wanted!" But your Higher Self whispers, "Wait. This isn't it."

Three weeks later, a completely unexpected opportunity appears that you couldn't have planned for—one that aligns with your deeper purpose in ways the first job never could. That's your Higher Self at work, seeing patterns and possibilities your conscious mind can't detect.

Key Characteristics:

It Sees the Bigger Picture: Your Higher Self operates from a broader perspective that extends beyond immediate personal concerns. Research on self-transcendent experiences shows that accessing this aspect of consciousness is associated with increased creativity, enhanced well-being, and a greater sense of meaning and purpose.[73] It's the part of you that can step back from the drama of daily life and see the larger patterns at play.

It Knows Things You Don't Know You Know: Studies of intuition suggest that your Higher Self processes information through pattern recognition and holistic understanding rather than linear analysis.[74] This aspect often provides insights that seem to come from beyond ordinary thinking—offering solutions your Outer Self couldn't generate through logic alone. You might call these insights, gut feelings, or simply "knowing."

Creativity Flows From Here: Research on creativity reveals that innovative ideas often emerge during states of relaxed awareness when conscious control is reduced.[75] Your Higher Self appears to be the source of creative insights and artistic inspiration that feel like gifts rather than personal achievements. Musicians, writers, and artists often describe their best work as "coming through them" rather than "from them."

It's Your Moral Compass: Studies indicate that moral reasoning involves brain networks associated with empathy, compassion, and concern for others' welfare.[76] Your Higher Self often generates wishes that serve not only personal well-being but also contribute to family, community, or global flourishing. It's the part of you that asks, "How does this serve the greater good?"

Wisdom Lives Here: Research on compassion and wisdom shows that these qualities are associated with specific neural networks and can be cultivated through practice. Your Higher Self naturally generates wishes that integrate your personal well-being with concern for others and alignment with ethical principles. It doesn't just ask "What do I want?" but "What serves the highest good for everyone involved?"

Understanding Instinct and Intuition: Which Self Is Speaking?

The words "instinct" and "intuition" are often used interchangeably, but neuroscience reveals they're actually three distinct phenomena arising from different aspects of consciousness—and knowing which Self is speaking can dramatically change how you respond.

Inner Self Instincts are your body's automatic protective responses based on past emotional experiences. When your stomach tightens at the thought of a promotion or you get a headache before a difficult conversation, that's your Inner Self speaking through the enteric nervous system—your body's "second brain" with over 100 million neurons. Your Inner Self stores "interoceptive memories" that trigger rapid, subconscious reactions designed to keep you safe, which is why you might feel inexplicably anxious in situations that remind your body of previous pain.

These instincts are reactive, rooted in protection, and often confuse past threats with present possibilities.

Outer Self Intuition operates through rapid pattern recognition in the prefrontal cortex, processing vast amounts of stored experience beneath conscious awareness. This is the "informed gut feeling" that emerges when your brain recognizes patterns it can't yet articulate—like a firefighter sensing danger before consciously identifying why. Research shows this cognitive intuition improves with experience; your brain becomes increasingly efficient at matching current situations against past experiences, which explains why experts often make better "gut decisions" than novices.

Higher Self Knowing is qualitatively different from both body-based instinct and cognitive intuition. This transpersonal wisdom arises when you access expanded states of consciousness—the sudden certainty that comes not from analysis or emotional reaction, but from a deeper source. It's the inexplicable knowing that arrives during meditation or creative flow states when the prefrontal cortex quiets. Unlike Inner Self instincts that create contraction and anxiety, Higher Self knowing typically feels expansive, calm, and certain—guiding you toward future alignment with your deepest purpose.

Integration and Alignment: When the Selves Work Together

The most effective wishes emerge when all three aspects of yourself are aligned and working together toward the same outcome. Research on internal coherence shows that when different aspects of personality are integrated rather than conflicted, people experience increased motivation, enhanced creativity, and greater success in achieving goals.[77]

Think of it this way:

Aligned wish: "I want to write a book" (Outer Self recognizes the goal) + "I feel energized and excited when I think about it" (Inner Self is on board) + "This serves my purpose and will help others" (Higher Self approves) = Powerful forward momentum

Misaligned wish: "I should write a book" (Outer Self thinks it's a good career move) + "I feel exhausted and anxious when I sit down to write" (Inner Self is resisting) + "I'm not sure why I'm really doing this" (Higher Self isn't engaged) = Struggle, procrastination, and eventual abandonment.

Fun-infused wish: "I want to learn Italian" (Outer Self sets the goal) + "I feel excited and playful when I practice—I'm watching Italian cooking shows and singing along to Italian songs!" (Inner Self is having fun) + "This connects me to my heritage and opens doors to deeper connections" (Higher Self sees the meaning) = Joyful, sustainable progress.

Notice the difference? When your Inner Self is having fun, wishes don't feel like work—they feel like play. And your subconscious will give you endless energy for play.

Think of it this way: Have you ever seen a neighbor walking a dog and the dog runs off? What does the neighbor usually do? They yell at the dog to come back. But that doesn't work. Instead, what does work is to get all excited and point in a different direction, and say, "Look, it's fun over here!" and the dog will happily go along.

Your Inner Self works the same way!

Freud believed a lot of our struggles come from inner battles—when hidden desires and conscious goals push against each other in our minds, making us feel stuck or divided. Jung, on the other hand, thought the path to healing is about bringing all parts of ourselves together and finding harmony, not just trying to control or fight against our inner feelings. Today, brain science supports this idea: real well-being comes from different parts of our minds—emotions, logic, and intuition—working together and communicating, not from one part trying to dominate the others.[78]

Identifying and Resolving Internal Conflicts

Many wishes fail because different aspects of yourself are working at cross-purposes. Learning to identify and resolve these internal conflicts is essential for effective wishing.

Common Sources of Internal Conflict:

Safety Concerns: Your Inner Self may resist wishes that feel threatening to security, comfort, or survival. Even positive changes can trigger subconscious fear if they involve uncertainty or risk. Research on change and adaptation shows that the nervous system often interprets novelty as potential threat, creating resistance even to desired outcomes.[79]

Example: You wish to start your own business, but every time you work on your business plan, you feel nauseous. Your Inner Self is saying, "But what if we can't pay the mortgage? Remember how scared we were when Dad lost his job?"

Identity Conflicts: Your Outer Self may resist wishes that conflict with your current self-image or social identity. Wishes for dramatic change can trigger identity confusion if they require becoming someone different. Studies of identity and behavior change show that lasting transformation requires updating your self-concept to align with desired changes.[80]

Example: You wish to become a public speaker, but you've always identified as "the quiet one." Your Outer Self asks, "If I'm not the quiet one anymore, who am I? Will my friends still like me?"

Value Misalignment: Your Higher Self may resist wishes that conflict with deeper values or spiritual principles. Research on values and motivation shows that goals aligned with intrinsic values create more satisfaction than those focused on external rewards.[81]

Example: You wish for a high-paying corporate job, but your Higher Self knows your deepest value is helping others. The money looks good on paper, but something feels hollow.

Past Trauma and Conditioning: Your Inner Self may resist wishes that remind it of previous disappointments or painful experiences. Research on trauma and healing shows that unresolved emotional wounds can significantly impact motivation and behavior patterns.[82]

Example: You wish for a romantic relationship, but your Inner Self remembers the devastating heartbreak from five years ago and keeps sabotaging potential connections to avoid that pain again.

Cosmic Collaboration and Metaphysics

Remember from Chapter 1 that Cosmic Collaboration is what happens in the sweet spot—where your intentions, actions, and energy meet opportunities, synchronicities, and responses from the wider universe. It's where what you CAN control works together with what you CAN'T control.

By now, you've learned how to expand your circle of control through understanding your Three Selves. You can align your Inner Self (emotions/body), Outer Self (conscious mind), and Higher Self (superconscious wisdom) to work together rather than at cross-purposes.

This internal alignment is a huge part of what you bring to the collaborative process.

But what about the OTHER side of the collaboration? What is that larger force or field you're collaborating WITH?

Let's step into the realm of metaphysics for a moment—not as abstract philosophy, but as a practical exploration of the mysterious forces that might be at play in your wishing process.

Throughout history, countless traditions have described a "web of life," a deeper order, or subtle forces at play behind the surface of everyday events. Some call it universal mind, collective superconscious, divine matrix, or simply "Upstairs." Metaphysics is the exploration of these ideas—asking questions about meaning, purpose, energy, and the invisible patterns linking us to each other and the world.

Modern science gives us powerful ways to understand the brain, the body, and behavior. But what if there's more to reality than what we can measure or touch? What if consciousness isn't just locked inside our heads but is part of a greater field that we all participate in? What if our deepest wishes don't just reflect our needs, but also help shape a reality that's always listening and responding in its own mysterious way?

Cosmic collaboration is about tapping into this wider field—where every thought, every intention, and every heartfelt hope sends ripples into the unseen fabric of existence. When we wish with this in mind, wishing isn't just personal or private: it's an act of participating in the creative, responsive universe.

Consider your own wish: what might shift if you saw it not just as a personal hope, but as a pulse of energy you send outward—a message the universe is capable of hearing and, perhaps, responding to in unexpected and mysterious ways?

In fiction, these ideas are often brought to life through symbolism, spirit guides, or miraculous interventions. But even outside of stories, we all know what it feels like to experience a meaningful coincidence, sudden inspiration, or help arriving at just the right moment. Whether these are signs, synchronicities, or simply reflections of our own hope, the metaphysical frame gives us permission to explore the possibility that reality is collaborative, creative, and alive.

Bridge to Fiction: Deus ex Machina

Writers are often cautioned about a plot device called Deus ex machina, a plot device where a seemingly unsolvable problem is unexpectedly and abruptly resolved by an unlikely or contrived event, character, or object. The term, which literally translates to "god from a machine," originated in ancient Greek theater. From an audience's perspective, it feels like the writer is cheating, offering a simple solution to the hero's problem. However, as you're learning throughout this book, in real life this "save the day" solution from "Upstairs" is often the result of integrated alignment with your Three Selves and your connection to an energy "out there."

From Understanding to Activation

Understanding the Three Selves framework is essential groundwork, but knowledge alone doesn't create alignment. The practical work of integrating these aspects of yourself—learning to recognize which Self is speaking, facilitating internal dialogue, and creating coherence among your Inner, Outer, and Higher Selves—requires dedicated practice and specific techniques.

The final chapters of this book provide comprehensive activation practices for working with your Three Selves at multiple levels. The Cosmic Wish Experiment demonstrates how to apply these principles in group settings, teams, and communities.

For now, simply becoming aware of your own internal multiplicity—noticing when different aspects of yourself are in harmony or conflict—is the crucial first step.

Meet the Scientists

The researchers whose work illuminates the Three Selves:

Sigmund Freud — Psychoanalysis and the structural model (Id, Ego, Superego)

Carl Jung — Collective unconscious, archetypes, and the integrating Self

Richard Schwartz — Internal Family Systems (IFS) therapy

Antonio Damasio — Neuroscience of emotion and bodily awareness in consciousness

Bessel van der Kolk — Trauma's effects on body, brain, and mind

(Full biographies in Appendix B)

Questions to Ponder

Reflect on your wish in light of the Three Selves:

- **Which aspect of yourself initiated your wish?** Was it your Inner Self's emotional desire, your Outer Self's rational recognition of a need, or your Higher Self's intuitive knowing?
- **How does each Self respond to your wish?** When you imagine your wish coming true, notice what your body feels (Inner Self), what your mind thinks (Outer Self), and what your spirit senses (Higher Self).
- **Where might internal conflicts exist?** Are there ways your wish might threaten your sense of safety, identity, or values?
- **What would alignment feel like?** Imagine all three aspects of yourself working together toward your wish. What would change in your experience?
- **What does each Self need?** Consider what would help your Inner Self feel safe, your Outer Self feel confident, and your Higher Self feel purposeful about your wish.
- **Have you ever experienced a "Deus ex machina" or Divine Intervention in real life?** How did it feel? Who or what intervened, and why?

Next: Motivation - What Drives Your Wishes Forward?

Understanding the Three Selves naturally leads to our next exploration: What truly motivates you to pursue your desires? In Chapter 7, we'll examine the complex landscape of human motivation, exploring not just what you want but also what you want to avoid, and the crucial distinction between surface desires and deeper needs. As we'll discover, motivation is far more nuanced than simply "wanting something"—and understanding these nuances is essential for sustaining the energy needed to bring wishes into reality.

Chapter 7: Motivation - What Drives Your Wishes Forward?

Now that you understand the different aspects of yourself that participate in wishing, a crucial question emerges: What truly motivates you to pursue your desires? That wish you made at the beginning of our journey—what would drive you to keep thinking about it, perhaps turning it into a goal and working toward it? And what might make you forget about it entirely?

Understanding motivation is essential because wishes without sustained motivation remain fantasies. You can have perfect clarity about what you want and complete internal alignment, but without authentic, sustainable motivation, even the most beautiful wishes will eventually fade into distant memories.

As we'll discover, motivation is far more nuanced than simply "wanting something." Drawing from frameworks used in storytelling and psychology, we'll explore how both what you want AND what you want to avoid create powerful motivational forces. We'll also examine the crucial distinction between what you think you want versus what you actually need—a difference that can make or break the effectiveness of your wishes. This exploration takes us into practical frameworks for understanding motivation, the neuroscience of desire and avoidance, and the profound relationship between surface desires and deeper needs.

94

The Motivation Matrix: Understanding the Four Drivers

One of the most practical frameworks for understanding motivation comes from recognizing that we're motivated not just by what we want,

	Want	Don't Want
Have		
	Nurture	Eliminate
Don't Have		
	Cultivate	Avoid

© DrawSuccess

but by four distinct categories that create a comprehensive picture of what drives human behavior. This Motivation Matrix, a concept I invented and copyrighted in my DrawSuccess program,[83] and highlighted in *The Hero's Playbook* and *Cosmic Wish Playbook*, is a simple tool to help identify the things to nurture, cultivate, eliminate, and avoid.

The Four Quadrants of Motivation:

Quadrant 1: Want + Have (Things to Nurture) The first quadrant involves things you want that you already have, at least to some degree. Your motivation here focuses on maintaining, protecting, or enhancing these positive aspects of your life. Research shows that gratitude and appreciation for existing blessings actually enhances motivation to attract more of the same.[84]

Examples for wishing:

- Wanting to deepen an already good relationship
- Seeking to expand a successful business or career you enjoy
- Desiring to enhance health when you're already reasonably healthy
- Wishing to grow spiritual practices you've already begun

Studies indicate that wishes built on existing foundations often succeed more readily because they don't require dramatic life changes that might trigger resistance.[85] Your motivation remains strong because you're already experiencing some satisfaction in these areas.

Quadrant 2: Want + Don't Have (Things to Cultivate) This quadrant represents the classic "goal-setting" space—things you want but don't currently have. This is where most people focus their wishing energy, and it can be powerfully motivating when approached skillfully. Research on approach motivation shows that moving toward desired outcomes activates reward systems in the brain and enhances both creativity and persistence.[86]

Examples for wishing:

- Wanting a romantic relationship when you're single
- Seeking financial abundance when struggling economically
- Desiring creative fulfillment when feeling stuck in unfulfilling work
- Wishing for healing when dealing with illness

However, studies also show that motivation in this quadrant can become problematic when it creates feelings of lack, desperation, or unworthiness.[87] The key is maintaining hope and excitement while avoiding attachment to specific timelines or methods.

Quadrant 3: Don't Want + Have (Things to Eliminate) This quadrant involves things you don't want that you currently have—patterns, circumstances, or experiences you'd like to eliminate or transform. Research on avoidance motivation reveals that moving away from unwanted situations can be powerfully motivating, though it requires careful handling to avoid creating more of what you're trying to escape.[88]

Examples for wishing:

- Wanting to end a toxic relationship you're currently in
- Seeking to eliminate debt or financial stress
- Desiring to overcome anxiety, depression, or limiting habits
- Wishing to transform work situations that drain your energy

Studies show that wishes focused on eliminating negatives work best when combined with positive visions of what you want instead.[89] Pure avoidance motivation often creates internal conflict and can inadvertently reinforce the very patterns you're trying to change.

Quadrant 4: Don't Want + Don't Have (Things to Avoid) This sneaky little quadrant represents things you don't want and don't currently have—and it's crucial for smart wishing. Research shows that acknowledging potential costs and concerns is essential for sustainable motivation.[90]

Here's why this matters: Sometimes what you're wishing FOR comes packaged with something you DON'T want. Being aware of these hidden trade-offs helps you wish more strategically—you can either prepare for them, find ways to minimize them, or build them into your wish from the start.

For example:

- Wishing for a high-powered job... but realizing it comes with stress you don't want
- Wishing for a committed relationship... but not wanting to give up your freedom
- Wishing for financial success... but not wanting the long hours away from family
- Wishing for fame... but not wanting the loss of privacy

The key is to identify these potential "don't wants" BEFORE you make your wish, so you can either accept them as part of the package or get creative about how to have what you want WITHOUT what you don't want.

The Neuroscience of Approach and Avoidance Motivation

We'll get more into Wishing and the Brain in the next chapter. Here, let's look at the connections between neuroscience and motivation and how "approach" motivation (moving toward desired outcomes) and "avoidance" motivation (moving away from unwanted circumstances) involve different brain systems with distinct characteristics and optimal applications.

Approach Motivation: The Brain's Reward Systems

Research on dopamine and reward prediction shows that approach motivation activates the brain's pleasure and learning centers, creating sustained energy for pursuing positive goals.[91] Studies indicate that when you focus on what you want rather than what you want to avoid, your brain literally becomes more creative, optimistic, and solution-focused.[92]

Effective Approach Motivation:

- Creates expansion, creativity, and openness to possibilities
- Enhances pattern recognition and opportunity awareness
- Builds energy and enthusiasm over time
- Supports long-term behavior change and growth
- Activates social connection and collaboration systems

Avoidance Motivation: The Brain's Protection Systems

Research on threat detection and stress response shows that avoidance motivation activates the brain's security and survival systems, creating focus and urgency but also potential tunnel vision.[93] What that means is that when we try to get away from something we don't want it might help us focus, but because it can increase stress, anxiety, and limited thinking it can make it difficult to see new solutions.

Characteristics of Avoidance Motivation:

- Creates focus, urgency, and immediate action
- Narrows attention to threats and problems
- Can generate stress and anxiety if sustained
- Effective for short-term behavior change
- May limit creativity and long-term vision

Optimal Integration: Using Both Systems Skillfully

Research shows that acknowledging what you want to avoid or change while focusing primary attention on what you want to create provides optimal motivational balance. The best way to stay motivated is to balance reaching for something good with avoiding what's bad.[94]

This is why the Motivation Matrix is so powerful for wishing—it helps you understand all four motivational drivers and use them consciously rather than being subconsciously driven by unexamined fears or desires.

Intrinsic vs. Extrinsic Motivation: The Foundation of Sustainable Wishing

One of the most important distinctions in motivation research involves the difference between intrinsic motivation (driven by internal satisfaction and fulfillment) and extrinsic motivation (driven by external rewards or consequences). Understanding this difference is crucial for creating wishes that maintain motivation over time.

Daniel Pink's research, synthesized in his book *Drive*, identifies autonomy, mastery, and purpose as the three key drivers of lasting motivation. Drawing from four decades of psychological studies, Pink demonstrates that when people's wishes and goals align with their inner sense of choice, growth, and meaningful contribution, their performance, creativity, and fulfillment skyrocket. Pink's AMP framework now serves as the benchmark in motivational science, affirming that authentic wishing is rooted in deep personal values and intrinsic reward.[95]

Intrinsic Motivation: The Engine of Sustainable Wishing

Research consistently shows that intrinsic motivation—engagement driven by inherent satisfaction, personal growth, and alignment with values—creates more sustainable behavior change and greater life satisfaction than extrinsic motivation.[96]

Self-Determination Theory identifies basic psychological needs that support intrinsic motivation.[97]

Autonomy: Feeling that your choices and actions arise from your own values and interests rather than external pressure or coercion. Wishes that honor your authentic preferences and align with your genuine interests maintain motivation more easily than those driven by "shoulds" or social expectations.

Competence: Experiencing yourself as capable of achieving desired outcomes through effort and skill development. Wishes that involve developing mastery, learning new abilities, or building on existing strengths often generate sustained motivation because they enhance your sense of effectiveness.

Relatedness: Feeling connected to others and contributing to relationships or communities that matter to you. Wishes that involve building connections, serving others, or contributing to causes larger than personal gain often maintain motivation because they fulfill fundamental needs for belonging and contribution.

The Courage to Wish: Brené Brown's research on vulnerability reveals an essential truth about intrinsic motivation: pursuing what you genuinely want requires courage. As Brown shows, daring to wish for something meaningful means stepping into uncertainty, risking disappointment, and embracing hope anyway. The act of wishing from authentic desire—rather than from external pressure or "shoulds"—makes us emotionally vulnerable. But this vulnerability isn't weakness; it's the birthplace of genuine motivation. When you wish from this place of courageous authenticity, you're tapping into the most sustainable form of motivation available. [98]

Enjoyment: Experiencing pleasure, fun, and positive emotion in the process itself. This is perhaps the most underappreciated driver of sustainable motivation. Research shows that activities we genuinely enjoy release dopamine and create self-sustaining motivation loops.[99] When wishes incorporate elements of play, creativity, and genuine enjoyment, they maintain momentum naturally—your Inner Self keeps giving you energy because the process itself feels rewarding.

This is why people can spend hours on hobbies they love without feeling drained, while forcing yourself to do something "good for you" that you hate eventually leads to burnout. If your wish doesn't have ANY element of fun or enjoyment built into it, your Inner Self will eventually sabotage it—no matter how "important" your Outer Self thinks it is.

Here's the beautiful secret about wishing: it's SUPPOSED to be fun. That's what makes it different from goals or obligations. Remember blowing out birthday candles as a child? Tossing coins in fountains? Those weren't grim tasks—they were delightful rituals filled with hope and playfulness. That childlike quality isn't frivolous—it's what makes wishing powerful. When you infuse your wishes with genuine joy and playfulness, you're not being silly—you're activating the most potent motivational force in the human brain.

Studies show that when wishes satisfy these needs—autonomy, competence, relatedness, and enjoyment—they tend to maintain motivation even through difficulties and setbacks.[100] Conversely, wishes driven primarily by external pressures often lose motivational power over time.

The Power of Purpose and Meaning

Research consistently shows that wishes connected to larger purposes and meaningful goals maintain motivation more effectively than those focused solely on personal gain or pleasure. Studies indicate that individuals who maintain strong sense of purpose live longer, healthier lives with greater life satisfaction.[101]

Viktor Frankl's research with Holocaust survivors revealed that humans can endure almost any suffering if they can find meaning in it. His work showed that people who maintained sense of purpose demonstrated greater resilience, better health outcomes, and stronger motivation to survive and thrive even in extreme circumstances.[102]

The Joy Factor: Why Fun Isn't Frivolous

There's a common misconception that if something is important, it should feel serious. That if you're really committed to a wish, you should be willing to suffer for it. But neuroscience reveals something different: sustainable motivation requires positive emotional energy, and joy is one of the most powerful forms of that energy.

When you're genuinely enjoying yourself—when the process feels playful, creative, and fun—your brain releases a cocktail of neurochemicals (dopamine, endorphins, oxytocin) that create what researchers call "intrinsic flow motivation"—energy that feels effortless and joyful rather than forced and depleting.[103]

This is why hobbies feel energizing while obligations feel draining, even if the hobby requires more effort. It's not about easy versus hard—it's about joy versus joylessness.

The Wishing Advantage: Here's what makes wishing special compared to goals or resolutions: wishing is inherently playful. The very act of wishing carries that childlike quality of hope, imagination, and possibility. Birthday candles, shooting stars, dandelion seeds, fountain coins—these rituals weren't designed to be grim exercises in discipline. They were (and are) meant to be delightful. (Get it? De-light-ful? Corny, I know. But I couldn't resist.)

When you strip the fun out of wishing and turn it into another obligation, another "should," another task to accomplish, you lose the magic that makes wishing powerful. Your Inner Self withdraws its support, and suddenly that wish feels like pushing a boulder uphill.

The solution? Build fun INTO your wish. Not as a reward for later, but as an essential ingredient NOW. If your wish to "get healthy" only involves punishing workouts you hate, find a form of movement that genuinely makes you smile. If your wish to "advance your career" feels like slogging through drudgery, find the aspects of your work that spark genuine curiosity and joy. If your wish to "be more creative" feels like forcing yourself through exercises, give yourself permission to play.

Here's the key: your Inner Self controls the energy you need, and it reserves that energy for experiences that feel genuinely rewarding. Build joy into your wish, and motivation becomes self-sustaining. Strip away the fun and treat it like another duty, and you'll face constant internal resistance.

Wants vs. Needs: The Storytelling Bridge to Deeper Understanding

One of the most profound insights from storytelling tradition involves the distinction between what characters want (surface desires) and what they need (deeper requirements for growth and fulfillment). This framework provides crucial insights for understanding and refining your own wishes.

Understanding the Want vs. Need Dynamic

In every compelling story, the protagonist begins by wanting something specific—often external and concrete. But as the story unfolds, we discover that what they really need is something deeper—usually internal growth, healing, or wisdom that would actually fulfill them. Research in psychology supports this narrative insight: surface desires often point toward deeper unmet needs.[104]

Examples of Want vs. Need in Stories:

- Luke Skywalker wanted to leave his farm and have adventures; he needed to find his purpose and become who he was meant to be
- In *A Love Story to the Universe*, the protagonist wanted success and recognition; she needed to learn she was already worthy of love
- Elizabeth Bennet wanted to avoid marriage; she needed to overcome prejudice and open her heart to genuine connection
- Elle Woods wanted to get married to her college sweetheart when she really needed to find her own voice.

Surface Want Examples and Potential Deeper Needs:

- Wanting a million dollars → Needing security, freedom, or ability to contribute meaningfully
- Wanting a romantic relationship → Needing to feel worthy of love or to heal capacity for intimacy
- Wanting career success → Needing to express authentic talents or make meaningful contribution
- Wanting others' approval → Needing to develop self-worth or authentic self-expression
- Wanting perfect health → Needing to feel safe in your body or free to pursue your purpose

Questions for Exploring Your Deeper Needs:

- If you received exactly what you're wishing for, what would that give you that you don't have now?

- What feelings or experiences are you really seeking through this wish?
- What deeper fears or concerns might this wish be addressing?
- How might receiving this wish serve not just you but others as well?
- What would you need to believe about yourself or life for this wish to feel less urgent?

Studies show that wishes aligned with deeper needs rather than surface wants tend to be more fulfilling when achieved and often manifest through unexpected but ultimately more satisfying pathways.[105]

Drawing from *A Love Story to the Universe* and other stories, we can see how the want vs. need dynamic plays out in character development and provides insights for our own wishing practices. In the novel, the protagonist's surface desire for professional success masked deeper needs for self-worth and authentic love. Only when she understood and addressed these deeper needs could she find genuine fulfillment.

This pattern appears consistently in compelling stories because it reflects a fundamental truth about human psychology: our conscious desires often point toward subconscious needs that require healing, growth, or wisdom for true satisfaction. Understanding this dynamic helps us approach our wishes with greater sophistication and effectiveness.[106]

Fear, Desire, and Misbelief: Hidden Motivational Forces

Effective wishing requires understanding not just what motivates you but also what might be subconsciously undermining your motivation. Three key factors—fear, desire, and misbelief—often operate beneath conscious awareness to either support or sabotage your wishes.

The Role of Fear in Motivation

Fear can be either a powerful motivational force or an imposing barrier, depending on how it's understood and managed. Research shows that moderate levels of concern can enhance motivation and performance, while overwhelming fear tends to shut down creativity and problem-solving abilities.[107]

Productive Fear: Concerns that motivate positive action

- Fear of Missing Out (FOMO)
- Fear of regret motivating you to pursue meaningful goals
- Fear of wasting your talents driving creative expression
- Fear of letting loved ones down enhancing commitment to growth
- Fear of missing opportunities encouraging openness to change

Destructive Fear: Concerns that paralyze or create resistance

- Fear of failure preventing you from trying
- Fear of success creating self-sabotage when progress occurs
- Fear of judgment limiting authentic self-expression
- Fear of change maintaining unsatisfying status quo

The Nature of Authentic Desire

Research on motivation distinguishes between authentic desires (arising from genuine values and interests) and conditioned desires (programmed by social expectations, past experiences, or subconscious patterns). Studies show that wishes based on authentic desires maintain motivation more effectively and create greater satisfaction when achieved.[108]

Identifying Authentic vs. Conditioned Desires:

- Authentic desires energize and inspire you when you think about them
- Conditioned desires feel heavy, obligatory, or anxiety-provoking
- Authentic desires align with your values and natural interests
- Conditioned desires serve others' expectations or past programming
- Authentic desires enhance your sense of aliveness and purpose
- Conditioned desires often involve comparison or competition with others

Understanding and Transforming Misbeliefs

Misbeliefs—subconscious assumptions about yourself, others, or how life works—often undermine motivation by creating internal conflict or resistance. Using a simple assessment to determine enneagrams, whether your own, that of others, or a character you might be writing about, can provide some valuable insight into misbeliefs.[109]

Research on cognitive therapy shows that identifying and transforming limiting beliefs can dramatically improve motivation and achievement.[110]

Common Misbeliefs That Undermine Wishing:

- "I'm not worthy of good things happening to me"
- "If I succeed, others will judge or reject me"
- "Getting what I want requires sacrificing what I value"
- "I can only be loved/accepted if I'm perfect/successful/helpful"
- "The universe is random and my wishes don't matter"
- "If I hope for something, I'll just be disappointed"

Transforming Misbeliefs Through Awareness and Evidence:

Studies show that misbeliefs change most effectively through a combination of conscious awareness and experiential evidence that contradicts limiting assumptions.[111] This process often involves:

- Identifying specific beliefs that create resistance to your wishes
- Examining evidence that supports and contradicts these beliefs
- Experimenting with acting as if more empowering beliefs were true
- Gradually building new patterns of thinking and behavior based on experience

Research on self-sabotage reveals that subconscious limiting beliefs are one of the primary reasons why people fail to achieve goals they consciously desire.[112]

Sustaining Motivation Over Time: Working with Natural Cycles

Research reveals that motivation naturally fluctuates, and understanding these cycles is crucial for sustaining long-term commitment to meaningful wishes.

Why Initial Enthusiasm Fades

Studies of behavior change reveal predictable patterns in how motivation changes over time. Initial enthusiasm for new goals typically fades within weeks or months due to several factors:

Novelty Habituation: Your brain's reward systems respond most strongly to new experiences. As pursuing your wish becomes routine, the neurochemical excitement naturally decreases. Research shows this is normal and doesn't indicate lack of commitment or authentic desire.[113]

Expectation vs. Reality Gaps: Initial motivation often involves idealized expectations about how pursuing wishes will feel. When reality includes mundane daily work, slow progress, or unexpected obstacles, motivation can decrease if expectations weren't realistic. Studies show that accurate expectations about the challenges involved actually enhance long-term motivation.[114]

A Spiritual Perspective of Fading Enthusiasm: Anthony de Mello

Psychotherapist, Jesuit priest, and spiritual teacher Anthony de Mello offered a radically different perspective on why enthusiasm fades—one that can transform how we approach our wishes entirely.

De Mello observed that we've been conditioned to believe we need certain things to be happy: success, recognition, possessions, relationships, achievements. This conditioning creates what he called "attachments"— beliefs that without something specific, we cannot be happy. The problem? When we pursue wishes from attachment rather than authentic desire, we're already setting ourselves up for disappointment.

"The tragedy of an attachment," de Mello wrote, "is that if its object is not attained it causes unhappiness. But if it is attained, it does not cause happiness—it merely causes a flash of pleasure followed by weariness, and it is always accompanied by the anxiety that you may lose the object of your attachment."[115]

This explains a phenomenon many experience but few understand: You pursue a wish with tremendous enthusiasm, achieve it, feel a brief surge of satisfaction... and then nothing. The happiness you expected doesn't materialize. Instead, you feel empty, restless, or immediately focused on the next thing you need to be happy. The motivation that once felt so compelling simply evaporates.

De Mello suggests that fading enthusiasm is often your consciousness recognizing the difference between attachment-driven desires (things you've been programmed to want) and authentic desires (things that genuinely align with your nature and purpose). When motivation fades, it might be wisdom rather than weakness—your deeper self recognizing that this particular wish emerged from conditioning rather than truth.

Understanding vs. Suppressing: A Different Approach to Fading Motivation

Rather than fighting to sustain motivation through willpower and techniques, de Mello advocates for a different approach: understanding. "Don't suppress desire," he said, "Understand it. Understand it. Don't seek to fulfill desire so much as to understand desire."

This means when motivation fades, instead of immediately trying to reignite it, pause and investigate:

Questions for understanding fading motivation:

- Is this wish based on authentic desire or conditioned attachment?
- Am I pursuing this because I genuinely want it, or because I believe I "should" want it?
- Does thinking about this wish energize me, or does it feel heavy and obligatory?
- Would I still want this if no one ever knew about it?

- Is this wish serving my authentic growth, or am I trying to prove something?

"If you understood, you'd simply drop the desire for it," de Mello explained. "This is another way of saying: If you woke up, you'd simply drop the desire for it." Sometimes the most important thing fading motivation teaches us is that we're chasing something we don't actually want—we've just been hypnotized into thinking we need it for happiness.

As de Mello taught, "Happiness is our natural state." We don't need to acquire it through achieving wishes; we need to drop the illusions that block our awareness of the happiness we already possess. When wishes emerge from this awakened state rather than from the belief that we're incomplete without them, motivation doesn't fade—it transforms into something more sustainable: the natural energy of authentic expression.

This awareness creates a paradox: When you stop believing you need something to be happy, you often discover what you genuinely want. And desires pursued from this place of freedom rather than attachment maintain their energy naturally—not because you're using techniques to sustain motivation, but because the wish emerges from your authentic nature rather than programmed conditioning.

The Balanced Approach: Psychology and Spirituality Together

The most sophisticated approach to sustaining motivation integrates both perspectives. Use psychological strategies to work with natural motivation cycles during authentic pursuits. Use spiritual awareness to recognize when fading enthusiasm signals attachment rather than authentic desire. And cultivate the wisdom to know the difference between a middle dip that requires perseverance and a wisdom signal that invites transformation.

As you work with your own wish, notice not just whether motivation is present or absent, but what quality of motivation you're experiencing. Is it the driven, anxious energy of attachment—the feeling that you must achieve this to be okay? Or is it the inspired, expansive energy of authentic desire—the natural expression of who you genuinely are?

The first type of motivation burns out. The second type renews itself.

What Motivates Each "Self"

Understanding the characteristics of each self is only half the equation for effective wishing. Equally important is recognizing what specifically motivates each aspect of your being, since each operates according to different reward systems.

Your Inner Self is motivated primarily by **pleasure, fun, and enjoyment**, safety and security, emotional connection and belonging, and creative self-expression. Think of your Inner Self like a child—it wants to play, not work. When a wish feels playful, joyful, and genuinely enjoyable, your Inner Self enthusiastically supports it with boundless energy. When it feels like drudgery or obligation, your Inner Self sabotages it—no matter how "good for you" your Outer Self insists it is. This is why turning something fun into a "should" is one of the fastest ways to kill your motivation for it. Your Outer Self responds to achievement and accomplishment, control and predictability, social status and recognition, and intellectual mastery. Your Higher Self is energized by service to others, spiritual growth, alignment with values and principles, and legacy or long-term impact.

When your wishes engage the motivational drivers of all three selves, you experience powerful internal alignment. When they don't, you'll likely face resistance or self-sabotage from the aspects that aren't getting their needs met.

Meet the Scientists

The researchers whose work illuminates motivation:

Anthony de Mello — Spiritual psychology and the nature of authentic desire

Daniel Pink — Autonomy, mastery, and purpose as core motivational drivers

Edward Deci & Richard Ryan — Self-Determination Theory

Gabrielle Oettingen — WOOP model (mental contrasting)

Albert Bandura — Self-efficacy and belief in one's abilities

Richard Davidson — Neuroscience of positive emotion and well-being

(Full biographies in Appendix B)

Questions to Ponder

As you reflect on your own wish and what motivates you to pursue it, consider these essential questions:

- **Where does your wish fit in the Motivation Matrix?** Consider all four quadrants: what you want that you have, want that you don't have, don't want that you have, and don't want that you don't have.
- **What's the difference between what you want and what you need?** Reflect on whether your surface desire points toward deeper needs for growth, healing, contribution, or authentic self-expression.
- **What fears, desires, and beliefs are influencing your motivation?** Notice both productive and destructive fears, authentic versus conditioned desires, and empowering versus limiting beliefs.
- **How much FUN is built into your wish?** Consider whether the process itself brings you joy and playfulness, or if you're treating it like another obligation. Your Inner Self powers what feels playful— not what feels like work.
- **How do you sustain motivation when initial enthusiasm fades?** Consider which strategies—values reconnection, progress recognition, social support, or others—most effectively restore your commitment.
- **What would complete motivational alignment look like?** Imagine feeling genuinely excited about your wish at surface levels while also recognizing how it serves your deeper needs and authentic growth.

Next: Wishing and the Brain: The Neuroscience of Conscious Intention

Understanding what motivates your wishes—the surface wants and deeper needs, the fears and desires, the beliefs that drive or derail your efforts—leads naturally to our next exploration: Where does all this motivation actually HAPPEN? What's occurring in your brain and nervous system when you wish effectively? In Chapter 8, we'll examine the specific neural networks, neurotransmitter systems, and neuroplastic changes that support both the experience of wishing and its potential manifestation in reality.

The journey from understanding motivation to exploring neurological foundations opens doorways to profound questions about the relationship between consciousness and brain function, the nature of neuroplasticity, and the possibility that human intention might interact with reality in ways that current neuroscience is only beginning to understand.

Chapter 8: Wishing and The Brain: The Neuroscience of Conscious Intention

Now that you understand who within you is wishing (Chapter 6) and the motivation behind the wishing, (Chapter 7), we turn to one of the most fascinating questions in our entire journey: What actually happens in your brain when you wish?

That wish you made at the beginning of this exploration isn't just a mental concept floating in some abstract space—it involves specific neural networks, neurotransmitter systems, and measurable brain changes that modern neuroscience can observe and understand.

When your Inner Self, Outer Self, and Higher Self align around a desire—when emotion, intention, and purpose work together—you're not just experiencing a subjective feeling. You're activating distinct patterns of brain activity, triggering specific neurochemical responses, and potentially creating structural changes in your neural architecture.

This chapter takes us into the cutting-edge research revealing how conscious intention, repeated practice, and hopeful thinking create literal changes in brain structure and function. We'll discover that effective wishing isn't just psychologically beneficial—it may literally rewire your brain in ways that enhance your capacity for creativity, resilience, and what some researchers suggest might be genuine consciousness-reality interaction.

Neuroplasticity and Wish Formation: How Repeated Wishing Rewires Your Brain

Stanford neuroscientist Andrew Huberman explains that one of the most revolutionary discoveries in modern neuroscience is neuroplasticity—the brain's capacity for change. Huberman's research shows that self-directed visualization, paired with periods of NSDR (non-sleep deep rest), directly reshapes neural circuits. Imagining a skill or goal activates almost the same pathways as performing it, which can accelerate learning, achievement, and healing. Dopamine, the brain's motivational signal, is released both during anticipation and progress—fueling persistence on the wishing journey. This turns wishing from a passive mental activity into an active brain-training practice that creates measurable change at any age.[116]

Neuroscience shows brain structure is always dynamic: billions of neurons connect, strengthen, weaken, disappear, or grow based on experience.[117]

How Wishing Creates Neural Pathways: Donald Hebb, a Canadian psychologist and neuroscientist, said, "Neurons that fire together, wire together."[118] When you repeatedly focus on specific wishes—especially using the Three P's (Peaceful, Positive, Purposeful)—network-level reorganization happens across your entire brain: not just a single region, but systems linked to attention, emotional regulation, social understanding, and imagination.[119] Research demonstrates that consciousness practices alter large-scale networks including the default mode network (mind-wandering and future thinking), executive control networks (attention and cognitive control), limbic emotional circuits (emotional regulation), and social brain networks (empathy and connection.[120]

Consistent, aligned wishing sculpts your brain architecture, expanding hope, creativity, and what scientists call "goal-directed attention."[121]

Frequency, Duration, and Intensity matter: The more you practice, the more your brain changes.[122] Just like with muscles, your brain builds patterns—and these patterns can serve you well or hold you back. How you wish really matters. The more you practice, the more your brain changes, but just like muscles, your mind can develop healthy or unhealthy habits—so the quality of your wishing practice is just as important as the quantity.[123]

Further, Joe Dispenza's work shows that intention paired with elevated emotion—measured in retreat data and brain scans—can foster changes in gene expression, immune function, and subjective wellbeing, suggesting that wishing may impact mind and body, right down to the cellular level.[124]

Neuroplasticity is bidirectional: positive, peaceful wishing grows new circuits—but repetitive anxiety or negativity can reinforce limitation. How you wish—your mindset and emotion—shapes your future brain.

The Default Mode Network: Your Brain's Wishing and Future-Thinking System

One of the most significant discoveries in neuroscience is the default mode network (DMN)—a constellation of regions such as the medial prefrontal cortex and posterior cingulate that lights up whenever your mind drifts inward. This "imagination system" fires whenever you're daydreaming, storytelling, or making wishes, helping you picture new possibilities.

The DMN is always "humming" with activity, especially during self-reflection, memory, and mental time travel. When you consciously wish, you activate networks for creative scenario-building, connecting wishes to your identity, mapping many possible futures, and integrating desires into your life story.[125]

Research links healthy DMN function to creativity, resilience, and psychological well-being, while disruptions are linked to depression and anxiety. Wishing practices engaging the DMN in positive, structured ways can support mental health.

Memory Reconsolidation

Wishing can even support personal healing. Neuroscience shows that memories aren't fixed—they're dynamic, and can be reshaped each time you recall them. Through conscious wishing and revisiting limiting beliefs or trauma, you can literally update memories, softening pain and rewriting your story with hope.[126] (We'll discuss the related concept of "Reverse Optimism" in Chapter 10).

Neuroplasticity and Trauma Healing:

Trauma imprints itself in brain anatomy—shrinking the hippocampus and heightening amygdala activity—but therapy, hope, and conscious wishing support healing, restoring regulation and expanding possibility.[127] [128]

Empowering Future Selves:

By constructing vivid, positive future scenarios, you lay the neural groundwork for growth, confidence, and resilience—making good things more likely to be noticed and realized. .[129]

Managing Desire and Disappointment:

Efficient wishing requires emotional flexibility, balancing passion for outcomes with secure detachment. Neural research shows that secure attachment styles and strong prefrontal-amygdala connections help you hold hope and composure through uncertainty, maintaining motivation and managing setbacks with grace.

Emotional Regulation and the Prefrontal Cortex: Managing Desire and Disappointment

Effective wishing requires sophisticated emotional regulation—the ability to maintain hope and enthusiasm while also accepting uncertainty and potential disappointment. Neuroscience research shows that certain parts of our brain help us balance our feelings, plan ahead, and adapt when things change. And we can get better at these skills with practice.

The Prefrontal Cortex and Executive Function

Research shows that the prefrontal cortex—particularly the medial and dorsolateral regions—plays crucial roles in emotional regulation, future planning, and what neuroscientists call "cognitive flexibility."[130] Studies indicate that when you practice peaceful, positive, and purposeful approaches to wishing, you strengthen these prefrontal regions and their connections to emotional centers like the amygdala.[131]

Building Tolerance for Uncertainty: One of the most important skills for effective wishing involves what researchers call "tolerance for ambiguity"—the ability to remain calm and hopeful despite not knowing when or how desired outcomes will occur. Neuroscience studies show that individuals with stronger prefrontal-amygdala connections demonstrate greater emotional stability during uncertain circumstances.[132] Regular meditation and mindfulness practices—which share many similarities with conscious wishing—can strengthen these neural pathways within weeks.[133]

The Neuroscience of Hope and Resilience: Research on hope and resilience reveals specific neural signatures associated with these positive states.[134] Studies show that hopeful individuals demonstrate increased activity in regions associated with goal-directed behavior, enhanced connectivity between emotional and executive brain areas, and greater activation of reward systems even before positive outcomes occur.[135] This suggests that hope and optimistic wishing may literally train the brain to recognize opportunities and maintain motivation during challenges.

Managing Attachment and Detachment: Advanced wishing practice requires balancing commitment to desired outcomes with acceptance of whatever unfolds. Neuroscience research on attachment styles and emotional regulation shows that "secure attachment"—the ability to invest fully while maintaining emotional stability regardless of outcomes—is associated with specific patterns of brain activation. Studies indicate that individuals with secure attachment demonstrate greater prefrontal control over emotional reactivity and more flexible responses to changing circumstances.

Mirror Neurons and Collective Consciousness: How Individual Wishes Affect Groups

One of the most intriguing aspects of wishing involves its social and collective dimensions. Research on mirror neurons and emotional contagion reveals specific brain mechanisms through which individual consciousness and intentions can influence group dynamics and collective outcomes. In other words,
our feelings and hopes can spread to others so what you wish for can really affect the people around you.[136]

The Discovery of Mirror Neurons

Neuroscience research has identified specialized neurons that fire both when you perform an action and when you observe others performing the same action. These "mirror neurons" appear to be fundamental to empathy, social learning, and what researchers call "emotional contagion"— the subconscious transmission of emotional states between individuals.

How Wishes Spread Through Groups: Studies show that emotions, attitudes, and even hopes can spread through social networks in measurable ways.[137] Research reveals that "we subconsciously mirror each other's movements to build rapport" and can "transmit stress or calm to others without speaking."[138] This suggests that when you practice peaceful, positive, and purposeful wishing, you may be influencing others in your environment toward similar states of hope and possibility.

Collective Intention and Group Synchronization: Emerging research on group meditation and collective intention suggests that when individuals focus together on shared outcomes, their brain activity can become synchronized in measurable ways.[139] Studies using EEG and other brain imaging technologies show that group practices can create "coherent field effects" where individual brain waves align and synchronize across participants.[140]

The Neuroscience of Empathy and Altruistic Wishes: Research on empathy and compassion reveals that wishing well for others activates specific neural networks associated with social connection and emotional resonance.[141]

Studies show that loving-kindness meditation—which involves directing positive intentions toward others—increases activity in areas associated with empathy while also enhancing personal well-being and social connection.[142] This suggests that altruistic wishing may be both neurologically optimal and collectively beneficial.

Social Brain Networks and Collective Flourishing: Neuroscience research reveals that humans have specialized "social brain networks" dedicated to understanding others' minds, coordinating group activities, and maintaining social cohesion. When you engage in conscious wishing that includes concern for collective well-being, you activate these social networks in ways that may support both individual and group flourishing.

The Integration of Brain Networks: When Wishing Becomes Effortless

Advanced wishing practice appears to involve the integration and harmonization of multiple brain networks that typically operate somewhat independently. Research on optimal performance states and transcendent experiences reveals specific patterns of neural integration that may correspond to what many traditions describe as effortless manifestation.

Sleep, Dreams, and Subconscious Processing: The Neuroscience of Nocturnal Wishing

Emerging research reveals that sleep and dreams play crucial roles in consolidating intentions, processing emotions, and potentially facilitating the kind of subconscious problem-solving that supports wish fulfillment.

Sleep as Neural Refinement Laboratory

Neuroscience research shows that sleep serves as a "consolidation laboratory" where the brain replays daily patterns, strengthens important neural connections, and integrates new learning.[143] The brain's replay of daily experiences during sleep could strengthen any intentions or wishes focused on during waking hours. This suggests that nighttime processing might be crucial for integrating spiritual guidance and consolidating wish-related neural patterns.

The Role of REM Sleep in Creative Problem-Solving: Research shows that REM sleep—the stage associated with vivid dreaming—plays crucial roles in creative problem-solving, emotional processing, and memory consolidation.[144] Studies reveal that people often wake with insights or solutions that weren't apparent while awake, suggesting that "the sleeping brain could be refining and clarifying" whatever challenges or desires were active during the day.[145]

Dream Incubation and Intention Setting: Some research suggests that setting specific intentions before sleep—including wishes or questions— can influence dream content and potentially lead to insights or solutions upon waking. Studies show that the dreaming brain continues to work on unresolved issues and may generate creative solutions through the novel recombination of memories and ideas.

Lucid Dreaming and Conscious Intention: Research on lucid dreaming—the ability to become conscious within dreams—reveals that some individuals can maintain awareness and even direct dream experiences. Studies show that "two-way communication is possible during a dream," suggesting that consciousness isn't limited to waking life.[146] [147] This research opens intriguing possibilities for using dream states as laboratories for exploring wishes and practicing optimal outcomes.

Network Integration and Coherent Brain States

Studies using advanced brain imaging reveal that during peak performance states—whether in athletics, creativity, or contemplative practice—different brain networks begin to function as integrated wholes rather than separate systems. When people are 'in the zone,' whether they're playing sports, creating, or meditating, different parts of their brain work together, making it easier to do their best.[148] Research shows that "consciousness may arise from brain-wide integration" where "neurons firing in separate regions—vision, sound, memory—become stitched together into one seamless experience."[149]

The Neuroscience of Flow and Effortless Action: Research on flow states—periods of effortless, optimal performance—shows specific patterns of brain activity that can apply to advanced wishing practice.[150] Studies indicate that during flow, there's decreased activity in the prefrontal cortex (called "transient hypofrontality"), reduced self-criticism and time awareness, and increased connectivity between creative and executive networks. This suggests that effective wishing may involve a balance between intention and surrender, effort and allowing.

Gamma Wave Coherence and The Default Network: Neuroscience research on sudden insight and "aha moments" reveals that breakthroughs often occur during bursts of gamma wave activity—high-frequency brain waves associated with binding together information from different brain regions. Studies show that "just before a breakthrough, the brain often enters a burst of gamma activity, a rhythm associated with integration across distant regions." This research suggests that optimal wishing states may involve similar patterns of whole-brain coherence.

Subconscious Decision-Making: How Your Brain Chooses Before You Know It

One of the most profound discoveries in neuroscience has revolutionary implications for understanding how wishes might actually manifest through subconscious behavioral choices. Research reveals that brain scans can sometimes detect decisions before you're consciously aware of making them, suggesting that your subconscious mind may be steering you toward desired outcomes through micro-decisions you don't even notice. This is where the Three Selves come together:

- Your **Outer (Conscious) Self** sets intentions and makes the wish.

- Your **Inner (Subconscious) Self** works "behind the scenes," nudging you in small, sometimes invisible ways toward that wish—by shaping attention, emotions, and countless tiny actions.
- Your **Higher Self** can infuse the process with purpose and meaning, guiding "chance" encounters or sudden nudges that feel intuitively right.

When all three selves are aligned in the wishing process—clear intention, heartfelt emotion, and a sense of meaning—the science suggests you're most likely to "move" toward your wishes, even before you consciously realize it.

The Haynes and Libet Experiments: Predicting Choices Before Awareness

Groundbreaking research by neuroscientists John-Dylan Haynes, Benjamin Libet, and colleagues has demonstrated that brain activity in the prefrontal and parietal lobes can predict decisions—such as whether to press a left or right button—up to 10-11 seconds before participants report becoming conscious of their choice.[151]

Studies using fMRI and EEG consistently show that "decisions arise gradually, shaped by subconscious activity that bubbles up into awareness." [152]

Implications for Wish Fulfillment: This research suggests that consciousness may be "the final stage in a longer chain—the moment the brain's hidden debate crosses a threshold." For wishing practice, this means that your subconscious mind might literally be making micro-decisions throughout each day that either support or undermine your conscious desires. These subconscious choices could involve:

- Which opportunities you notice or ignore
- How you respond to potential pathways toward your wishes
- What risks you're willing to take or avoid
- Which people you're drawn to connect with
- How you interpret ambiguous situations

The Critical Importance of Subconscious Alignment: These findings provide neurological validation for the Three Selves framework explored in Chapter 6. If your subconscious mind is making decisions before your conscious awareness, then having your Inner Self (subconscious) truly aligned with your wishes becomes absolutely crucial. Research suggests that internal conflicts between conscious desires and subconscious fears or beliefs could literally sabotage wish fulfillment through thousands of subtle, often-invisible choices you never consciously recognize.

Free Will and Conscious Influence: Importantly, this research doesn't eliminate free will but rather reveals it as more nuanced than previously understood. Studies suggest that consciousness may serve as an "editor" or "veto" function—you may not consciously initiate every micro-decision, but you can become aware of subconscious patterns and consciously influence them through practices like:

- **Mindfulness training** to increase awareness of subconscious behavioral patterns
- **Values clarification** to align subconscious decision-making with conscious priorities
- **Repetitive visualization** that programs subconscious pattern recognition toward desired outcomes

Programming the Subconscious Decision-Maker: Research on neuroplasticity suggests that repeated conscious practice can gradually influence subconscious processing patterns. When you consistently practice peaceful, positive, and purposeful wishing, you may be literally training your subconscious mind to recognize and move toward opportunities that serve your conscious intentions. This could explain why some individuals seem to "naturally" attract desired outcomes—their subconscious decision-making systems have been trained to support their conscious wishes through thousands of small choices that collectively create significant life changes.

James Doty's Manifestation Neuroscience: Scientific Understanding of Intention

Leading neuroscientist James Doty, Director of the Center for Compassion and Altruism Research at Stanford University, has conducted groundbreaking research on the neuroscience of manifestation and conscious intention.

Doty's research demonstrates that intention-setting activates the brain's salience network—particularly the reticular activating system (RAS)—which primes individuals to notice and respond to hidden opportunities. Repeated visualization combined with strong emotional engagement forges new neural connections and supports goal-directed breakthroughs. Through daily repetition, relaxation, and explicit visualization, Doty's protocols train the subconscious to act as a 'pattern matcher' for dreams and wishes. Program participants in clinical and popular studies reported measurable changes in motivation, noticing more aligned opportunities and making choices subconsciously that further their intentions.[153]

The Neuroscience of Positive Emotions and Approach Motivation

Research on positive emotions and approach motivation provides crucial insights into why the "positive" component of the Three P's is neurologically essential for effective wishing.

The Broaden-and-Build Effect

Barbara Fredrickson's groundbreaking research reveals that positive emotions trigger what's called the "broaden-and-build" effect: positive feelings broaden your options and build lasting resources.[154] Studies show that positive emotions enhance cognitive flexibility, increase openness to new experiences, and improve both physical health and social relationships.[155]

135

Approach vs. Avoidance Neural Systems: Neuroscience research reveals that the brain has distinct systems for approach motivation (moving toward desired outcomes) and avoidance motivation (moving away from threats).[156] Studies show that approach motivation activates left prefrontal regions associated with goal-directed behavior, enhanced creativity, and social connection, while avoidance motivation activates right prefrontal regions associated with withdrawal and threat-detection.

Dopamine and Reward Prediction: Research on the neurotransmitter dopamine reveals that this "motivation molecule" doesn't actually create pleasure but drives the anticipation and pursuit of rewards.[157] Studies show that dopamine levels spike highest not when you receive something you want, but when you expect you might receive it.[158] This suggests that hopeful, optimistic wishing may create optimal neurochemical conditions for sustained motivation and opportunity recognition.

Optimism and Neuroplasticity: Research on optimism shows that positive expectations about the future enhance both motivation and actual outcomes. Studies indicate that optimistic individuals demonstrate increased neuroplasticity, better stress resilience, and enhanced immune function. However, research also shows that effective optimism must be grounded in realistic assessment rather than naive fantasy—supporting the importance of realistic, positive wishing.

Bridge To Fiction: Inside Out's Brilliant Brain Lessons

Pixar's *Inside Out* films offer two of the most accessible and accurate depictions of how brain function shapes behavior, wishes, and even our capacity for hope. In the first film, when 11-year-old Riley moves to San Francisco, we watch her brain's "control center" struggle as Joy and Sadness get lost in long-term memory. What follows is a powerful illustration of neuroplasticity in action: as Riley's personality islands crumble—her love of hockey, her goofiness, her family connection—we see how brain disruption literally changes behavior. Riley becomes withdrawn, makes poor decisions, and eventually runs away. But here's the fascinating question the film raises: Did Riley lose her capacity to wish during this neurological crisis? When her brain's emotional regulation system broke down and her prefrontal cortex couldn't access positive memories or imagine positive futures, wishing became neurologically impossible. She couldn't envision a happy outcome, couldn't feel hope, couldn't imagine herself thriving in her new home. Only when Joy and Sadness work together—when Riley's brain networks reintegrate and her emotional regulation returns—can she begin wishing again.

Inside Out 2 takes this neuroscience even deeper by showing what happens during puberty when new emotions arrive—literally depicting how the teenage brain develops new neural networks and capabilities. When Anxiety takes over Riley's headquarters and removes her "Sense of Self" (built from core beliefs accumulated over thirteen years), we witness something profound: Riley becomes unable to make authentic choices that reflect who she truly is. With her Sense of Self gone, she can't access the neural foundation that connects her values, memories, and identity— the very framework needed for purposeful wishing. Anxiety tries to build "a better Riley" by planting new beliefs, but without the integration of all her emotions working together, Riley loses herself. She betrays her best friends, pretends to like things she doesn't, and behaves in ways that feel hollow and disconnected. The film brilliantly demonstrates that effective wishing requires more than just wanting something—it demands a coherent sense of self, integrated emotional regulation, and the neurological capacity to imagine and move toward positive futures. When any of these brain functions are disrupted, our ability to wish authentically disappears, no matter how hard we try.

Meet the Scientists

The researchers whose work illuminates the neuroscience of wishing:

James Doty — Neuroscience of manifestation and intention

Marcus Raichle — Default Mode Network discovery

Barbara Fredrickson — Broaden-and-build theory of positive emotions

Richard Davidson — Meditation's effects on brain circuitry

Sara Lazar — Mindfulness and brain structural changes

Antonio Damasio — Body-centered theory of consciousness

Karim Nader — Memory reconsolidation

Marco Iacoboni — Mirror neuron systems

Joe Dispenza — Integration of neuroscience, epigenetics, and mental rehearsal

(Full biographies in Appendix B)

Questions to Ponder

As you consider the neuroscience of your own wishing practice, reflect on these questions:

- **How has your brain changed through your wishing practices?** Notice any shifts in your capacity for hope, creativity, emotional regulation, or resilience that might reflect neuroplastic changes.

- **What old neural patterns might you need to rewire?** Consider limiting beliefs, anxiety patterns, or habitual negative thinking that could benefit from conscious rewiring through peaceful, positive, and purposeful practice.

- **How do you want to train your brain for more effective wishing?** Reflect on which neural networks—default mode, executive control, emotional regulation, social cognition—you might want to strengthen through practice.

- **What role does sleep and subconscious processing play in your wishing?** Notice whether insights, solutions, or shifts in perspective occur during rest periods, dreams, or upon waking.

- **How do your individual wishes affect others around you?** Consider whether your emotional states, hope levels, and positive intentions influence family members, colleagues, or community members through emotional contagion and mirror neuron systems.

- **What does optimal brain integration feel like in your wishing practice?** Reflect on moments when wishing feels effortless, inspired, or deeply harmonious—times when different aspects of your consciousness seem to work together seamlessly.

Next, The Three Ps: Peaceful, Positive, and Purposeful

In Chapter 9, we'll move from brain science to practical application as we delve into "The Three P's"—practical frameworks for focusing intention, and taking inspired action.

This exploration will reveal how to harness the insights we've discovered while avoiding the common pitfalls that derail even well-motivated wishes. We'll explain that effective wishing requires a paradoxical combination of passionate engagement and wise surrender—a dance between human effort and cosmic assistance, the nature of surrender and control, and the mysterious process by which conscious intention becomes lived reality.

Chapter 9: The Three P's of a Cosmic Wish - Peaceful, Positive, and Purposeful

Now that you understand who within you is wishing, what motivates those different aspects, and how it works in the brain, we arrive at one of the most practical questions in our entire exploration: How do you actually make wishes more effectively? That wish you made at the beginning of our journey—how can you approach it in a way that maximizes both your psychological well-being and the likelihood of positive outcomes?

In Chapter 1, I identified three essential qualities that distinguish effective wishing from mere hoping, fantasizing, or wishful thinking, aka "The Three P's of a Cosmic Wish"—Peaceful, Positive, and Purposeful. We'll explain in this chapter that these aren't just nice ideas but are actually backed by neurological and psychological science as optimal states for both personal well-being and what many would call manifestation.

Note: The 3 P's work best when your nervous system feels fundamentally safe. If you're dealing with trauma, ongoing stress, or mental health challenges, please consider working with qualified professionals alongside these practices.

Peaceful: The Neurological Foundation of Effective Wishing

Your nervous system state fundamentally determines your brain's capacity for the kind of thinking, feeling, and perceiving that supports effective wishing. Richard Davidson's landmark research at the University of Wisconsin used MRI scans to demonstrate structural changes in the brains of long-term meditators, including increased activity in prefrontal regions related to attention and emotional regulation. Davidson found that compassion, gratitude, and mindfulness rewire neural connections for stress resilience, improved mood, and even immune function.[159]

Jon Kabat-Zinn's creation of Mindfulness-Based Stress Reduction (MBSR) at the University of Massachusetts Medical School introduced an empirically tested framework for reducing stress and cultivating inner calm. Studies on MBSR demonstrate how mindfulness stabilizes attention, lessens habitual stress reactions, and fosters a mindfulness-mediated stress response that supports non-reactive awareness and sustainable well-being.[160]

Stephen Porges's Polyvagal Theory clarifies the physiological roots of peace. By explaining how the vagus nerve regulates safety, connection, and calm through its "social engagement system," Porges provides the neurological foundation for what we experience as inner ease and trust. Peaceful states activate the parasympathetic, ventral vagal branch—the so-called "rest and digest" system—which optimizes conditions for healing, creativity, learning, and growth.[161] [162]

Together, Davidson's neuroscience, Kabat-Zinn's mindfulness research, and Porges's neurophysiology converge on one finding: when the body feels safe, the brain becomes capable of the creativity, intuition, and cognitive flexibility essential for effective wishing.

The Neuroscience of Peaceful States

Research shows that peaceful states arise when sympathetic arousal subsides and parasympathetic regulation predominates. Kabat-Zinn's participants in long-term MBSR programs report sustained reductions in anxiety, improved emotional balance, and enduring experiences of inner calm even a year after practice.[163] When a person's nervous system feels safe and calm, Porges's model predicts increased social receptivity and the neurochemical conditions for trust, cooperation, and insight. These findings explain why peace is not simply an absence of stress but a distinct neurophysiological mode that makes clarity and intuition possible.

Peaceful Wishing Characteristics

Calm Body and Regulated Breathing: Research on heart rate variability shows that coherent breathing—slow, deep, rhythmic patterns in sync with vagal activity—creates optimal conditions for emotional regulation and cognitive performance. This coherence enhances the clarity and intuition behind every wish.[164]

Present-Moment Awareness: Studies by Kabat-Zinn demonstrate that training attention in the present moment activates the prefrontal cortex while reducing amygdala reactivity.[165] This presence supports both creativity and problem-solving by quieting stress hormone responses.

Trust in the Process: Attachment and resilience studies show that trust and safety states—correlating with Porges's ventral vagal activation—reduce cortisol and enhance immune function. Trustful wishing encourages openness to unexpected outcomes.

Inner Quiet: Kabat-Zinn and Davidson both demonstrate that mental quiet supports intuitive insight and authentic motivation; inner stillness is not inactivity but an optimized state for growth. Long-term mindfulness practitioners show enhanced connectivity between prefrontal and insula regions linked with self-awareness and compassion.

In essence, to be peaceful is to create neurobiological conditions of safety and presence that prime the mind for possibility—making this state the foundation for positive and purposeful wishing.

Positive: The Emotional Chemistry of Attraction

Emotional state directly influences brain function, perception, and behavior in ways that dramatically affect the likelihood of positive outcomes. Research reveals that positive emotions don't just feel good—they literally broaden awareness, enhance creativity, and help you recognize opportunities you'd miss in negative states.

The Neuroscience of Positive Emotions

Barbara Fredrickson's broaden-and-build theory shows that positive emotions expand cognitive flexibility and deepen interpersonal connection, fostering the "upward spirals" of resilience and resource-building necessary for wishing.[166] When people experience joy, gratitude, or love, their attention literally *broadens*—measurable through eye-tracking and fMRI—and over time they *build* adaptability, creativity, and psychological strength.[167]

Jonathan Haidt's research on moral emotions extends this science to feelings like gratitude, elevation, and admiration.[168] Haidt found that witnessing acts of kindness or virtue evokes "elevation"—an emotion that opens the chest, warms the heart, and activates affiliative impulses fueled by oxytocin and serotonin. These responses motivate altruistic action, trust, and social bonding—the same qualities that sustain joyful, prosocial wishing.

Together, Fredrickson's and Haidt's frameworks reveal positive emotion as both a neurological and moral amplifier: it widens perspective and deepens connection, making the wish process inherently relational and growth-oriented.

Wishing FOR vs. Wishing AGAINST: The Science of Positive Framing

Here's something crucial about the "Positive" in the Three P's: you must wish FOR what you want, not AGAINST what you don't want. This isn't just semantics—it's neuroscience.

Research on goal framing shows that your brain literally processes "stop the violence" differently than "create peace." While the first might draw crowds to a protest, it also activates stress responses and narrows thinking. But when you add a "for" statement you activate creativity and expand possibilities toward POSITIVE change. [169]

This is why successful social movements focus on what they're FOR, not just what they're AGAINST. The civil rights movement articulated beloved community. The environmental movement gains traction by promoting clean energy futures, not just opposing fossil fuels.

When you wish FOR something positive, your brain becomes a solution-detector. When you wish AGAINST something negative, your brain becomes a threat-scanner.

For more on reframing wishes positively, see the Wish Circle examples at: https://cosmicwishexperiment.com/wish-circle-examples/

Positive Wishing Characteristics

Fun, Joy, and Playfulness: Positive doesn't just mean "not negative"—it includes the active presence of joy, delight, and playfulness. Research shows that positive emotions like joy activate approach motivation systems and broaden creative thinking. Your Inner Self responds powerfully to wishes that feel genuinely fun and enjoyable. When wishing feels like play rather than work, you tap into sustainable motivation that doesn't require willpower to maintain.

Genuine Enthusiasm: Authentic enthusiasm activates dopamine reward networks that sustain motivation and persistence. Studies show that wishes fueled by true excitement maintain creative momentum longer than obligation-driven efforts.[170]

Gratitude for Present Circumstances: Haidt and Fredrickson both found that gratitude enhances psychological well-being and social bonding, shifting focus from scarcity to abundance.[171] This attitude amplifies the broaden-and-build cycle by linking contentment with creative possibility.

Optimism About Possibilities: Research demonstrates that positive expectations activate brain regions associated with planning and reward.[172] Optimistic individuals persist through uncertainty and perceive resources others miss. Albert Bandura's studies on self-efficacy confirm that confidence in one's ability transforms wishing into effective action.[173]

Focus on Desired Outcomes: Neuroscience shows that the reticular activating system prioritizes information consistent with dominant mental images.[174] By focusing on the desired state rather than avoiding fears, the mind becomes a collaborative partner in manifestation.

Positive Intent for All: Haidt linked elevation and compassion with increased oxytocin, fostering trust and kindness. Research confirms that collective welfare intensifies fulfillment and creates wishes aligned with greater meaning. [175]

Purposeful: The Power of Aligned Intention

Goals connected to meaning, service, or authentic values foster greater resilience and satisfaction. Alignment with deeper meaning and purpose amplifies the effectiveness of wishes in ways that purely self-focused desires cannot match. Research consistently shows that goals connected to transcendent purposes generate more sustained motivation, greater life satisfaction, and often more successful outcomes than those serving only personal gain.

The Neuroscience of Purpose

Stephen Porges's Polyvagal Theory shows that our experiences of social engagement, trust, and meaning depend on activation of the ventral vagal system—a state of physiological safety that supports both connection and proactive intention.[176] [177] Only when we feel safe, both in body and community, can the mind sustain purpose-driven, future-oriented motivation needed for effective wishing. Purposeful intentions, then, are not just "mental" but are rooted in the nervous system's ongoing regulation of openness, curiosity, and moral engagement.

Jonathan Haidt's science of "moral emotions" demonstrates that feelings such as awe, elevation, and reverence—elicited by purposeful living and prosocial behavior—draw us beyond personal gratification into self-transcendence and collective flourishing. Haidt's work shows that our brains are wired for meaning: acting on higher values triggers neurochemical states of fulfillment and persistence unavailable to narrowly self-serving goals.

Purposeful Wishing Characteristics

Clear, Specific Intentions: Research on goal-setting shows that well-defined objectives—especially those oriented toward meaningful outcomes—activate goal-directed networks and are more likely to be achieved.[178]

Values Alignment: Goals and wishes closely aligned with authentic personal values and principles draw on deeper motivational circuits in the brain and provide lasting satisfaction.[179]

Service to Others: Porges found that social engagement and service to others enhance vagal tone and promote physiological states of trust, which, in turn, support long-term motivation and resilience. Research on altruism confirms that acting for benefits beyond the self sustains motivation and satisfaction.[180]

Spiritual and Transcendent Connection: Haidt's work highlights how self-transcendent emotions—such as awe, reverence, and gratitude for larger purposes—are linked to moral vision, persistence, and community engagement.[181] Wishing from a spiritual or transcendent source often generates commitment, deep fulfillment, and a sense of being part of something much larger than oneself.

Long-term Vision: Purposeful wishes typically involve consideration of broader impact—how present goals will shape both immediate and future well-being for self and community.[182]

149

Expanded Benefits of Purposeful Wishing

Enhanced Social Support: Polyvagal integration shows that purposeful, service-oriented goals invite more effective collaboration and support.[183]

Improved Opportunity Recognition: When people operate from aligned purposes, their brains are primed to notice and act on opportunities that further their goals.

Persistence and Resilience: Both Porges and Haidt found that states of moral engagement and physiological safety generate resilience, allowing breakthroughs even through adversity.

Alignment with Natural and Social Systems: Meaningful, value-aligned wishing appears to synchronize not just with personal goals, but also with communal, cultural, and (some traditions suggest) evolutionary forces—amplifying impact in ways that purely individualistic efforts cannot.

Purpose, then, is not merely an add-on to wishing—it is the motivational and neurobiological engine that empowers sustained, meaningful, and socially connected success.

Integration: How the Three P's Work Together

The most effective wishing occurs when peaceful, positive, and purposeful qualities are integrated rather than pursued separately.

Research on optimal functioning shows that these states enhance each other synergistically, creating conditions that are greater than the sum of their individual effects.

Peaceful + Positive = Relaxed Optimism

The combination of peace and positivity creates what researchers call "relaxed optimism"—a state of confident expectation without anxiety or forcing.[184] Studies show that this combination optimizes both creative problem-solving and emotional resilience. When you're both peaceful and positive about your wishes, you can maintain hope and enthusiasm while remaining open to unexpected pathways and timing.

Positive + Purposeful = Inspired Motivation

Research indicates that the combination of positive emotions and purposeful intentions creates particularly sustainable motivation.[185] Studies show that when wishes serve both personal fulfillment and larger purposes, they generate what researchers call "inspired motivation"— energy that feels effortless and joyful rather than forced or difficult. This combination appears to activate reward systems in ways that purely personal or purely altruistic goals do not.

Peaceful + Purposeful = Surrendered Commitment

The integration of peace and purpose creates what might be called "surrendered commitment"—total dedication to worthy outcomes combined with acceptance of whatever unfolds. Research on psychological flexibility and adaptive goal adjustment shows that this combination reduces anxiety while maintaining motivation, often leading to better outcomes than either passive hoping or controlling effort alone.[186] [187] [188]

So far in this chapter, we've explored each of the Three P's individually—how Peaceful states calm your nervous system, how Positive emotions broaden your perception and build resilience, and how Purposeful alignment engages your brain's deepest motivational centers. But here's where it gets really interesting: when you combine all three qualities and practice them consistently over time, something extraordinary happens.

Studies of peak performance, flow states, and transcendent experiences reveal common characteristics that emerge when peaceful, positive, and purposeful energies work together.[189] [190]

- **Effortless Action**: Your behavior feels inspired and natural rather than forced
- **Enhanced Intuition**: You access insights and guidance beyond ordinary thinking
- **Synchronicity Recognition**: You notice meaningful coincidences and opportunities more readily
- **Sustainable Motivation**: Your energy maintains itself rather than depleting over time
- **Expanded Awareness**: You perceive both practical details and larger patterns simultaneously
- **Social Magnetism**: You naturally attract assistance, resources, and collaboration

From Force to Power: A New Way to Understand Wishing

One of the most intriguing bridges between psychology, spirituality, and the science of consciousness comes from psychiatrist Dr. David R. Hawkins. Over decades of research (summarized in his book *Power vs. Force*.[191]) Hawkins mapped human consciousness on a scale from 1 to 1000—from the lowest emotional states of shame and fear all the way up to the highest frequencies of love, peace, and enlightenment.[192]

His central discovery? Emotions below a certain threshold operate as force—they deplete your energy, narrow your focus, and require constant effort to maintain. Emotions above that threshold operate as power—they replenish your energy, expand your awareness, and flow naturally.

Think about it: When you're stuck in fear, anger, or pride, how much energy does it take just to get through the day? You're pushing, controlling, manipulating. It's exhausting. But when you're in acceptance, gratitude, or peace? Things start to flow. Doors open. People show up to help. You're collaborating with reality instead of fighting it.

Recent neuroscience research supports this framework. Studies on psychophysiological coherence demonstrate that optimal emotional and cognitive states emerge when different aspects of our nervous system work in harmony. Research on emotional consciousness shows that increased emotional coherence directly correlates with improved well-being.[193]

Level	Scale
Enlightenment	700–1,000
Peace	600
Joy	540
Love	500
Reason	400
Acceptance	350
Willingness	310
Neutrality	250
Courage	200
Pride	175
Anger	150
Desire	125
Fear	100
Grief	75
Apathy	50
Guilt	30
Shame	20

POWER

FORCE

Source: David Hawkins Power vs. Force

Where the Three P's Live on the Consciousness Scale

Here's what makes the Three P's framework so powerful—each quality corresponds to a specific range on Hawkins' consciousness map:

Peaceful aligns with the highest levels of consciousness (600 and above)—what Hawkins called the frequencies of serenity, inner peace, and unity. When you're truly peaceful, you're not just calm; you're operating from a state of high coherence where different aspects of yourself work in harmony.[194]

Positive corresponds to the broad emotional range between acceptance and love (roughly 350-500 on Hawkins' scale). This is where gratitude lives. Where optimism restores flow. Where you can see possibilities instead of just problems. Research on positive emotions and hope shows this is the sweet spot for building resilience and recognizing opportunities.

Purposeful operates in the mid-to-high levels of reason and integrity (400 and above). This is where your intentions harmonize with ethical alignment and service to others. You're not just chasing what you want—you're aligned with something that matters beyond yourself. Studies show that having a sense of purpose literally adds years to your life and increases overall well-being.

Together, the Three P's move your wishing from *force* to *power*. From trying to command reality to consciously collaborating with it. In Chapter 11 we'll get into the downside and dark side of wishing, explaining the harmful impact of "force" wishes, not only to the wisher but also to the larger cosmos. And in Chapter 12 we'll discuss collective wishing and how the best, most effective leaders know how to harness the higher-level energies on Hawkins' scale.

The Eight-Week Transformation: From Temporary States to Lasting Traits

Here's the really good news: when you practice the Three P's together and sustain them over time (as in the eight-week program we'll explore later in this book), research across neuroscience, psychophysiology, and consciousness studies shows something remarkable happens.

Day by day, wish by wish, you're strengthening neural and energetic pathways. And around week five or six? Many people report a shift. Peace and joy stop being something they have to *try* to feel and start becoming their natural resting state. This is what Hawkins meant when he talked about moving up the consciousness scale—not as a one-time leap, but as a gradual elevation through consistent practice.

Over time, you're not merely wishing *for* change. You're *becoming* the elevated energy from which change naturally emerges.

That's the essence of moving from Force to Power. From effortful wishing to effortless creation. From trying to make things happen to allowing them to unfold.

And that's when wishing becomes truly cosmic.

What Just Moved Into Your Circle of Control

Remember at the beginning of this book when we distinguished wishes from goals? Goals, we said, are within your control. Wishes involve Cosmic Collaboration—forces beyond your direct influence.
But here's what's shifted after everything you've learned in Chapters 1-9:

You've just brought a MASSIVE amount INTO your control.

Through understanding the neuroscience, psychology, and inner mechanics of wishing, you now control:

Your inner state (the 3 P's—Peaceful, Positive, Purposeful)
Your brain's neural pathways (through conscious practice and repetition)
Your emotional alignment (understanding and working with all Three Selves)
Your subconscious programming (recognizing and shifting limiting beliefs)
Your daily actions (taking steps aligned with your wishes)

Your response to obstacles (maintaining alignment even when challenged)

This is enormous. Most people think wishing is almost entirely out of their control—just luck, or "the universe's decision." But you now understand that you command a significant portion of the wishing equation through these inner practices.[195]

This distinction reflects what psychologist Julian Rotter called the Locus of Control — the sense of whether life events are primarily determined by one's own actions or by external forces. Decades of follow-up studies show that people with a balanced internal locus of control — those who take responsibility without demanding total control — report higher psychological well-being and stronger motivation.

Later research by Paulhus (1983) expanded Rotter's model, showing that balanced internal control — confidence without perfectionism — correlates with reduced anxiety and higher life satisfaction.[196]

What Remains Outside Your Control:

Even masters of cosmic wishing don't control everything. What remains in the realm of Cosmic Collaboration includes:

Other people's choices (free will isn't yours to command)
The timing of responses (when manifestation occurs)
External circumstances (economy, weather, global events)
The exact path wishes take to manifestation

And that's exactly as it should be. These elements require collaboration with something larger than yourself—call it the cosmos, collective consciousness, divine intelligence, or quantum field. You've learned to master YOUR part. Now let's explore how to skillfully work with what remains beyond your direct control.

That's where the Four Responses come in...

Bridge To Fiction: Marielle's Moment Of Truth

In the *We Meet Again* trilogy, protagonist Marielle faces her darkest moment when Dante—the love of her lives across multiple incarnations—ends their relationship to protect her from danger. She collapses in grief, crying for hours, feeling utterly lost and alone. But then something extraordinary happens.

After allowing herself to fully feel the pain, Marielle makes a choice. She goes to the gym, summoning her inner and outer strength with each muscle movement and drip of sweat. She transforms her loft into "Kairos"—Greek for the opportune moment when conditions align perfectly—creating an operations headquarters for her mission. The significance of this shift cannot be overstated: Marielle moves from reactive victim to proactive hero.

She recognizes that while she's always had difficulty asking for help, this quest isn't personal—it's global. "With or without these two men," she declares, "she will fulfill her destiny."

This is the Three P's in action. Peaceful: She processes her emotions and finds her center. Positive: She channels devastating loss into determined action. Purposeful: She connects her personal pain to a larger mission that serves humanity. Marielle's transformation demonstrates that the Three P's aren't about denying difficulty or pretending everything is fine—they're about aligning your inner state so you can move forward with clarity, strength, and authentic motivation even in the face of heartbreak.

Meet the Scientists

The researchers whose work illuminates the Three P's:

Jon Kabat-Zinn — Mindfulness-Based Stress Reduction (MBSR)

Jonathan Haidt — Moral emotions and prosocial behavior

Stephen Porges — Polyvagal Theory

Barbara Fredrickson — Broaden-and-build theory of positive emotions

Richard Davidson — Meditation and brain rewiring

(Full biographies in Appendix B)

Questions to Ponder

As you consider applying the Three P's to your own wish, reflect on these essential questions:

- **How peaceful do you feel when you think about your wish?** Notice whether your desire creates calm anticipation or anxiety and stress. Consider what might help you approach your wish more peacefully.

- **What positive emotions does your wish generate?** Reflect on whether thinking about your desire creates genuine enthusiasm, gratitude, and optimism, or whether it feels heavy, obligatory, or anxiety-provoking.
- **How does your wish connect to larger purposes?** Consider how your desire serves not just personal fulfillment but also contributes to family, community, or universal well-being.
- **Where might you be attached to specific outcomes or methods?** Notice any areas where you're demanding particular timelines, specific pathways, or exact results rather than remaining open to unexpected possibilities.
- **How could you cultivate more of each P in relation to your wish?** Identify specific practices—breathing, gratitude, values clarification, detachment exercises—that might enhance your peaceful, positive, and purposeful approach.
- **What would it feel like to wish from complete Three P integration?** Imagine approaching your desire with complete peace, authentic positivity, and clear purpose while remaining open to outcomes that serve your highest good.
- **Which aspects of your wish feel within your control, and which feel outside it?** Make two lists: what you can directly influence (your preparation, actions, attitude, skills) and what requires cosmic collaboration (other people's responses, timing, external circumstances). Does this clarity change how you approach the wish?
- **What did you previously think was "out of your control" that you now realize you CAN influence?** Reflect on how learning about the 3 P's, neuroplasticity, and the Three Selves has expanded

what you understand to be within your power. What does this shift mean for your wishing practice?

- **Where might you be trying to control things that are genuinely outside your circle?** Consider whether you're attempting to force timing, control other people's choices, or demand specific pathways. How might releasing this control actually enhance your wish's potential?

Next: The Four Responses

Understanding how to approach wishes with peaceful, positive, and purposeful states leads naturally to our next discussion in Chapter 10: The Four Responses—the different ways that the universe appears to interact with human wishes, from direct fulfillment to unexpected alternatives that serve deeper needs.

This exploration will take us beyond motivation, the brain, and the 3 Ps to exploring consciousness-reality interaction doorways and ponder some of the most profound questions in contemporary science: the nature of consciousness, the relationship between mind and matter, and the possibility that human intention might be more powerful—and reality more responsive—than current scientific paradigms suggest.

Chapter 10: The Four Responses

Now that you understand the key factors within your expanded circle of control—your inner state, alignment, Three Selves, neuroplasticity, and conscious actions—let's explore the impact of cosmic collaboration on the outcome.

Cosmic Collaboration

Remember from Chapter 1 when we introduced the concept that goals are in your control, prayers are outside your control, and wishes are a bit of both?

Now, something has changed: Your circle of control has expanded dramatically. Through understanding the science of wishing, you now know how to influence far more than you realized:

- You can shift your internal state through the 3 P's
- You can align your Three Selves to work together
- You can rewire your brain through neuroplasticity
- You can understand and harness your motivation
- You can consciously engage with the entire wishing process

That's the power of understanding the science - you've maximized what's in YOUR control.

Cosmic Collaboration is what happens when you've done YOUR part expertly, and now you collaborate with the forces beyond you—where your maximized intentions, actions, and energy meet opportunities, synchronicities, and responses from the wider universe.

Where an ordinary wish just hopes, a cosmic wish ENGAGES—moving with both mastery of what you control and openness to what you don't.

Cosmic Collaboration transcends faith and belief and is supported by solid science in a variety of areas, including: Neuroscience, Cognitive Psychology, Social Psychology, Quantum Physics, Complexity Science, Cosmology, Anthropology, Philosophy of Mind, Behavioral Economics, Health Sciences, as well as the more "fringe" studies of Parapsychology and Consciousness Studies, and Information Theory.

The Four Responses

Once you've maximized your part—aligning your inner state, engaging your Three Selves, and taking purposeful action—wishes unfold in patterns. Through studying wishes across cultures, timeframes, and contexts, we observe that outcomes consistently fall into four distinct categories: YES, NO, WAIT, or SOMETHING BETTER.

These aren't arbitrary. They're the ways reality responds to intention. Whether you understand these responses as coming from the universe, divine intelligence, the quantum field, collective consciousness, or simply as the natural unfolding of complex systems—the patterns remain consistent.

What matters is recognizing that once you've done your part, the collaborative process continues. And understanding these four response patterns helps you work skillfully with whatever unfolds. Let's look at each response and see how even a "no" might serve you, just as a "yes" might not be what you actually need.

Bridge to Fiction: The Team "Upstairs"

In the fictional world of A Love Story to the Universe, I introduce what I call a team "Upstairs" comprised of Guides and Traffic Angels who help coordinate meaningful encounters on earth. In the story, the team meets three Wish Fairies who take them to the magical realm of Astraea where wishes are gathered, sorted, and answered.

Is that really how it works? I have no idea. But it sure was fun thinking – and writing – about it!

Response 1: YES - Receiving What's Wished For

The most straightforward response to a wish is direct fulfillment—when reality seems to align with conscious intention in ways that feel both meaningful and magical. Research suggests several mechanisms through which "YES" responses might occur, ranging from well-understood psychological processes to cutting-edge investigations into consciousness-reality interaction.

The Neuroscience of Synchronicity

Have you ever thought of someone right before they texted you? Or stumbled upon exactly the book you needed at just the right moment? These meaningful coincidences might be more than random chance.

Carl Jung, the Swiss psychiatrist who founded analytical psychology, spent decades studying what he called "synchronicity"—moments when your inner world and outer events line up in ways that feel significant, even though there's no obvious cause-and-effect connection.[197] He wasn't talking about wishful thinking. Jung partnered with Nobel Prize-winning physicist Wolfgang Pauli to bring serious scientific investigation to these experiences. Their 1952 work suggested something radical: maybe meaningful connections between mind and world don't always need a causal explanation. Sometimes, connection itself is the mechanism.[198]

Modern research backs this up. Recent studies tracking people's daily experiences found that those who notice and pay attention to meaningful coincidences report higher creativity and greater life satisfaction— suggesting these moments matter in measurable ways.[199]

What's happening in the brain when we experience synchronicity?

Dr. Marcus Raichle discovered something fascinating: when your brain isn't focused on a specific task—like when you're daydreaming or in a relaxed state—it doesn't just shut off. Instead, it activates what he called the "default mode network," a sophisticated pattern-recognition system that continuously scans your environment for meaningful connections.[200]

165

Think of it like having a brilliant detective working in the background of your mind, connecting dots you didn't even know existed.

Dr. Emmanuel Stamatakis and his team at Cambridge University took this further. They found that people with stronger default mode network activity are better at automatic information processing—they spot patterns and opportunities faster, often without consciously trying. Their brains naturally detect meaningful coincidences that others might miss entirely.[201]

This means when you make a wish and then notice synchronicities appearing, your brain might be doing exactly what it's designed to do: recognizing genuine patterns and opportunities that align with your intentions.

Choice Architecture and Decision-Making

Here's something surprising: having more options doesn't always help you get what you want.

Psychologist Sheena Iyengar discovered this through fascinating research on choice. In one famous study, she set up a jam-tasting booth at a grocery store. When she offered 24 varieties, people stopped to look—but only 3% bought anything. When she offered just 6 varieties, 30% of people made a purchase. Too many choices actually paralyzed people instead of empowering them.[202] [203] [204]

This "choice overload" reveals something crucial about how "YES" responses work:

Focus your wish. When you scatter your attention across multiple contradictory desires—"I want to move to the city" AND "I want to buy land in the country"—you dilute your intention. Your brain gets confused signals. The universe gets mixed messages. "YES" responses typically come to wishes that are singular and clear, not competing and conflicting.

Commit to one clear direction. Rather than keeping every possible option open "just in case," effective wishers choose a path and pursue it with full commitment—while staying flexible about *how* it unfolds. This doesn't mean rigidity; it means clarity.

Trust the collaborative process. Iyengar's research showed that in some contexts, people actually make better decisions when they collaborate with trusted others rather than going it completely alone. Similarly, cosmic wishes work best when you're clear about *what* you want while remaining open to wisdom beyond your own.

The bottom line? Making one consistent, focused wish and staying with it tends to be far more effective than generating a new wish for every opportunity that appears. Clarity creates momentum. Scattered attention creates confusion.

The Baader-Meinhof Phenomenon: When Conscious Intention Meets Selective Attention

Ever decided you want a red Jeep, and suddenly you see red Jeeps everywhere?

That's the Baader-Meinhof phenomenon (also called the frequency illusion), and it's one of the most fascinating intersections between brain science and wishing. It perfectly demonstrates why both skeptics AND believers can look at the same experience and both be right.[205]

Here's what happens: You make a wish—let's say you want to start a business in sustainable fashion. Suddenly, everywhere you turn, you're noticing articles about eco-friendly fabrics, running into people who mention their clothing startups, seeing social media posts about sustainable design. It feels like the universe is conspiring to help you.

The skeptic says: "Those opportunities were always there. Your brain is just noticing them now because you've primed your attention. It's selective perception—nothing magical."

The believer says: "Focused intention creates synchronicities. The universe is responding to my wish and bringing opportunities to me."

Here's the wild part: both might be true.
Your reticular activating system (the brain's pattern-recognition filter) absolutely does start prioritizing information related to your conscious intentions. That's neuroscience. But why does this matter for wishing? Because whether the opportunities were "always there" or whether your intention somehow attracted them, the result is the same: you now see pathways you couldn't see before.[206] [207]

The moment you make a cosmic wish with clear intention, your brain becomes a highly sophisticated opportunity-detection system. And suddenly, doors that were invisible become obvious. Resources you overlooked become available. People who could help appear in your path.

Magic? Science? Does it matter? You're getting results either way.

Intuitive Decision-Making and "YES Moments"

Have you ever had a moment where you just *knew* something was right—before you could explain why?

Maybe you walked into a networking event and felt instantly drawn to talk to one specific person, who turned out to be exactly the connection you needed. Or you "randomly" decided to take a different route home and stumbled upon the perfect apartment for rent. These "YES moments" aren't just lucky coincidences—they're your brain doing sophisticated work behind the scenes.

Nobel Prize winner Dr. Daniel Kahneman revolutionized our understanding of how the mind makes decisions. He discovered that we actually think in two different ways: System 1 (fast, automatic, intuitive) and System 2 (slow, deliberate, analytical). When you make a wish and then experience a "YES moment"—that flash of recognition that says this is it—you're using System 1 thinking powered by your default mode network. It's your brain rapidly processing patterns and making connections before your conscious mind even catches up.[208]

But here's what's really fascinating: those gut feelings aren't random.

Dr. Giorgio Gronchi and his colleagues studied the neural foundations of intuition and discovered that what feels like a sudden "knowing" is actually your subconscious mind conducting incredibly sophisticated real-time analysis. Your brain is constantly processing vast amounts of environmental information—subtle cues, patterns, opportunities—that never reach your conscious awareness. Then, when all that subconscious processing identifies something important, it surfaces as an intuitive hunch or gut feeling. You're not imagining these moments; your brain genuinely detected something real.

And some people are naturally better at this than others.

Research by Dr. Vatansever and colleagues revealed something remarkable: people who demonstrate superior intuitive decision-making have stronger connectivity between their default mode network and their hippocampus (the brain's memory center). In other words, some brains are simply better wired to notice and act on synchronistic opportunities that align with their conscious intentions. The really exciting news? This appears to be a trainable skill. You can actually strengthen your brain's ability to recognize "YES moments" through practice.[209]

What this means for your wishes: When you set a clear intention and then start noticing opportunities that feel *right*, trust that feeling. Your subconscious mind has been working overtime, scanning your environment for patterns and possibilities that match your wish. Those intuitive nudges are your brain's way of saying, "Pay attention—this matters."

The Blue Balloon Phenomenon: When Reality Seems to Respond to Your Thoughts

Imagine: You're driving home from work, and out of nowhere, the thought of a blue balloon pops into your mind. Not because you're planning a party. Not because you just saw one. Just... a blue balloon. Random. You pull into your driveway and there, caught in your fence, is an actual blue balloon.

What just happened?

This phenomenon—let's call it the "Blue Balloon Phenomenon"— represents one of the most intriguing intersections between consciousness and reality. And before you dismiss it as pure coincidence, the scientific explanations are more fascinating than you might expect.

Your Body Knows Before You Do

Organizations like the Institute of Noetic Sciences explore the frontiers of consciousness research, investigating questions about mind-matter interaction that lie beyond conventional neuroscience. While their findings are considered preliminary by mainstream science, they represent an ongoing inquiry into the deeper nature of consciousness. Wha they learned is that basically your body knows things before your conscious mind catches up. They've documented that heart rate, skin conductance, pupil dilation, and brain activity often shift *in advance* of emotional stimuli that are selected completely at random. Their advice? "Have you ever noticed your body giving you information before your mind caught up? Did you listen? The more we practice tuning into these pre-feelings, the more we may discover about the untapped wisdom within us" (Institute of Noetic Sciences.[210]

These subtle physiological signals might externalize through meaningful symbols, coincidences—or even instinctive wishes—reflecting your mind's intuitive dialogue with its environment.

So what's really going on with that blue balloon? Science offers three compelling explanations:

Explanation 1: Your Subconscious Received a Message
"You sensed it before you knew it."

Maybe your peripheral vision caught a glimpse of blue movement as you turned onto your street. Maybe you subconsciously heard something rustling in your fence. Your brilliant subconscious mind processed these subtle environmental cues and bubbled the information up to consciousness as the thought "blue balloon."

The science backing this up is remarkable:

Dr. Antoine Bechara's Iowa Gambling Task showed that our bodies respond to optimal choices before our conscious minds understand what's happening. Participants showed measurable skin conductance responses that predicted advantageous decisions seconds before they consciously knew which strategy worked best. Your subconscious is constantly processing information your conscious mind hasn't caught up to yet.[211]

Dr. Dean Radin documented "presentiment" effects—measurable physiological responses to future emotional stimuli that occur several seconds before the stimulus appears. In controlled laboratory studies, participants' autonomic nervous systems showed changes that correlated with randomly-selected future images. Something in us appears to sense what's coming.[212]

Dr. Julia Mossbridge's meta-analyses found statistical evidence that human physiology can detect future random events. The effects are small but consistent across multiple studies, suggesting that precognitive abilities might be far more common than we thought.[213]

For the blue balloon: This explanation relies on sophisticated but entirely natural information processing. No magic required—just your incredibly powerful subconscious mind doing what it does best.

Explanation 2: Your Consciousness Influenced Reality
"Your focused thought made it more likely."

Now we venture into controversial territory: What if your consciousness somehow influenced physical reality? What if thinking about the blue balloon actually increased the probability of one appearing?

Before you roll your eyes, consider this research:

The Global Consciousness Project provides some of the most robust evidence that human consciousness might influence physical systems. Dr. Roger Nelson's research at Princeton shows statistically significant deviations from randomness in quantum random number generators during events that capture global attention—major disasters, New Year's celebrations, moments when millions of minds focus on the same thing. The odds against chance? 10 trillion to one. These findings suggest that collective consciousness can measurably affect physical systems.[214]

Roger Penrose and Stuart Hameroff's quantum consciousness theories propose that consciousness operates at quantum levels within neural microtubules. If consciousness functions quantum mechanically, it might theoretically influence quantum probability fields in ways that could affect where objects (like balloons) end up.[215]

Dr. William Tiller's research on "intention-imprinted devices" demonstrates that focused human intention can influence the properties of physical spaces. His experiments show that intention can alter the pH of water and the behavior of biological systems, creating what he calls "conditioned environments" where subsequent manifestation becomes more likely.[216]

For the blue balloon: Your conscious focus on "blue balloon" might have influenced quantum probability fields through mechanisms we don't yet understand. If consciousness operates at quantum levels, your intention could have subtly shifted the complex system of factors that determine where objects end up.

Explanation 3: It Was Always There

"Your attention system was primed to notice it."

The third explanation relies on well-established cognitive neuroscience: the balloon was already in your environment, but it only registered in consciousness after your attention system was primed to notice it. Remember the Baader-Meinhof phenomenon we discussed earlier? This is similar.

Your Reticular Activating System (RAS) serves as your brain's filtering mechanism, determining which of the millions of sensory inputs you receive actually reach conscious awareness. Until you think "blue balloon," your RAS isn't prioritizing blue balloon-related information. But once that thought surfaces—whether from genuine precognition or random mental noise—you suddenly become a blue-balloon-detection machine. What was invisible becomes obvious.[217]

Dr. Daniel Simons' famous research on inattentional blindness showed that people can completely miss a person in a gorilla suit walking through a basketball game when they're focused on counting passes. We literally don't see what we're not looking for—until suddenly, we do.[218]

For the blue balloon: It might have been there for hours or even days, rustling in your fence. But your brain filtered it out as irrelevant background information—until the moment your RAS decided it mattered.

The science of psychophysics—which studies the relationship between physical stimuli and mental perception—examines these phenomena, with research showing that expectation actually lowers sensory detection thresholds, making us more sensitive to stimuli we're anticipating. For example, experiments demonstrate that primed expectation can both accelerate conscious awareness of faint stimuli and increase the likelihood that anticipated events are noticed—a finding that clarifies how wishes, anticipation, and reality sometimes seem to align in mysterious ways.[219] [220]

The Truth? Maybe All Three

Here's what makes this really interesting: these explanations aren't mutually exclusive. They might all be operating simultaneously in a sophisticated consciousness-reality feedback loop:

1. Your subconscious picks up subtle cues (precognition/intuition)
2. Your focused attention primes your RAS to notice balloon-related stimuli (selective attention)
3. Your consciousness potentially influences probability fields at quantum levels (manifestation)

The result? A seemingly magical synchronicity that represents the sophisticated integration of multiple consciousness systems operating across different levels of reality.

The Quantum Connection: Zero-Point Field Interactions

Moving into even more speculative (but scientifically grounded) territory, some consciousness researchers propose that intention might influence physical systems through quantum field interactions—the fluctuating quantum energy that exists in apparently "empty" space. While highly speculative, this provides a potential physical mechanism for how focused intention could influence material reality.

For readers interested in exploring the quantum mechanics of consciousness further:

- Dean Radin's research on intention effects on quantum random number generators.[221]
- William Tiller's work on how focused intention influences material systems.[222] [223]
- Stuart Kauffman's complexity science framework on the "adjacent possible."[224]

Why This Matters for Cosmic Collaboration

The Blue Balloon Phenomenon challenges conventional scientific understanding because it suggests consciousness might function as more than a passive observer of reality. If these effects are real—and the research suggests they might be—it would fundamentally change what we know about the relationship between mind and matter.

Dr. Amit Goswami and other consciousness researchers argue that such phenomena point toward a "consciousness-based reality" where observation doesn't merely detect pre-existing conditions but actively participates in creating what is observed. While controversial, this perspective continues to attract serious scientific investigation discussed in the next chapter.[225]

This is especially important for understanding wishing and Cosmic Collaboration. When you make a wish, who—or what—are you connecting with? Is it:

- Your own subconscious wisdom?
- A quantum field of possibility?
- A universe that responds to consciousness?
- All of the above?

The Blue Balloon Phenomenon suggests that the boundary between art and science, between mind and matter, between wisher and cosmos, might be far more permeable than we ever imagined.

And that's not woo-woo—that's where cutting-edge science is pointing.

Bridge To Fiction: Dan Brown's Secret Of Secrets

In fact, IONS directly advised Dan Brown for his novel *Secret of Secret* — making it serve as a powerful "bridge to fiction" connection between art and science. In it, he integrates metaphysical theories with established science to build mainstream curiosity into topics covered in this book on wishing.

In addition to touching on the concept of presentiment, Brown's book delves into the theory of "nonlocal consciousness": the idea consciousness can extend beyond the brain.[226] This can explain everything from near-death-experiences to lucid dreaming, and more. As we will explore later, such experiences invite us to question where intuition ends and intention begins.

Confirmation and Selective Attention: Your Brain Rewires to See What You're Wishing For

Here's something remarkable: expectation doesn't just influence how you interpret what you see—it actually changes what you see in the first place.

Dr. Thomas Ramsøy's research on creativity and the default mode network revealed that when people expect to see certain things, their visual cortex becomes pre-activated *before* the stimulus even appears. Your brain literally starts preparing to perceive what you're looking for. Expectation alters perception itself, not just your interpretation of it.[227]

Translation: When you make a wish and hold that intention, your brain starts scanning for it before it even appears.

Dr. Li and colleagues studied default mode network connectivity during social situations and discovered that when people hold specific intentions or wishes, they subconsciously increase their sensitivity to environmental cues and opportunities related to those intentions. This explains why wishers often report remarkable "coincidences" that perfectly align with their stated goals—it's not magic, it's neuroscience. Your brain literally becomes more sensitive to relevant environmental information.[228]

Think of it like this: You wish to start a podcast, and suddenly you're "randomly" meeting people who mention podcasting equipment, overhearing conversations about audio editing, noticing articles about successful podcasters. Were these opportunities always there? Probably. But now your brain is tuned to the frequency that picks them up.

Dr. Schacter and colleagues' research on "constructive episodic simulation" adds another layer: when you vividly imagine future scenarios—like really visualizing your wish coming true—you activate the same neural networks involved in memory and perception. This creates neurological conditions that enhance your ability to recognize related environmental opportunities when they actually arise. You're essentially training your brain to spot the wish when it shows up.[229]

But there's something crucial that many manifestation teachings skip, as illustrated in the following fictional "case study."

Bridge to Fiction Case Study: When "YES" Arrives with Unexpected Lessons

Sarah had been wishing for a promotion for two years. She visualized it, she aligned her Three Selves, she took purposeful action. Then it happened—she got the promotion. Her wish received a clear "YES."

But within three months, Sarah was exhausted, overwhelmed, and questioning everything. The promotion came with unexpected challenges: a difficult team dynamic she hadn't anticipated, travel that strained her relationships, and pressure that triggered anxiety she thought she'd resolved years ago.

Was this really a "YES"? Yes—but not the simple one she'd imagined.

This is what many people miss about "YES" responses: they often arrive with unexpected challenges, hidden lessons, or growth requirements you didn't see coming. Remember the Motivation Matrix and Quadrant 4 in Chapter 7, the thing you Don't Want + Don't Have? This is what happened with Sarah. The universe (or your subconscious wisdom, or cosmic intelligence—pick your framework) sometimes knows that getting what you want requires becoming someone who can handle it.

Questions to ask when your wish receives a "YES":
- What am I learning beyond the initial joy?
- What skills is this "YES" requiring me to develop?
- What parts of myself is this wish revealing that need attention?

- How is this "YES" different from what I imagined—and why might that difference matter?
- What if this "YES" is exactly what I needed, even if it's not exactly what I wanted?

Sarah eventually realized her promotion was teaching her boundaries, delegation, and authentic leadership—skills she'd been avoiding. The "YES" wasn't just about the title. It was about who she needed to become to truly deserve it.

This is cosmic collaboration in action: Your wish gets granted, but the universe adds curriculum you didn't realize you signed up for.

Response 2: NO - When Reality Says No

You did your best. You aligned your Three Selves. You took purposeful action. You visualized, hoped, worked for it. And reality said no. The job went to someone else. The relationship ended. The opportunity vanished. The dream crashed.

When we wish, the last thing we want is a "no" response. It hurts.

Your initial reaction to NO doesn't feel like wisdom or protection or cosmic guidance. It feels like rejection. Like failure. Like the universe doesn't care about you or your wishes. And in that moment, it's supposed to feel that way. You're grieving the loss of what you wanted.

But here's what most people often don't realize about NO responses: they're not endings. They're information.

"No" responses aren't endings: They're information.

Have you ever looked back on something you desperately wanted but didn't get—and felt overwhelming relief? Maybe you were devastated when you didn't get that job, only to realize six months later it would have been a nightmare. Or you were heartbroken when that relationship ended, only to meet someone far better suited to you. That's not just hindsight— it's what we call Reverse Optimism: the ability to look back and recognize the hidden gifts in rejection.

The Dalai Lama captured this perfectly: "Sometimes not getting what you want is a wonderful stroke of luck." And how many country songs celebrate "unanswered prayers"—when you're grateful your wish *didn't* come true?

But here's what most people miss: There is actual science explaining why blocked wishes often serve you better than granted ones.

When NO Protects You from the Wrong Wish

Dr. Tim Kasser's research reveals something crucial: **not all wishes are created equal**. His decades of studies show that wishes rooted in extrinsic motivation—external validation, material acquisition, social comparison, status—consistently lead to decreased happiness and increased anxiety, *even when achieved*. Meanwhile, wishes aligned with intrinsic values—

personal growth, meaningful relationships, contribution to others—create lasting satisfaction.

Think about it: You wish for the corner office, the fancy title, the impressive LinkedIn profile. You get it—and you're miserable. Why? Because you were chasing what you thought you *should* want rather than what would actually fulfill you.

A NO response might be your subconscious or superconscious (Inner Self or Higher Self) wisdom – or the universe, or cosmic intelligence—whatever framework resonates with you protecting you from pursuing something that would never truly satisfy. It's redirecting your energy toward what matters.

This is where Reverse Optimism becomes powerful.
The formula works like this:
"If _____ hadn't happened, then _____ wouldn't have happened."
Or: *"If _____ HAD happened, then _____ would/might have happened, and that wouldn't have been good."*

NO as Teacher, Not Rejection
Dr. Angela Duckworth's research on grit and perseverance shows that successful individuals learn to distinguish between adaptive persistence and maladaptive stubbornness—understanding when NO responses signal the need for strategic changes rather than just increased effort.[230]

Dr. Carol Dweck's research on growth mindset and shows that how you interpret rejection determines everything. People who view blocked wishes as learning opportunities—rather than personal failures—demonstrate enhanced resilience, creativity, and eventual goal achievement. The NO isn't ending your story; it's editing it.[231] [232]

Author Mark Manson captured this paradox perfectly in one of my favorite quotes: "Happiness is solving problems." Research on the PERMA model confirms this—accomplishment and the process of working toward mastery create well-being, not just achieving the end result. The NO isn't taking away your happiness; it's giving you a meaningful problem to solve. And solving meaningful problems is precisely what creates lasting fulfillment.

Dr. Kevin Ochsner's neuroscience research on cognitive reappraisal adds another layer: when you learn to reframe potentially negative events, you're literally rewiring your brain. Brain imaging shows that successful reappraisal increases communication between your prefrontal control regions and emotional processing centers. You're building emotional intelligence every time you work skillfully with a NO.

Dr. Barbara Fredrickson's "broaden-and-build" theory suggests that positive reframing doesn't merely make people feel better—it actually expands their awareness of possibilities and builds psychological resources for future challenges.[233]

And here's where it gets fascinating: Dr. Richard Tedeschi and Dr. Lawrence Calhoun's research on post-traumatic growth reveals that people who extract meaning from major setbacks often report *greater life satisfaction* than those whose early wishes were easily fulfilled. The struggle—the NO—built something in them that the easy YES never could.

Resilience and Meaning-Making

Sometimes, wishing for something doesn't go as planned. According to Dr. Martin Seligman's research, what truly matters isn't whether we get what we want right away—it's how we explain setbacks to ourselves. People who see obstacles as specific and temporary ("This was just today—I can try again!") bounce back better than those who believe disappointment means they'll never succeed.[234]

As Dr. Viktor Frankl famously said:

> *Those who have a "why" to live, can bear with almost any "how."*
> *Viktor Frankl*

Frankl's work—rooted in the hardest experiences imaginable—shows that finding meaning helps us keep going, even when things are tough. So, when you get a "NO" in response to a wish, treat it as a clue: sometimes the answer points you toward what truly matters, helping you find your deeper purpose. Quotes and science like these remind us: hope and meaning are powerful tools for resilience. Every "no" is a chance to reframe, learn, and move closer to what really lights you up.

Here's something fascinating about NO responses: Sometimes what we desperately want would actually harm us—we just can't see it yet.

Bridge to Fiction: When "NO" Protects Us: The Three Justins Paradox

Perhaps the most intriguing aspect of "NO" responses lies in what might be called the "Three Justins Paradox"—the recognition that getting what we want can sometimes be worse than not getting it.

This example comes from *A Love Story to the Universe*, where three eleven-year-old boys, all named Justin, are each wishing for bicycles on their birthdays. Justin #1, from a loving but financially struggling family, wishes for any bicycle. Justin #2, from a middle-class household, wishes for a bike to help him get to his dog-walking job. Justin #3, from a wealthy family, wishes for the "Optibike Everest 300 Mile Range Adventure E-Bike."

The paradox emerges when we consider potential outcomes. Justin #3 might get his expensive bike only to have it stolen, feel inadequate when a rival gets an even better model, or suffer an accident due to the bike's power and complexity. Meanwhile, Justin #1's "unanswered prayer" might lead to a neighbor helping him fix up a discarded bicycle, creating a lifelong friendship and teaching valuable repair skills.

This echoes the classic Christmas Story dilemma: the boy who desperately wants a BB gun despite everyone warning "you'll shoot your eye out." Sometimes the very thing we desire most intensely carries hidden dangers that our conscious mind cannot foresee but some deeper intelligence recognizes and protects us from.

187

Bridge to Fiction: The Exquisiteness of Contrast

In *A Love Story to the Universe*, there's a character named CC from the planet Lofton, where all wishes come true instantly. Think about flying and you can fly. Sound magical? It is. But CC shares something profound after arriving in Astraea: "I didn't understand the exquisiteness of not getting your wish until I got here. Now I embrace the beauty of contrast. **You can only see fireflies in the dark.**"

That's the hidden gift of NO. Without contrast—without disappointment, redirection, delay—we can't appreciate the YES when it arrives. We can't develop resilience, wisdom, or depth. We can't become the version of ourselves capable of handling what we truly desire.

Bridge to Fiction Case Study: When Michael Got His NO (And Discovered His YES)

Michael spent three years wishing to open his own restaurant. He had the business plan, the perfect location scouted, investors lined up. Then everything fell apart in the final month—permits denied, investors pulled out, the location went to someone else. Complete, devastating NO.

For six months, he was bitter. He felt like the universe had betrayed him, like all his work meant nothing. But during that time, something shifted. He started teaching cooking classes from his home—something he'd never considered. He discovered he loved teaching more than the idea of running a restaurant. The classes grew. People kept asking for more. Within a year, he'd built an online cooking education business that gave him flexibility, creativity, and income he never would have had with a restaurant.

Looking back with Reverse Optimism, Michael realized: *If that restaurant had happened, I never would have discovered teaching. I would have been trapped in 80-hour weeks managing staff and inventory instead of doing what I actually love.*

The NO revealed the deeper truth. His want didn't match his need. He didn't need to run a restaurant. His need was more aligned with sharing his passion for cooking in a way. The wish was pointing in the right direction, and his "no" response led him to a better option that gave him freedom and connection.

This is cosmic collaboration at work: Your conscious mind wanted one thing, but your subconscious or superconscious wisdom (or the universe) knew something better was possible—something you couldn't even see yet.

Questions to Ask When Your Wish Receives a NO:

- What was I actually seeking beneath this specific wish? (Freedom? Recognition? Security? Connection?)
- Was this wish rooted in intrinsic or extrinsic motivation? (Would it have genuinely fulfilled me, or just looked good to others?)
- What's being revealed about my deeper needs or values?
- How might this NO be protecting me from something I can't see yet?

- What would Reverse Optimism look like here? ("If this HAD happened, then..." Or perhaps, "Because this happened, THAT happened.)
- What might be trying to emerge instead?

Remember: A NO isn't the universe rejecting you. It's reality offering information. Maybe the timing is wrong. Maybe you're not ready. Maybe there's a better path you haven't considered. Maybe you're being protected from something that would ultimately hurt you.

The question isn't whether to accept the NO—it's how to work *with* it.

Response 3: WAIT - Navigating Uncertainty and Delay

WAIT might be the hardest response of all.

At least with NO, you know where you stand. You can grieve, adjust, move on. And YES—well, YES is what you wanted. But WAIT? WAIT is limbo. It's checking your email seventeen times a day. It's the "did they ghost me or are they just busy?" of wish responses. It's lying awake at 3 a.m. wondering if you should keep hoping or give up.

WAIT means: not yet. Maybe. Things are aligning. Or maybe they're not. You don't know. And that not-knowing? That's what makes WAIT so unbearable.

Why Your Brain Hates Uncertainty

There's a reason WAIT feels so uncomfortable: your brain literally hates not knowing.

When the outcome of your wish is unclear, your brain goes into scanning mode. It's constantly looking for signals: Is this going to work out? Should I keep hoping? Should I give up? This creates that restless, can't-settle feeling—like waiting for the other shoe to drop.

Your nervous system is asking: Should I keep investing energy here? Or protect myself from disappointment?

Here's what's fascinating: that uncomfortable feeling during WAIT isn't just anxiety. It's actually your brain on high alert, primed to spot opportunities. Think of it like your internal radar is turned up to maximum sensitivity. You're ready to recognize and respond the moment something shifts—even if it doesn't feel that way.

And here's the part that changes everything: those physical sensations you're feeling? The butterflies, the restlessness, the heightened awareness? Research shows your brain decides whether to label those sensations as "anxiety" or "excitement."[235] Think about it: Waiting for test results feels almost identical to waiting for a surprise party. Same elevated heart rate. Same alertness. Same butterflies. The difference? How you interpret the feeling.

You have more control over that interpretation than you think.

191

The Marshmallow Test: When WAIT Pays Off

In the 1960s, Stanford researchers ran a simple but revealing experiment.[236] They put a marshmallow in front of young children and said: "You can eat this now, or wait 15 minutes and get two marshmallows."

Some kids waited. Some didn't.

The researchers tracked these children for decades. The ones who could delay gratification? They had better grades, better health, more successful careers, better relationships. The ability to WAIT—to resist immediate gratification for something better later—turned out to be one of the strongest predictors of life success.

Here's what this tells us about WAIT as a wish response: **The delay often leads to something better.**

Getting one marshmallow now feels satisfying in the moment. But two marshmallows later? That's objectively better. The kids who could tolerate the discomfort of waiting got the bigger reward. Not just in the experiment—but throughout their lives.

WAIT isn't punishment. It's often the pathway to the better outcome.

The Wisdom of Timing: What You Can't Control

Here's what you need to understand about WAIT: **The timeline is not in your control.**

Some wishes respond in minutes—like finding that parking space. Others take months or years. The timeline doesn't indicate whether you're "doing it right" or whether cosmic collaboration is working. It simply reflects the complexity of what needs to align.

The ancient Greeks understood this. They had two different words for time: *chronos* and *kairos*.

Chronos is clock time—seconds, minutes, hours ticking by. It's what you measure on your watch.

Kairos is the right time—the opportune moment when everything aligns. Research on kairos timing [237] suggests that wishes fulfilled at their "right time" are typically more satisfying and sustainable than those achieved through force or rushing.

Think about pregnancy. You can't make a baby develop faster just because you're impatient. Nine months is nine months. Dr. Malcolm Gladwell's research on timing effect shows that many phenomena—from biological development to social change—involve precise timing requirements that cannot be artificially accelerated without compromising quality.[238]

Some things just take the time they take.

Your role during WAIT isn't to control WHEN. It's to maintain your alignment WHILE the timing unfolds.

Two Kinds of WAIT: Internal vs. External Readiness

When you're stuck in WAIT, there are usually two things happening: either **you're not ready yet**, or **the world isn't ready yet**. Sometimes it's both.

When YOU'RE not ready: Think of it like a checklist of prerequisites. You want to launch your business, but you haven't yet developed the skills, built the network, saved the capital, or learned the lessons you'll need to succeed. The WAIT isn't arbitrary—it's the time required to check off those boxes. If you complete that checklist in six months, your wish might manifest quickly. But if it takes you three years to gain the necessary experience, build the right relationships, and develop the required expertise, then the wish won't—and shouldn't—happen until then.

Research on goal hierarchies shows that complex achievements require completing sub-goals in sequence.[239] You can't skip steps. The entrepreneur who tries to launch before developing basic business skills usually fails. The writer who publishes before learning craft usually regrets it. WAIT gives you time to become the person who can handle what you're wishing for.

When THE WORLD isn't ready: Sometimes you're completely prepared, but the cultural moment hasn't arrived yet. Malcolm Gladwell's research on tipping points reveals that ideas, products, and movements require specific cultural conditions to take hold. You can have the best idea at the wrong time, and it goes nowhere. The same idea five years later? It transforms the world.

Think about innovations that failed initially but succeeded later—not because the innovation changed, but because culture caught up. Electric cars existed for decades before Tesla made them desirable. Video calling technology existed long before COVID made Zoom essential. The technology was ready. The world wasn't.

Patience is NOT Passive: Here's what's crucial: WAIT doesn't mean sit around hoping. It means **be productive while you wait**. Dr. Carol Dweck's research on growth mindset shows that people who use waiting periods for skill development, relationship building, and learning dramatically outperform those who simply wait passively for circumstances to change.

If you're waiting for internal readiness—work the checklist. Build the skills. Make the connections. Gain the experience. Do the hard inner work. The WAIT is your preparation time.

If you're waiting for external readiness—keep creating, keep building, keep refining. Stay visible. Nurture your community. When the cultural moment arrives, you want to be positioned and ready.

The worst thing you can do during WAIT is nothing.

How to Navigate WAIT Emotionally

Beyond being productive, you also need strategies for managing the emotional toll of uncertainty.

Stay connected to your future self. Dr. Hal Hershfield's research on "future self" visualization shows that people who can vividly imagine their future selves handle waiting periods far better.[240] They're not just gritting their teeth through delay—they're maintaining a clear vision of where they're heading. Picture yourself six months from now, a year from now, with the wish fulfilled. Keep that future self real and present, even as you wait. However, "buyer beware." We'll explore how visualization can go awry in Chapter 11: The Pitfalls and Problems in Wishing.

Make if-then plans for the hard moments. Dr. Peter Gollwitzer's research on implementation intentions reveals that people who create specific if-then plans for managing uncertainty show greater emotional stability than those who just try to "wait it out." For example: "If I start obsessively checking my email, then I'll go for a walk." "If I feel anxious about the timeline, then I'll review my vision board." These pre-planned responses create psychological scaffolding that supports you during ambiguous periods.

Practice present-moment awareness. Dr. Judson Brewer's mindfulness research shows that staying grounded in the present moment significantly reduces the psychological distress of uncertain outcomes. When you catch yourself spiraling into "what if" thinking, bring yourself back to what's actually happening right now. Not the imagined future. Not the feared outcome. Just now.

Find meaning in the waiting itself. Dr. Shigehiro Oishi's research on meaning-making during uncertainty demonstrates that people who see waiting periods as opportunities for growth experience higher well-being and are more likely to achieve their goals. What if this WAIT is preparing you? Teaching you something essential? Building patience, resilience, or trust you'll need later?

The waiting isn't wasted time. It's part of the process.

Questions to Ask When Your Wish Gets WAIT:

- Am I waiting for internal readiness or external readiness? (What's my checklist? Or is the world not ready yet?)
- What can I do NOW to work my checklist? (Skills to build, connections to make, experience to gain?)
- Am I being productive or just passive? (What action is available in this moment?)
- Can I reframe this restless feeling as anticipation rather than anxiety?
- Am I trusting the process, or exhausting myself trying to control the timeline?
- What if this delay is allowing something essential to develop—either in me or in the circumstances?
- How might I look back on this waiting period with gratitude once the wish unfolds?
- What would it look like to see this WAIT as part of the gift rather than an obstacle to it?

Remember: WAIT isn't the universe ignoring you. It's not a test of your worthiness. It's the complexity of reality aligning in ways you can't see yet. Things are happening beneath the surface—connections forming, skills developing, circumstances shifting—that need time to unfold.

The question isn't whether to wait—it's how to wait skillfully: with productivity, presence, and trust in the timing you can't control.

Response 4: SOMETHING BETTER – Recognizing and Accepting Unexpected Gifts

Sometimes the universe says yes—just not to what you asked for.

You wished for the job in New York but got offered an even better position in Austin. You hoped to reconnect with an old friend but met someone new who became your business partner. You wanted your book published by a specific press, but a different publisher offered you a three-book deal with more creative freedom.

In that moment, you realize: **I didn't get what I wanted. I got something better.**

Sometimes this recognition is instant—the moment you see the alternative, you know it's superior. The relief is immediate. The gratitude flows naturally. You can't believe you almost missed this by being so fixated on your original wish.

Other times, the recognition takes longer. You're disappointed at first. You mourn what didn't happen. But gradually—maybe in weeks, maybe in months—you start to see it. The thing you got instead? It's actually better. Not just different. Not just "good enough." Actually, objectively, surprisingly BETTER.

This is the SOMETHING BETTER response. And it's one of the most powerful—and most challenging—responses to recognize and embrace.

Why We Sometimes Resist "Better"

If something is genuinely better, why would we resist it? The psychology reveals several fascinating reasons:

The "I know what I want" stubbornness. There's a particular kind of ego investment in being RIGHT about what you need. Accepting something better means admitting you didn't actually know what was best for you. For some people, that feels like failure rather than gift.

You literally can't see it. Remember the Reticular Activating System from Chapter 8?[241] Your brain filters reality based on what you're looking for. If you're scanning for a red car, you might miss the perfect blue one. If you're fixated on one specific outcome, your brain might not even register the better alternative—even when it's right in front of you.

Attachment to the story you've been telling. You've already told everyone you're moving to New York. You've imagined the apartment, the coffee shop you'd frequent, the life you'd build there. Austin wasn't in your narrative. Sometimes we resist better opportunities because they require us to rewrite the story we've been living into.

Dr. Steven Hayes' research on psychological flexibility shows that people who can hold their goals lightly while staying committed to their values demonstrate greater well-being and achievement than those who rigidly cling to specific outcomes.[242] This is why the phrase "this or something better" isn't just spiritual bypassing—it's practical wisdom backed by science.

The Science of Recognizing Better: Why We're Bad at Predicting Happiness

Here's something fascinating: We're remarkably bad at knowing what will actually make us happy.

Dr. Dan Gilbert's research on "affective forecasting"[243] reveals that humans consistently misjudge both the intensity and duration of their emotional responses to future events. We overestimate how happy achievements will make us and how devastated disappointments will leave us. We think we know what we want, but our predictions about what will fulfill us are often wildly inaccurate.

Dr. Timothy Wilson's studies on the "impact bias" show that people systematically overestimate the emotional impact of both positive and negative events. That corner office you're convinced will change your life? Research suggests it probably won't affect your baseline happiness nearly as much as you think. Meanwhile, the opportunity you're dismissing as "not quite right" might actually be exactly what serves your deeper needs.

This is why SOMETHING BETTER responses are so valuable: reality sometimes has access to information about what will actually fulfill you that your conscious mind doesn't possess.

The "Wrong Question" Phenomenon

Sometimes we get SOMETHING BETTER because we were asking for a solution when we actually needed to address the underlying cause. Remember from Chapter 7 how we explored the difference between wants and needs? This is where that distinction becomes crucial in understanding why the universe sometimes gives us something we didn't ask for.

This also connects directly to the framework in my book *Five Reasons Why Bad Things Happen*—we might be trying to fix a symptom when the real issue requires deeper attention – so we can get to the "why" and fix not just the symptom but also the cause.

You wished for more money, but what you actually needed was to heal your relationship with abundance and worthiness. You wished for a romantic relationship, but what you actually needed was to develop self-love first. You wished for the promotion, but what you actually needed was courage to start your own business.

SOMETHING BETTER often appears when cosmic intelligence recognizes the deeper need beneath your surface request—when you were asking for what you *wanted* but got what you actually *needed*.

What "SOMETHING BETTER" Actually Looks Like

Beyond Your Imagination: Things You Didn't Know to Ask For

The most magical SOMETHING BETTER responses involve opportunities you couldn't have imagined because you didn't know they existed. You wished for a new job and ended up discovering a career path you'd never heard of. You wished to travel and stumbled into a community that became your chosen family. You wished for healing and found a spiritual practice that transformed your entire worldview.

These are the moments when you realize the limitations of your own imagination. The universe showed you possibilities beyond your conscious awareness.

The Timing Twist

Sometimes you get your original wish later—but by then, you don't want it anymore. You've grown. You've changed. What seemed essential six months ago now feels irrelevant or even limiting.

This is SOMETHING BETTER through personal evolution. You became someone who needed something different.

The Compound Effect

One SOMETHING BETTER often leads to a cascade of unexpected goodness. The job rejection led to the road trip that led to the conversation that led to the opportunity that changed everything. This is why tracking your wishes matters—you can see the chain of responses that wouldn't have happened if you'd gotten your original wish.

Better for More Than Just You

Sometimes SOMETHING BETTER serves a greater good beyond your individual desire. Your business didn't work out, which meant you were available to help your sister through her crisis. Your relationship ended, freeing both of you to find more aligned partnerships. Your project failed, but the skills you developed became valuable to a cause larger than yourself.

This is where cosmic collaboration reveals its most profound dimension: your wishes participating in patterns of benefit beyond what you can see.

The Worthiness Piece: Opening to Receive

Dr. Kristin Neff's research on self-compassion reveals something crucial: people with low self-worth often sabotage opportunities that are "too good" because they don't believe they deserve them. They literally cannot receive SOMETHING BETTER because their internal narrative says they're not worthy.[244]

The Gratitude Paradox

Here's something counterintuitive: Being genuinely grateful for what you already have actually opens you to receive more. Dr. Robert Emmons' extensive research on gratitude shows that people who practice regular appreciation experience greater life satisfaction, stronger relationships, and yes—more opportunities appearing in their lives.

It's not about "attracting abundance" through positive thinking. It's about training your brain to recognize and receive opportunities when they appear. Gratitude literally rewires your reticular activating system to notice possibilities you'd otherwise miss.

Opening to What You Didn't Know to Ask For

Sometimes SOMETHING BETTER requires you to release your grip on the specific outcome and simply hold the intention for what truly serves you. This isn't passive hoping—it's active trust combined with continued aligned action.

The practice sounds simple: "This or something better." But it requires genuine surrender, not just lip service. It means being willing to be surprised, to be wrong about what you need, to receive gifts in unexpected wrapping.

The Connection Between WAIT and SOMETHING BETTER

Sometimes WAIT is actually preparing you to recognize or receive SOMETHING BETTER.

Maybe you're not ready yet—you need skills, wisdom, healing, or maturity to handle what's coming. Maybe circumstances aren't aligned yet—other people, resources, or opportunities need time to come together. Maybe your original wish needs to evolve before the better alternative can become visible.

WAIT and SOMETHING BETTER are intimate partners in cosmic collaboration. The delay isn't punishment—it's preparation for the gift you didn't know was possible.

How to Work With SOMETHING BETTER
Celebrate It!
When you recognize a SOMETHING BETTER response, celebrate it immediately. Don't spend time mourning what you didn't get. This teaches your brain to recognize and welcome these responses faster.

Reframe Your Language
Instead of: "I didn't get what I wanted, but at least I got X."
Try: "I got Y, which is actually better because [specific reasons]."
This isn't toxic positivity—it's accurate assessment. Name specifically why this alternative serves you better.

Questions to Ask
- How is this alternative better than my original wish?
- What would I have missed if I'd gotten exactly what I asked for?

- What deeper need is this fulfilling that I didn't consciously recognize?
- How has this surprised me in positive ways?
- What is this teaching me about trusting cosmic collaboration?
- In what ways might this serve others beyond just me?
- How might this be preparing me for something even greater?

Trust the Pattern

Once you start recognizing SOMETHING BETTER responses, they become easier to spot. You develop a kind of sixth sense for recognizing when reality is offering you an upgrade, even when it doesn't match your original specifications.

This is the ultimate skill in cosmic wishing: the ability to stay focused on your deeper intentions while remaining radically open to how they manifest.

Bridge to Fiction: The Role of the Upstairs

A Love Story to the Universe is told from the point of view of a team "Upstairs," populated by Spirit Guides, Traffic Angels, and Wish Fairies doing their best to assist a human named Nelle. The following is an excerpt where the character questions the dynamic of fate, free will, and divine intervention.

> Then she wonders: *Who writes our story anyway?* Is it fate? Free will? A Divine force? Or is it all random, and we just have to decide how to react? Was Shakespeare right?

Are we all just performing a role written by someone else? Is everything predestined?

The others fade into the background as Nelle tries to solve the mystery. She can feel them hovering above her, ready to nudge her if she goes too far off track. In fact, her experience with them is that they can even get somewhat forceful, like persistent Border Collies forcefully knocking her onto the right path if necessary.

Remember the definition of Cosmic at the beginning of this book?
b) of, relating to, or concerned with abstract spiritual or metaphysical ideas; cosmic wisdom.

Many of you reading this book feel this otherworldly presence in your life. Others may define it as the collective superconscious or using theories from quantum physics. Whichever approach, it's worth considering the role of this "force" in aligning us with "something better" to either get us back on track with the life lessons we signed up for or perhaps to take us on an even more elevated path.

Einstein said it best:

> "You find it strange that I consider the comprehensibility of the world ... as a miracle or as an eternal mystery. Well, a priori, one should expect a chaotic world, which cannot be grasped by the mind in any way... That is the 'miracle'

which is constantly reinforced as our knowledge expands."[245]

Integration: Working with The Four Responses

Now that you understand each of the Four Responses, here's the real skill: learning to work with *all* of them skillfully.

The Feedback Loop: Each Response Teaches You Something

Think of the Four Responses as a conversation with reality. YES tells you what's working. NO shows you what needs to shift. WAIT teaches you patience and preparation. SOMETHING BETTER reveals possibilities you couldn't see.

Dr. John Dunlosky's research on metacognition—basically, thinking about your own thinking—shows something fascinating: People who learn from *all four types* of responses achieve more, bounce back faster, and feel more satisfied with life than people who just keep using the same wishing strategies no matter what happens.[246]

The key capabilities? Pattern recognition (spotting which response you're getting), emotional regulation (staying steady regardless of outcomes), cognitive flexibility (adjusting your approach based on feedback), and meaning-making (finding the wisdom in each experience).

Dr. Angela Duckworth's research on "deliberate practice" backs this up.[247] People who treat wishing like a learnable skill—tracking patterns, identifying what works, adjusting their approach—get significantly better results over time than those who rely on pure persistence or positive thinking alone.

And Dr. Peter Gollwitzer's studies on "implementation intentions" show that people who pre-plan their responses to different outcomes ("If I get a NO, then I'll...") stay more emotionally stable and motivated than those who just react spontaneously.[248]

Staying Steady: How to Accept Any Response

Here's the truth: cosmic wishing works best when you can genuinely be okay with *any* of the Four Responses.

Not fake okay. Not "I'll pretend I'm fine while I'm actually bitter." Actually, genuinely okay—because you trust that each response serves you somehow.

The research on equanimity (inner stability regardless of what happens) reveals specific practices that help:

Mindfulness: Dr. Judson Brewer's studies show that people who develop mindfulness skills—the ability to observe what's happening without immediately reacting—report greater life satisfaction and achievement even when they experience multiple disappointments.[249]

Radical Acceptance: Dr. Tara Brach's work shows that practicing present-moment awareness helps you meet any result—pleasant or unpleasant—without getting stuck in resistance or desperation. Brain imaging studies show this actually changes how your prefrontal cortex and emotional centers communicate.

Self-Compassion: Dr. Kristin Neff's research reveals something crucial: treating yourself with kindness regardless of outcomes doesn't reduce your motivation—it actually *enhances* it by reducing the emotional toll of setbacks.[250]

Psychological Flexibility: Dr. Steven Hayes' Acceptance and Commitment Therapy research demonstrates that the ability to stay open to all possible outcomes while maintaining clear values is a learnable skill. People who develop this capacity often find that the *process* of wish pursuit becomes as satisfying as the outcomes.[251]

Why Your Wishes Seem to Come True (The Science)

Before we wrap up the Four Responses, let's address the obvious question: Do wishes actually *work*? Or are we just seeing what we want to see?

The scientific answer is: **Both.**

The Placebo Effect: Research shows that when people believe something will help them, their brains release actual pain-relieving chemicals, their immune systems function better, and their symptoms improve—even when they received a sugar pill.[252] Your beliefs create measurable physical changes.

Self-Fulfilling Prophecy: Social psychology research shows that when you expect positive results, you subconsciously adjust your behavior in ways that make those results more likely. You notice relevant opportunities more readily. You make choices that align with your desired outcomes. Your wish doesn't magically alter reality—but it definitely influences how you interact with reality.

Confirmation Bias: Here's the tricky part: People naturally remember the times wishes came true more than the times they didn't.[253] This makes wishing feel more reliable than it might actually be. But some researchers argue this "bias" might actually be *adaptive*—maintaining hope and motivation even in uncertain circumstances keeps you moving forward.

What Your Response Patterns Reveal About You

Here's something interesting: If you track your wishes over time, you'll probably notice patterns in which responses you tend to get. These patterns aren't random—they reveal something about your beliefs, your readiness, and your growth edge.

Mostly YES responses? Dr. Carol Dweck's research suggests you might have strong self-efficacy and trust in your environment. But watch out— easy achievement might mean you're not challenging yourself enough. The real growth happens when you wish for things that stretch you.

211

Mostly NO responses? Dr. Martin Seligman's research on explanatory style shows this often reflects subconscious beliefs about unworthiness or impossibility. The good news? These belief patterns can be changed through cognitive work, often leading to dramatic improvements in outcomes.[254]

Mostly WAIT responses? Dr. Daniel Siegel's research suggests you may be developing patience, trust, and tolerance for uncertainty—valuable capacities that often precede major breakthroughs. Extended waiting periods frequently indicate that larger systemic changes are preparing to emerge.

The Bottom Line: Learning to recognize *which* response you're getting—and what it's trying to teach you—transforms wishing from blind hope into conscious collaboration.

Meet the Scientists

The researchers whose work illuminates the Four Responses:

Carl Jung — Synchronicity theory
Marcus Raichle — Default mode network
Martin Seligman — Learned optimism
Viktor Frankl — Logotherapy and meaning-making
Daniel Kahneman — Intuitive decision-making (System 1/System 2)
Daniel Simons & Christopher Chabris — Inattentional blindness
Daryl Bem — Precognition experiments

Kevin Ochsner — Cognitive reappraisal neuroscience

Richard Tedeschi & Lawrence Calhoun — Post-traumatic growth theory

(Full biographies in Appendix B)

Questions to Ponder:

- Which type of response do you experience most often with your wishes? What patterns do you notice in terms of timing, content, or emotional state when making the wish? How might these patterns reflect your underlying beliefs about worthiness, possibility, or trust in reality's responsiveness?

- How do you typically react to "NO" or "WAIT" responses? Do you tend toward persistence, giving up, or exploring alternatives? What might this reveal about your relationship with uncertainty, control, and trust in beneficial outcomes even when they don't match your original preferences?

- Can you identify times when "SOMETHING BETTER" emerged from blocked wishes? How might these experiences inform your current approach to wish fulfillment, goal flexibility, and openness to unexpected possibilities that serve your deeper needs and values?

- What might the Blue Balloon Phenomenon represent in your own experience? Have you noticed instances where consciousness and reality seemed to interact in ways that challenged conventional explanations of coincidence and causation?

- How could developing greater pattern recognition about your wish responses enhance both your goal achievement and your overall life satisfaction? What would it look like to approach wish practice as a learnable skill rather than a matter of luck or fixed ability?

- Based on your response patterns, what areas of personal development might deserve attention? How might your wish experiences be providing feedback about beliefs, strategies, or life directions that could benefit from conscious examination and potential adjustment?

Next: The Pitfalls and Problems in Wishing

Chapter 11 will explore the fascinating intersection between personal wishing and collective transformation—discovering how consciousness might operate not just individually but collectively to influence the course of human and planetary evolution. We'll investigate everything from prayer circles to global meditation events, from social movements to environmental healing initiatives, exploring the emerging science of how collective intention might shape reality on scales far beyond individual experience.

Chapter 11: The Pitfalls and Problems in Wishing

By now, wishing probably feels a lot more nuanced and meaningful than it did when you first picked up this book. Early chapters nudged us beyond childhood dandelion puffs and birthday candles, inviting us into a space where science, philosophy, and personal experience all mingle.

Yet even powerful tools can cast shadows. And here's where things get interesting: What happens when people take these practices too far—or forget why they wished in the first place? Where are the hidden pitfalls, the addictive patterns, or moments we lose sight of wisdom and ethics?

Let's explore the side of wishing that isn't always glitter and light.

How Wishing Can Go Wrong

Wishing, at its best, is a force for clarity, motivation, and heart-centered action. But the very tools that help us create our future can also turn sideways—especially when science and soul fall out of sync.

Sometimes, wishing becomes more about getting what we want than understanding why we want it in the first place. If we push our dreams at all costs, ignore the signals of body wisdom, or sidestep lessons meant for our growth, the result isn't always happiness—it can be exhaustion, frustration, or confusion.

The brain's dopamine system, for example, rewards us for anticipating good outcomes, driving creativity and boldness.[255] But those same anticipation circuits can fuel addictive patterns if we chase "the next big wish" instead of savoring what's present.

Wishing also faces ethical dilemmas. What happens when our desires clash with someone else's well-being? Jon Kabat-Zinn's work in mindfulness reminds us that intentions should be paired with non-harming, care, and awareness.[256] Daniel Kahneman and Jonathan Haidt show that good intentions aren't enough—ethics and empathy must guide our choices.[257]

Most importantly, the problem isn't with wishing itself—but with how, why, and for whom we wish. Overreaching, ignoring lessons, or giving up entirely can each trigger distinct forms of suffering. Let's dig deeper into the most common pitfalls—so your wishes keep you moving forward, not stuck or out of balance.

The Toxic Manifestation Epidemic

Before exploring the hidden shadows of wishing, it's crucial to address the cultural damage caused by modern manifestation teachings that equate "Cosmic Collaboration" with personal blame.

The "Secret" Shadow

Popular manifestation movements—most notably "The Secret"—introduced millions of people to ideas about optimism, intention, and personal power. For many, these teachings opened doors to understanding that mindset matters, that focus influences outcomes, and that we're not merely passive recipients of fate. These are genuine benefits worth acknowledging.

The problem isn't that these teachings are entirely wrong—it's that they're incomplete. By treating the "Law of Attraction" as the supreme, all-encompassing principle of reality, they can lead to what psychologists now call "manifestation trauma"—the deep shame and self-blame people internalize when life doesn't conform to their positive thoughts.[258]

Also, focusing on conscious wants isn't always the most effective or enriching approach. As discussed in earlier chapters, wants don't always align with needs, and if you don't take into account the "will" of the Three Selves, you might be going in the wrong direction.

Beyond the Law of Attraction: The Bigger Picture

When we look at what science actually reveals about how outcomes unfold, we find something far more fascinating—and more empowering—than "thoughts become things."

Causality is fundamental: research shows that our brains evolved to detect causal relationships between our actions and their outcomes.[259] We're wired to understand that effort creates results, that choices have consequences, and that what we *do* matters as much as—often more than—what we merely think about. The psychology of causation reveals that humans naturally track how our actions influence outcomes,[260] which is why planning, preparation, and persistence consistently outperform passive visualization.

Even more compelling is what complexity science and systems theory teach us: outcomes emerge from dynamic interactions between multiple factors—your actions, other people's choices, environmental conditions, timing, and countless variables operating at different scales.[261] Complex systems create "emergent properties"—results that couldn't be predicted by looking at any single factor in isolation.[262]

Your life isn't just the product of your thoughts; it's an emergent phenomenon arising from a vast web of causality and interconnection. As complexity researchers put it: "At each level of complexity, entirely new properties appear. Psychology is not applied biology, nor is biology applied chemistry"—meaning higher-order outcomes can't be reduced to simple cause-and-effect thinking like "positive thoughts create positive results."

This more complete understanding doesn't diminish the power of intention—it *enriches* it. When you recognize the Law of Purpose (your deeper calling), the Law of Karma (actions rippling through time), the Law of Timing (readiness—both yours and the world's), and the Law of Interconnection (your wishes unfolding within a vast network of other people's free will and choices), you're not working with less power. You're working with **reality as it actually is**—complex, alive, responsive, and far more interesting than a cosmic vending machine.

The Toxic Message

The manifestation movement's greatest limitation isn't just its incomplete view of causality. It's the victim-blaming that emerges when people believe they create *everything* through their thoughts. The toxic message is clear: "You create your own reality completely. If something bad happens, you attracted it through your thoughts or vibration."

This approach:

- Victim-blames people facing trauma, illness, or systemic oppression.[263]
- Fosters shame and self-doubt when life naturally presents adversity
- Bypasses the wisdom of cosmic intelligence, which sometimes protects us with delays or redirection
- Ignores complexity—genetics, environment, social systems, collective karma, and the reality that you're not the only force at work in the universe

Scientific reality paints a clearer picture: Dr. Martin Seligman's research on learned helplessness shows that when people believe they have total control over uncontrollable events, they're much more likely to experience depression and anxiety. The manifestation movement doesn't just oversimplify reality—it sets people up for psychological harm when reality inevitably proves more complex than their vision boards suggested.[264]

219

The "Leap Before You're Ready" Trap

Beyond the psychological harm, manifestation teachings can lead to measurably dangerous financial decisions. *The Secret* (published in 2006, just before the 2008 financial crisis) encouraged a "leap now, build your wings later" mentality that appealed to millions—but what happens when magical thinking meets major life decisions?

Recent research reveals the tangible consequences. In a 2023 study published in *Personality and Social Psychology Bulletin*, psychologists Lucas Dixon, Matthew Hornsey, and Nicole Hartley developed the first scientific scale to measure manifestation beliefs and tracked real-world outcomes.[265] Their findings are striking:

People who believe strongly in manifestation are:

- 1.42 times more likely to have declared bankruptcy
- 1.33 times more likely to invest in high-risk cryptocurrency
- 1.28 times more likely to have been victims of fraud
- Significantly more prone to "get rich quick" schemes

The researchers found that manifestation believers consistently overestimate their likelihood of achieving unlikely success and underestimate the timeframe needed—a dangerous combination when making financial commitments. (How many people bought outrageous mortgages after *The Secret* came out, believing the universe would "provide"?)

Here's the crucial distinction: Remember from Chapter 1 that wishes, by definition, involve outcomes beyond your direct control—that's what makes them wishes rather than goals. The problem with "leap before you're ready" thinking isn't the leap itself. It's confusing *what you control* (your inner state, your preparation, your aligned action) with *what you're wishing for* (the outcome, the cosmic response, the universe's collaboration).

When you sign a mortgage you can't afford, you're not making a cosmic wish—you're making a legally binding commitment that's entirely within the goal category. You've taken what should have stayed in the realm of "I wish for financial abundance" and forced it into "I will make this specific thing happen through sheer belief." That's not cosmic collaboration— that's magical thinking applied to contract law.

The neuroscience and psychology we covered in earlier chapters— understanding your Three Selves, building sustainable neural pathways, aligning with genuine purpose—these *do* work because they help you control what's actually controllable: your inner state, your actions, your readiness. But leaping without preparation, signing contracts you can't afford, or making irreversible decisions based on "feeling aligned" alone? That's treating a wish like a guarantee, and the universe doesn't work on our demand.

A Word About Control

The distinction this book makes is that while not everything is in your control, the more you apply the sciences we discussed—neuroscience, psychology, psychophysiology, complexity science and so many more—the more control you have, not only over the outcome to your wishes, but also how to handle the responses in a way that will increase your power.

Spiritual Bypassing & Toxic Positivity

"Spiritual bypassing"—a term coined by Dr. John Welwood—describes the habit of using spiritual ideas to dodge emotional work, deny responsibility, or gloss over life's real challenges. This looks like detachment, denial of pain, or using spiritual slogans to rationalize inaction.

"Toxic positivity" is even more insidious—a relentless insistence on optimism, which dismisses legitimate grief, anger, or fear:[266][267]

- Emotional suppression
- Shame and invalidation of difficult feelings
- Failure to solve actual problems or take necessary action

As Brené Brown's research on shame, resilience, and wholeheartedness shows, confronting disappointment, failure, or the vulnerability of openly wishing can trigger deep feelings of inadequacy or self-doubt. Brown reminds us that true growth is possible only when we acknowledge our feelings honestly and foster compassion for ourselves and others, transforming shame into courage, connection, and renewed motivation.[268][269]

Both cause harm by shutting down authentic emotional processing and making negative emotions unacceptable.

Privilege Blindness

A further issue is privilege blindness: "Everyone can manifest abundance if they just believe." This sentiment dismisses systemic inequities and blames individuals for circumstances beyond their control:[270] [271]

- Ignores social and economic obstacles
- Implies equal opportunity for all, which is demonstrably untrue
- Perpetuates blame, shame, and exclusion rather than support or understanding

Dr. John Welwood and other researchers highlight that spiritual and manifestation teachings are harmful when they bypass necessary emotional development, deny systemic barriers, or avoid facing discomfort head-on.[272]

Main Risks and Pitfalls

Now, let's get specific. Below are the most common ways that wishing can fall short or even get in the way of true fulfillment. Each pitfall draws from research and psychological insight—so you'll see not just what can go wrong, but why it happens.

Manipulating Outcomes

When wishing morphs into control—trying to bend others to your will or force situations—it can lead to conflict and disappointment. Research in mindfulness ethics[273] and social safety demonstrates how genuine intent and compassion make wishing powerful—while manipulation erodes trust.[274] [275] [276]

Stripping the Fun Out of Wishing:

One of the fastest ways to kill a wish is to turn it into another obligation. When you strip all the joy, playfulness, and fun out of wishing and treat it like a grim task to accomplish, your Inner Self withdraws its energy. The "should" energy repels sustainable motivation. As discussed in Chapter 7, Research on intrinsic motivation shows that when activities lose their inherent enjoyment, people experience decreased engagement and increased burnout. Remember: wishing is supposed to be delightful. The moment it becomes another item on your productivity checklist, another thing you're forcing yourself to do "correctly," you've lost the magic that makes wishing powerful. If your wish doesn't have ANY element of genuine enjoyment built into it, your subconscious will sabotage it—no matter how noble or "good for you" it seems.

Manifestation Addiction: Dopamine Loops If manifesting becomes a habit—always seeking more, chasing a high—it can trap us in cycles of anticipation and letdown.[277] Daniel Gilbert's work on affective forecasting shows many misjudge how happy a wish will make them, only to be caught wanting something else.[278] (All the more reason to understand the Four Responses!)

Bypassing Wisdom and Lessons Sometimes, people wish for outcomes that shortcut important life lessons—money without budgeting, relationships without healing, or recognition without genuine contribution.

Ethical Blind Spots Even well-intended wishes can ignore values, readiness, or the impact on others. Daniel Kahneman's research and Jonathan Haidt's work on moral emotions highlight how easy it is to overlook consequences—especially when focused only on a goal.[279]

Bridge to Fiction: When Wishing Stopped

In *A Love Story to the Universe*, the Wish Fairies face three existential crises—all caused by humans who stopped wishing. Each crisis reveals what happens when the connection between human consciousness and Cosmic Collaboration breaks down.

During the Black Plague, people lost confidence in their ability to make wishes. "It was a dark time in heaven and on Earth," as DD explains. Even the Wish Fairies "had given up hope and were ready to close down Astraea for good." The solution? A brilliant Wish Fairy named Aristella inspired humans with a new ritual: blowing on dandelions, where "people all over puffed on the blowball, they made a wish and imagined their loved ones' souls ascending into heaven with love."

Then there was Zabelê, the Brazilian girl who jumped seven waves on New Year's Eve, making seven wishes that all came true. The Hundredth Monkey Effect kicked in—when enough people witnessed her luck but couldn't replicate it, they didn't just stop wishing. They stopped believing in the *possibility* of wishing themselves.

And Nelle? She created a whole other level of havoc in Astraea because deep down, she didn't feel worthy. The scoreboard in Astraea ticked from 79 to 80—entering the DANGER ZONE toward "Total system shutdown."

The message from Astraea is clear: wishing isn't just a personal practice. It's essential to the Cosmic Collaboration between human consciousness and universal intelligence.

But what does science say happens when people stop wishing?

The Dark Side of NOT Wishing

The fictional crisis in Astraea reflects real psychological phenomena. When people stop wishing—stop hoping, imagining better futures, and engaging with possibility—it can lead to paralysis, passivity, and learned helplessness. Martin Seligman's studies demonstrate that hope and agency aren't luxuries—they're lifelines for motivation and change.[280] Without them, both individuals and communities struggle to thrive.

Each risk is an opportunity to reflect, recalibrate, and reconnect. Up next: practical steps to safeguard your wishing power, so it moves life forward in positive, healthy ways.

Safeguarding Your Wishing Power: Practical Steps

If you're looking to make wishing a lasting, positive force in your life, here are some research-backed practices and reflection tools to keep things healthy, ethical, and growth-oriented.

Practice Ethical Self-Check Before every major wish, pause for a self-assessment. Ask: Is this wish aligned with my core values? Does it honor consent and the well-being of others? Am I ready for what comes next? Tools from the fields of mindfulness and ethics give practical strategies for checking your intentions.[281]

Watch Out for Anticipation Addiction It's easy to slip into cycles of wishing for "the next big thing"—especially when reward centers in your brain crave novelty. Keep a gratitude journal, ground yourself in the present, and reflect on why a wish matters instead of just chasing more.

Honor the Lessons, Don't Bypass Them Remember: lasting change asks for patience and reflection. Viktor Frankl's logotherapy[282] as well as Antonio Damasio's research on body wisdom show genuine growth almost never skips the "hard stuff." Use setbacks as signals to pause and check your assumptions.[283]

If You've Given Up on Wishing—Restart Small A sense of learned helplessness is more common than you'd think. Start tiny: wish for a moment of delight, gratitude, or growth. Those first, modest steps can rekindle hope and agency, helping motivation and resilience return.

Connect to Your Inner Self Wisdom

Remember from the chapter on the Three Selves: your Inner Self isn't just a keeper of emotions and memories—it's also the source of profound body wisdom. Neuroscientist Antonio Damasio's somatic marker hypothesis shows that feelings and bodily sensations often guide better decisions than logic alone.[284]

Whenever you make a wish, check in. Are your Inner Self's emotions and physical sensations aligned with your Outer Self's rational plans and your Higher Self's intuition? Practice mindful movement, tune into your felt sense before setting intentions, and let your body point out internal conflicts or old patterns that might be holding you back.

Real alignment, as explored in the Three Selves chapter, happens when you listen beyond the mind—so every wish is supported by the full wisdom of your being..[285]

With these habits, wishing stays a source of joy and growth—instead of becoming a trap. Use the science, pause for reflection, and let hope walk with wisdom as you progress forward.

Meet The Scientists

The researchers whose work illuminates the pitfalls and problems in wishing:

Martin Seligman — Positive psychology and learned helplessness
Viktor Frankl — Logotherapy and meaning-making

Antonio Damasio — Body-centered consciousness and somatic markers

Daniel Gilbert — Affective forecasting and happiness prediction

Jon Kabat-Zinn — Mindfulness-Based Stress Reduction (MBSR)

Daniel Kahneman — Intuitive decision-making (System 1/System 2)

Jonathan Haidt — Moral emotions and prosocial behavior

John Welwood — Spiritual bypassing

Lucas J. Dixon, Matthew J. Hornsey, and Nicole Hartley — Manifestation beliefs and real-world consequences

(Full biographies in Appendix B)

Questions to Ponder:

- **Which pitfall resonates most with your past wishing experiences?** Have you ever fallen into manifestation addiction, spiritual bypassing, or the "leap before you're ready" trap? What did those experiences teach you about the difference between cosmic collaboration and magical thinking?

- **How has toxic positivity or victim-blaming affected your relationship with wishing?** Have you ever blamed yourself for outcomes beyond your control, or felt shame when positive thinking wasn't enough? How might understanding the complexity of causation—rather than oversimplified "Law of Attraction"—change how you approach both success and setbacks?

- **Where might you be trying to control rather than collaborate?** Are there wishes where you're attempting to manipulate outcomes or force results rather than holding intention while remaining open to cosmic timing and wisdom? What would it look like to release control without releasing hope?

- **Have you lost the joy in your wishing practice?** If wishing has become another obligation or productivity metric, what would it take to restore the playfulness and delight? How might your Inner Self be signaling withdrawal of energy when wishes feel like "shoulds"?

- **What lessons might your blocked or delayed wishes be offering?** Rather than viewing obstacles as failures of manifestation, what growth, preparation, or redirection might the universe be inviting? How could you honor the wisdom in "not yet" without falling into learned helplessness?

- **How does your body wisdom inform your wishes?** When you check in with your Inner Self before setting intentions, what do physical sensations and emotions reveal about true alignment versus surface desires? What practices might help you develop this somatic intelligence for more authentic wishing?

Next: Collective Wishing and Emergent Change

As you reflect on the shadow side of wishing and the ways personal intention can go astray, it's important to remember that wishing does not occur in isolation. Every hope and dream you nurture exists within a larger collective—community, culture, and even global consciousness. Just as individual wishes shape personal trajectories, shared intentions have the power to transform teams, organizations, and entire societies. In the next chapter, we'll explore what happens when wishes ripple outward: how individuals, groups, and communities align around common desires, and why the science reveals that collective wishing doesn't just amplify results—it multiplies possibility. Let's discover how joining forces with others can bring your wishes to life in ways greater and more meaningful than you might ever imagine.

Chapter 12: Collective Wishing for Cooperative Change

Remember that wish you made at the very beginning of this book? Over the past eleven chapters, we've explored how to turn your wish into a cosmic wish by aligning the Three Selves, clarifying motivations, fears, and misbeliefs, understanding brain circuitry, navigating the Four Responses, mastering the 3 P's, and discovering the transformative power of storytelling.

Now, let's take that further and look at wishes on a larger scale.

What happens when aligned individuals come together around shared intentions? The science reveals something remarkable: the power doesn't just add up---it multiplies exponentially. Some wishes naturally involve others. Some wishes ARE about creating change beyond the individual--- in teams, organizations, communities, even globally. This chapter explores WHY collective wishing works and what it means for creating meaningful change.

But first, an important question: should you even share your wishes with others?

When to Share Your Wishes (And When to Keep Them Private)

Should you tell people about your wishes, or keep them private? According to neuroscience and psychology research, the answer is more nuanced than you might expect.

The Premature Satisfaction Problem

Dr. Andrew Huberman's neuroscience research reveals a critical insight: when you tell people about your goals before taking action, your brain releases dopamine---the same neurotransmitter associated with achievement. This creates a "post-goal" state where your brain believes progress has been made simply through declaration, reducing motivation to actually take action.[286]

Derek Sivers popularized this research in his TED talk, demonstrating that people who announced their goals were significantly less likely to achieve them than those who kept intentions private.[287]

The social recognition creates what psychologists call "social reality"--- your brain treats the acknowledgment as partial completion of the goal itself. This relationship between public commitment and reduced follow-through has been reproduced in behavioral research summarized by NPR's shots segment "What's the Best Way to Achieve a New Goal?"[288]

This demonstrates in practice the effect Peter Gollwitzer identified in implementation-intention research that premature verbalization can replace action-driven momentum.[289]

Keep Your Wishes Private When:

The wish is new and unformed --- You're still gaining clarity, your Three Selves aren't aligned, or you haven't taken concrete action yet. Research on implementation intentions reveals that premature disclosure—before you've formed genuine commitment—significantly reduces follow-through.

Sharing would invite judgment --- Family or friends have been discouraging (or they just wouldn't understand), the wish challenges others' expectations, or you're vulnerable to being talked out of it.

Sharing could trigger jealousy or competition --- Others might want similar things and see you as competition, or their own subconscious resistance could create energetic interference with your manifestation, even if they consciously wish you well!

The wish is deeply personal or spiritual --- It involves inner transformation, your relationship with your Higher Self, or soul growth. Studies on intrinsic motivation show that external validation can undermine internally-driven pursuits.[290]

You notice a desire for external validation --- You want to prove something or seek approval. Research on extrinsic vs. intrinsic motivation shows wishes driven by external validation have lower completion rates. **However, there's a crucial distinction between seeking approval**

(extrinsic validation) and receiving supportive accountability (strategic partnership). In fact, participants with regular accountability check-ins showed 65% goal completion on average rising to 95% when weekly follow-ups were scheduled.[291] [292]

This finding is central to Self-Determination Theory, which demonstrates how external evaluation reduces intrinsic motivation by diminishing self-direction.[293]

Share Your Wishes Strategically When:

You have supportive accountability partners --- They have a track record of encouraging without judgment and understand the Four Responses. Studies on accountability partnerships show significantly increased goal achievement with constructive support. Plus, when they have something to gain by your achievements, it can be a win-win! Research on positive goal interdependence shows that when individuals perceive their goals as aligned---where your success supports theirs---they naturally work to facilitate each other's achievements.[294] [295]

You've already taken initial action --- Huberman's protocol: Share goals only after you've begun behavioral implementation and established initial neural pathways through action.[296]

You're with people who can (and want to) actively help --- They have resources, connections, or expertise you need. Social capital research shows strategic disclosure to potential allies significantly increases resource access.

You're participating in aligned Wish Circles or support groups ---
The group understands cosmic wishing principles and practices the 3 P's. Research on group intention suggests aligned group focus can amplify individual intention effects.[297]

The Conscious Disclosure Practice
Before sharing a wish, ask yourself:
1. Have I taken at least one concrete action toward this wish?
2. Am I sharing to get help/accountability or approval/validation?
3. Will this person's response affect my commitment?
4. Do I feel more excited about sharing or doing the actual work?
5. Is this person capable of holding space for all Four Responses?

If YES to questions 1, 2, and 5, and NO to 3 and 4: Share strategically. If not: Keep it private until your neural commitment is stronger than your need for external validation.

Who Should You Tell? Distinguishing Yaysayers from Naysayers

The science is clear: it matters who you share your wishes with. Yaysayers---those who offer encouragement, support, and constructive feedback---help boost your motivation and increase your likelihood of realizing your wishes. Naysayers---those who criticize, doubt, or dismiss---can erode confidence, fuel self-doubt, and sometimes prevent you from taking action.[298 299 300]

How can you recognize a Yaysayer? They...

- Encourage your growth
- Offer nonjudgmental support
- Celebrate your achievements
- Never undermine your confidence or focus
- Help you keep calm and focused during times of uncertainty

Research shows that sharing wishes with respected, supportive individuals enhances persistence and performance. In contrast, negative reactions from naysayers or indifferent people can undermine your commitment and progress. Social support actually acts as a psychological buffer, reinforcing your belief in success, while negative feedback can activate stress responses and reduce your chances of pursuing your goals. [301] [302] [303]

Whenever possible, choose to disclose your wishes to proven supporters, mentors, or friends who will nurture your growth. Save your most vulnerable dreams for those who earn your trust, not those likely to dampen your enthusiasm. [304] [305]

Once you've chosen supporters wisely, you're better equipped to protect your wish's inner potential. This selective approach isn't just practical; it's essential for cultivating the Three Ps---your wish's peace, positivity, and purpose.

Integration with the 3 P's

Peaceful: Intentional privacy maintains your inner peace by avoiding others' projections, doubts, or unwanted advice.

Positive: Sharing only with truly supportive people protects the positive emotional state essential for effective wishing.

Purposeful: Conscious disclosure decisions keep you focused on authentic purpose rather than external validation.

Remember: The cosmic collaboration happens between you, your Three Selves, and universal intelligence. Sometimes the most powerful thing you can do is keep that sacred conversation private until it's strong enough to withstand the noise of the external world. Selective secrecy isn't withholding---it's gestation; a wish kept in quiet trust gathers coherence before it learns to fly.

Now, when you ARE ready to share your wishes---when you've chosen your supporters wisely and taken those initial actions---something extraordinary becomes possible: collective wishing.

The Collective Subconscious: We're More Connected Than We Think

The Inner Self from Chapter 6---that subconscious, emotional aspect of consciousness---connects to something larger. Carl Jung called it the "collective unconscious," a term he used to describe the deepest layer of the unconscious mind shared by all human beings, containing archetypes and inherited psychic structures that transcend individual experience. The terminology matters here. Jung used 'collective unconscious,' but in English, 'unconscious' literally means 'not conscious'—knocked out, brain not working. Since Freud and Jung used both 'subconscious' (das Unterbewusste) and 'unconscious' (das Unbewusste) somewhat interchangeably, this creates confusion. So to be clear: when I say 'Collective Subconscious,' I'm referring to the shared field connecting the subconscious awareness in all of us.

The Collective Subconscious isn't metaphysical speculation; it's neuroscience. Research on mirror neurons reveals that specific brain cells fire both when we perform an action and when we observe someone else performing that same action, creating a neural basis for empathy and social connection.[306]

Studies on emotional contagion by psychologists Elaine Hatfield and John Cacioppo demonstrate that emotions spread through social networks like wildfire, with people unconsciously mimicking and synchronizing their emotional states with those around them.[307]

Even more remarkably, research on neurological synchronization shows that when people come together in aligned activities---singing, breathing, sharing emotional states---their brain waves literally synchronize. Uri Hasson's research at Princeton using fMRI scanning revealed that during effective communication, the brain patterns of speakers and listeners begin to couple and align, with the listener's brain activity mirroring the speaker's with only a slight delay.[308] Studies of group meditation show that participants' brain waves synchronize in ways that create measurable coherence in the surrounding electromagnetic field.[309]

This explains why one person's positive energy can shift an entire room, or why one aligned catalyst can transform a team's culture. Everyone's swimming in an invisible sea of shared subconscious energy. What each person contributes to that sea---the alignment cultivated through the 3

P's, the clarity gained through understanding the Three Selves---creates ripples extending far beyond the individual.

When groups align their intentions, something measurable happens. Research by psychologist Christakis and political scientist Fowler on social contagion demonstrates that behaviors and emotional states spread through networks up to three degrees of separation---your friend's friend's friend can influence your happiness, health behaviors, and life choices.[310]

Individual cosmic wishes don't exist in isolation. They interact with and influence the collective field in ways both subtle and profound.

The Science of Amplification

What if our intuition about future events isn't just psychological pattern recognition, but something more? Parapsychologist Dean Radin has conducted studies suggesting physiological responses can occur seconds before a stimulus is presented. While his work is debated within the scientific community, it invites us to consider whether consciousness might interact with time in ways we don't yet fully understand.

More established research shows clear amplification effects. Studies on coordinated group activities---from sports teams to musical ensembles to military units---demonstrate that synchronized action creates enhanced performance outcomes beyond what individual skill levels would predict. Research by organizational psychologist Anita Woolley shows that collective intelligence emerges when groups achieve high levels of social sensitivity and turn-taking in communication, creating a "group IQ" that exceeds the capabilities of the smartest individual member.

The mathematics of alignment reveals something fascinating: 1+1+1 doesn't equal 3 when it comes to aligned intention. Network science demonstrates that connections between nodes create exponential rather than linear increases in system capability. When three people align their efforts, they create not just three units of power but three individuals plus three relationships (A-B, B-C, A-C), yielding six potential interaction effects. Add a fourth person, and the relationship count jumps to six. This exponential growth explains why aligned teams consistently outperform collections of talented individuals working in parallel.

Research on tipping points by physicist Duncan Watts and sociologist Malcolm Gladwell demonstrates that you don't need everyone aligned to create massive change---often just 10-25% of a population adopting a new behavior can tip an entire system into transformation.[311]

In consciousness research, the Maharishi Effect shows that when even 1% of a population reaches coherence through Transcendental Meditation, collective stress indicators drop, and peace indicators rise. Decades of studies reported reductions in crime and conflict when a small threshold of people practiced synchronized meditation. This principle mirrors Hawkins' findings that higher-calibrating individuals measurably uplift the collective through resonance fields of consciousness.[312]

These findings have profound implications for collective wishing: even a minority of aligned individuals can catalyze transformation throughout larger groups.

The Three Levels of Collective Wishing

Collective wishing operates at three distinct but interconnected levels, each building on and amplifying the previous.

Level 1: Individual Wishes Aligned with Larger Purpose

At this level, personal wishes serve or connect to something bigger. When someone wishes to "excel in my role" while understanding that their role serves their company's mission to provide clean water in developing countries, their individual wish plugs into collective energy. The wish remains personal---focused on individual growth and contribution---but it aligns with and draws power from a larger purpose. Research on goal interdependence by psychologist Morton Deutsch shows that when individuals perceive their personal goals as contributing to collective success, motivation and performance both increase significantly.[313]

Level 2: Team-Level Collective Wishes

Small groups of 3-12 people sharing a common intention represent the sweet spot of collective wishing. This is where Wish Circles come alive--- intimate gatherings where aligned individuals amplify each other's intentions through shared practice. Research by organizational psychologist Richard Hackman demonstrates that teams of this size can maintain the high levels of communication, trust, and psychological safety necessary for genuine alignment while avoiding the coordination challenges of larger groups.[314] At this level, team members aren't just pursuing parallel individual goals---they're creating shared intentions that transcend any single person's wishes. A product development team wishing to "create something that genuinely helps people" operates as a collective consciousness, with individual contributions flowing into a unified creative force.

Level 3: Organizational and Community-Level Wishes

Large-scale unified intentions---whether company-wide, community-wide, or even global---require leadership, structure, and clear communication to maintain coherence. Historical examples like the Civil Rights Movement demonstrate that when thousands or millions of people align around a shared vision, transformation becomes possible that no individual or small group could achieve alone. Research by political scientist Elinor Ostrom on collective action shows that even large groups can successfully manage shared resources and pursue common goals when they establish clear communication channels, shared principles, and mechanisms for addressing free-riders.[315]

The power emerges when all three levels align simultaneously: individuals pursuing personal wishes that connect to team intentions that serve organizational or community transformation. This creates what complexity scientists call "coherence across scales"---alignment from the micro to the macro level that generates remarkable collective capability.

The Three Selves at Scale

The Three Selves framework doesn't disappear when we move to groups. In fact, it scales up in fascinating ways. Just as individuals need to align their Inner Self (subconscious/emotional), Outer Self (conscious/strategic), and Higher Self (purpose/wisdom), organizations develop collective versions of these three aspects.

The organizational Inner Self manifests as emotional culture---the shared feelings, unspoken norms, and subconscious patterns that shape how people experience work together. Research by Sigal Barsade and Olivia O'Neill on emotional culture shows that these collective emotional patterns significantly influence productivity, creativity, and employee wellbeing, often more powerfully than official policies or stated values.[316]

The organizational Outer Self appears in structures, strategies, and conscious operations---the visible systems, processes, and plans that guide collective action. This is the realm of engineering, strategic plans, and documented processes and procedures.

The organizational Higher Self emerges in purpose, values, and vision--- the transcendent reason for the organization's existence beyond profit or survival. Companies like Patagonia, with its mission to "save our home planet," exemplify organizations where Higher Self purpose permeates decision-making at all levels.

The magic happens when individual alignment meets collective alignment: when each person has integrated their three selves AND the organization has aligned its collective Inner, Outer, and Higher selves. This creates what organizational theorists call "strategic coherence"---a state where individual actions naturally serve collective purpose because alignment exists at every level simultaneously.

Understanding how the Three Selves scale up naturally leads to questions about motivation—how do groups stay energized and committed to shared wishes?

Collective Motivation

The motivation drivers from Chapter 7 operate at group level in ways both similar to and different from individual motivation. Self-Determination Theory, developed by Edward Deci and Richard Ryan, identifies three fundamental psychological needs that drive human motivation: autonomy (feeling in control of one's choices), competence (feeling effective and capable), and relatedness (feeling connected to others).[317] These needs don't disappear in groups---they transform.

At collective scale, autonomy becomes shared agency---the team's sense that they have real influence over their direction and methods. Research by management scholar Amy Edmondson on team psychological safety shows that groups perform best when members feel safe to take risks, voice concerns, and make decisions without fear of punishment or humiliation.[318]

Competence transforms into collective efficacy---the group's shared belief in their ability to achieve challenging goals together. Research by organizational psychologist Albert Bandura demonstrates that teams with high collective efficacy persist longer, set more ambitious goals, and achieve better outcomes than teams lacking this shared confidence.[319]

Relatedness deepens into what sociologists call "communitas"---the intense feeling of social connection and shared identity that emerges in

245

aligned groups. Research on high-performing teams shows that this sense of "we're in this together" predicts team success more reliably than individual talent levels.

The challenge lies in creating shared motivation that honors individual drivers. People come to teams with different motivational profiles---some driven by achievement, others by affiliation, still others by autonomy or purpose. Collective wishing works when the shared intention creates space for diverse motivational needs while channeling them toward unified goals.

Collective Fears, Desires, and Misbeliefs

Earlier chapters explored how fears, desires, and misbeliefs impact wishing at the individual level. These same forces operate at the collective level--- and understanding them unlocks the key to creating aligned, powerful groups.

Teams and organizations develop collective patterns that live in the group's subconscious and become incredibly powerful. Collective fears manifest as shared anxieties that shape group behavior below conscious awareness. A team might collectively fear failure ("our launches always fail"), vulnerability ("showing weakness means getting fired"), or change ("new processes always make things worse").

Research by organizational psychologist William Kahn on psychological safety demonstrates that these collective fears create defensive routines that block creativity, prevent honest communication, and sabotage performance.

However, by applying the lessons of the Four Responses, including the message that "NO" responses aren't endings, they're information, they're more likely to do a "post-mortem" analysis of what went wrong to create stronger, longer-lasting improvements.

Collective desires represent what groups want together---which can harmonize with or conflict against individual wishes. A sales team might collectively desire to "crush the competition" while individual members want to maintain work-life balance and avoid aggressive tactics. Research on goal conflict by psychologist Robert Emmons shows that when collective and individual desires misalign, motivation deteriorates and performance suffers.[320]

Collective misbeliefs are the stories groups tell themselves that aren't true: "We're not innovative," "That's just how things work here," "We can't compete with larger companies." Research on organizational identity by management scholar Blake Ashforth reveals that these shared self-concepts become self-fulfilling prophecies, with groups unconsciously acting in ways that confirm their limiting beliefs about themselves.[321]

The opportunity emerges when groups become aware of these patterns and consciously transform them. Research on appreciative inquiry by organizational development scholar David Cooperrider demonstrates that when teams examine their collective assumptions and deliberately

247

reframe limiting beliefs into empowering narratives, breakthrough becomes possible. A team that shifts from "we always struggle with innovation" to "we're learning to innovate more effectively" opens space for new behaviors and outcomes.

This examination isn't comfortable. It requires courage to surface and discuss collective fears, acknowledge conflicting desires, and challenge cherished misbeliefs. But groups that do this work---that bring collective subconscious patterns into conscious awareness---tap into extraordinary transformative power.

The 3 P's for Groups

The 3 P's---Peaceful, Positive, Purposeful---become the foundation for collective alignment, supported by robust research across organizational psychology and neuroscience. These principles are especially potent in Wish Circles, where groups gather with the explicit intention to support each other's cosmic wishes.

Peaceful at collective scale means creating the conditions for collective calm and psychological safety. Amy Edmondson's research at Harvard demonstrates that teams perform best when members feel safe to take interpersonal risks---admitting mistakes, asking questions, challenging ideas---without fear of embarrassment or punishment.

This collective peace doesn't mean avoiding conflict; it means wishing for productive conflict. Neuroscience research shows that when teams feel psychologically safe, members' brains shift from threat-detection mode (amygdala activation) to learning mode (prefrontal cortex engagement), enabling creativity and complex problem-solving.[322]

Positive means maintaining collective optimism and appreciation without sliding into toxic positivity that denies reality. Research by positive organizational psychologist Barbara Fredrickson on the "broaden-and-build" theory of positive emotions shows that when groups maintain a ratio of approximately 3:1 positive to negative interactions, they build resources, expand creative thinking, and achieve better outcomes.[323]

But this positivity must be genuine---research on emotional labor by sociologist Arlie Hochschild warns that mandatory cheerfulness leads to toxic positivity, producing exhaustion and cynicism.

Purposeful means groups clarify and maintain shared purpose that transcends immediate tasks. Simon Sinek's research on inspirational leadership demonstrates that organizations that clearly articulate their "why"---their deeper purpose beyond profit---attract more committed employees, inspire greater innovation, and achieve more sustainable success.[324] Research on meaningful work by organizational psychologist Amy Wrzesniewski shows that when employees connect their daily tasks to larger purpose, engagement and satisfaction increase dramatically.

Why does addressing collective fears (from the previous section) become necessary BEFORE achieving collective 3 P's? Because unexamined fears create the opposite of peace, lurking anxieties poison positivity, and hidden misbeliefs obscure purpose. Groups must surface and transform their shadow patterns to create genuine conditions for the 3 P's to flourish.

The Four Responses as a Group

Groups collectively experience YES, NO, WAIT, and SOMETHING BETTER in ways that create unique challenges and opportunities for maintaining alignment.

When a team receives a **YES**---their project gets funded, their proposal wins approval, their product succeeds---collective celebration amplifies individual joy. Research on shared victories shows that groups that properly acknowledge success build collective efficacy and momentum for future efforts.[325]

NO creates collective disappointment that can either fragment or strengthen teams. Research on team resilience by organizational psychologist Gretchen Spreitzer demonstrates that groups maintain cohesion through failure when they: (1) collectively process the disappointment rather than blaming individuals, (2) extract learning from the experience, and (3) recommit to shared purpose rather than abandoning it.[326]

WAIT tests collective patience and faith. Research on goal pursuit by psychologist Gabriele Oettingen shows that groups navigate uncertainty more successfully when they practice "mental contrasting"--- simultaneously holding both the desired future and current obstacles in awareness. This balanced perspective prevents both naive optimism and premature abandonment during waiting periods.

SOMETHING BETTER reveals group wisdom that transcends individual perspectives. Sometimes what emerges differs from what anyone originally envisioned but serves the collective good more fully. Research on collective intelligence by MIT professor Thomas Malone shows that diverse groups often generate solutions superior to what any individual member could have conceived alone.[327]

The Role of Leadership in Collective Wishing

This kind of collective alignment requires true leadership---what researchers call "alignment architecture." Effective leaders don't force compliance (which kills intrinsic motivation and genuine alignment). Instead, they create conditions where alignment can flourish.

Leaders as Alignment Architects

The leader's primary job becomes creating conditions for alignment rather than commanding specific behaviors. Research on transformational leadership by organizational psychologist Bernard Bass demonstrates that leaders who inspire through vision, model desired behaviors, and support individual development create more engaged, innovative, and successful teams than those who rely on transactional rewards and punishments.[328]

Leaders model the 3 P's first---they embody the peaceful, positive, purposeful presence that sets the tone. Research on emotional contagion in organizations shows that leaders' emotional states spread more rapidly and powerfully than those of other team members, making leaders' self-regulation crucial for collective wellbeing.[329]

Alignment architecture requires specific practices: creating clear communication channels, establishing shared principles and values, facilitating regular alignment check-ins, and making space for both collective practices and individual Three Selves work. Research on high-reliability organizations by management scholars Karl Weick and Kathleen Sutcliffe reveals that successful teams maintain alignment through consistent attention to these structural and cultural elements.

Forced Compliance vs. Genuine Alignment

Research on intrinsic versus extrinsic motivation at organizational scale reveals a crucial distinction. When leaders mandate positivity, demand alignment, or force enthusiasm, they trigger reactance---psychological resistance to perceived freedom threats. People comply outwardly while disconnecting inwardly, creating what organizational theorist Chris Argyris called "skilled incompetence"---the ability to follow rules while undermining their intent.

This distinction echoes psychiatrist David Hawkins' mapping of consciousness levels in his work *Power vs. Force*. Hawkins identified that emotions and states below a certain threshold operate as force---they deplete energy, narrow focus, and require constant effort to maintain.

Emotions above that threshold operate as power---they replenish energy, expand awareness, and flow naturally.

Leaders who try to force alignment through mandates and control operate from the lower frequencies Hawkins described, exhausting themselves and their teams. Leaders who cultivate genuine alignment by supporting autonomy, competence, and connection operate from the higher frequencies of power---creating sustainable, self-reinforcing positive change.[330]

Genuine alignment emerges when people CHOOSE to commit because they find personal meaning in collective purpose. Research on self-determination theory shows that when organizations support autonomy (choice), competence (growth), and relatedness (connection), intrinsic motivation flourishes and performance excels.[331]

The difference shows up in organizational culture research. Studies comparing employee engagement across companies reveal that organizations with mandated culture programs achieve lower engagement than those that invite participation and honor individual choice within shared frameworks.

How Leaders Model the 3 P's

Leaders create **Peaceful** conditions through psychological safety. Amy Edmondson's research identifies specific leader behaviors that build safety: admitting their own mistakes, asking questions rather than always having answers, and responding to failures as learning opportunities rather than occasions for punishment.[332]

Leaders maintain **Positive** through realistic optimism---what psychologist Sandra Schneider calls "flexible optimism" that acknowledges challenges while maintaining confidence in the team's ability to address them. This differs dramatically from toxic positivity that denies problems or mandatory cheerfulness that exhausts people through emotional labor.

Leaders clarify **Purposeful** by articulating and regularly reconnecting teams to compelling purpose. Research by Wharton professor Adam Grant shows that even brief reminders of how work serves others or contributes to meaningful goals significantly increases motivation and performance.[333]

The leader sets the emotional tone for the entire organization. Research by business professor Sigal Barsade on emotional contagion in organizations demonstrates that leaders' emotional states---whether anxiety, enthusiasm, calm, or frustration---spread rapidly through teams and shape collective emotional culture.[334]

Leadership Practices That Create Coherence

Specific leadership practices create neurological and emotional coherence across teams. **Regular collective practices**---team meetings conducted with intention, shared rituals that mark transitions and achievements, alignment check-ins that assess whether actions serve purpose---create the structural container for ongoing alignment.

Transparency about challenges maintains trust and reality-testing. When leaders acknowledge NO responses (setbacks, rejections, obstacles) and WAIT periods (uncertainty, resource constraints, timing issues), teams learn to navigate difficulty without losing faith or fragmenting. Research on organizational transparency by management scholar Sim Sitkin shows that leaders who acknowledge challenges early and honestly maintain higher trust and better problem-solving than those who hide difficulties.[335]

Celebrating wins together amplifies YES responses and builds collective efficacy. Research on positive organizational scholarship demonstrates that teams that regularly acknowledge and celebrate successes---both large milestones and small victories---maintain higher morale, stronger cohesion, and better subsequent performance.

Making space for individual Three Selves work within collective context honors that collective alignment requires individual alignment. Leaders who provide time, resources, and psychological permission for team members to do their own inner work---clarifying personal values, processing emotions, connecting to Higher Self wisdom---strengthen rather than distract from collective purpose.

When Leadership Is Absent

Research reveals what happens when there's no clear leadership. Without alignment architecture, groups default to what organizational theorists call "entropy"---gradual drift toward disorder, fragmentation, and lowest-common-denominator behavior. Studies on leaderless groups show increased diffusion of responsibility (everyone assumes someone else will act), susceptibility to groupthink (conformity pressure overrides critical thinking), and difficulty maintaining focus on long-term goals.

Teams need alignment architects. Research on self-managing teams shows that even groups without formal hierarchical leaders require someone to hold the "meta" role---attending to group process, facilitating alignment, and ensuring practices that maintain coherence. Without intentional alignment practices, even talented, well-intentioned individuals struggle to create and sustain collective power.

The danger of leaderless "flat" structures without intentional alignment practices has become clear in organizational research. Companies that eliminate hierarchy without replacing it with robust alignment infrastructure often experience greater rather than less dysfunction.

Possibilities Emerge when Aligned

When individuals align wishes with collective purpose, when teams embody the 3 P's together, when organizations consciously transform collective patterns---extraordinary things become possible.

At team level, transformation manifests as flow. Research by psychologist Mihaly Csikszentmihalyi on group flow shows that teams move from struggle to effortless coordination, with members experiencing enhanced creativity, deeper engagement, and greater satisfaction.[336]

Shared victories feel more meaningful. Challenges become collaborative problem-solving rather than blame-shifting. Research on collective joy and psychological flow demonstrates that aligned teams genuinely ENJOY the work more---fun becomes both catalyst and consequence of alignment.

At organizational level, companies become living systems rather than mechanical structures. Innovation accelerates when alignment frees cognitive resources previously consumed by internal friction. Research on organizational agility shows that aligned companies respond to market changes faster and more creatively than fragmented competitors. Customer and client impact multiplies because alignment creates authenticity---people can sense when an organization's actions genuinely match its values. The organization itself becomes a force for positive change, both in its immediate domain and through ripple effects into the broader community.

At community and global level, aligned collective intention becomes one of the most powerful forces on the planet. Historical examples demonstrate this truth: the Civil Rights Movement transformed societal structures that had persisted for centuries. Environmental activism has created policy changes affecting billions of people. Modern possibilities include climate action, social justice movements, and technological breakthroughs that address global challenges.

The alignment ripples outward. Research on social change by political scientist Sidney Tarrow shows that successful movements create demonstration effects---other groups see what's possible and organize their own transformation efforts.[337] Every aligned team becomes a proof of concept. Every transformed organization becomes a beacon. This is how the world actually changes: through the exponential power of aligned collective wishing spreading from group to group, organization to organization, community to community.

What About Skeptics?

One of the most common questions when bringing collective wishing into organizational settings is: "What do we do about the skeptics? The doubters and cynics among us who could poison the well and bring everybody down?"[338] [339]

While everyone in public groups joins willingly, if you're leading an organizational or corporate wish program, not everyone may participate so eagerly.

The instinct might be to exclude them, force them, or try to convert them. But research in group decision-making and organizational psychology reveals a counterintuitive lesson: authentic skeptics actually strengthen collective wishing practices by fostering curiosity, epistemic vigilance, and open-mindedness.[340] [341] [342]

When positioned correctly, skeptics can serve as Measurement Keepers, Reality Testers, and Research Liaisons—roles that ground your practice in scientific rigor while protecting against groupthink and social loafing. Their questioning isn't obstruction; it's the rigorous scrutiny at the heart of effective science and creative collaboration.[343]

The key is understanding the difference between authentic skepticism (which improves group outcomes) and cynicism (which harms collaborative energy):

- Skeptics are open-minded, adaptive, and constantly seek evidence before drawing conclusions.[344]
- Cynics, on the other hand, are persistently distrustful, pessimistic, and disengaged—they often perform worse on decision tasks and inhibit group trust and performance.[345]

For a complete guide on how to include skeptics in organizational wish circles—including roles, science, and protocols – and a note to those skeptics out there reading this book —see The Skeptic's Gift: Harnessing Dissent in Collective Wishing (And A Note To Skeptics) in the Appendix.

Your Role in Cooperative Change

Individual transformation through cosmic wishing opens the door to collective transformation. The principles explored throughout this book---the Three Selves, the 3 P's, understanding motivation, navigating the Four Responses---scale up beautifully when applied to teams and organizations.

Whether someone leads formally or simply wants to catalyze positive change, the foundation remains the same. The science---neuroscience,

259

psychology, organizational research---provides solid ground. The *Cosmic Wish Playbook* provides the practices. Understanding the WHY reveals what's truly possible.

Collective wishing isn't wishful thinking---it's how human consciousness works, how social change happens, and how individual wishes become part of something transformative. The science confirms this is real.

The question becomes: what will be created when aligned individuals come together? What becomes possible when your cosmic wish joins with others in a Wish Circle? Think of the impact. Creating positive change together ranks among the most meaningful human experiences. Individual wishes can ripple outward, transforming not just personal lives but teams, organizations, communities, and the world itself.

Every person who understands these principles becomes a potential catalyst. Every team that practices collective alignment becomes a demonstration of what's possible. The world changes one aligned group at a time---and that alignment begins with individuals who've done their own inner work and now understand how to create coherence at larger scales.

What will you create?

Meet the Scientists

The researchers whose work illuminates collective wishing:

Amy Edmondson — Psychological safety and team performance
Nicholas Christakis & James Fowler — Social contagion

Malcolm Gladwell — Tipping points

Simon Sinek — Purposeful leadership

Dean Radin — Collective consciousness effects

Elinor Ostrom — Collective action

Carl Jung — Collective unconscious

Uri Hasson — Neural synchronization during communication

David Hawkins — Consciousness levels (Power vs. Force)

(Full biographies in Appendix B)

Questions to Ponder

- **How does your personal wish connect to collective transformation?** Beyond surface alignment, what deeper purpose does your individual desire serve in the larger web of human consciousness and cosmic evolution? How might recognizing this connection shift both your commitment to the wish and your responsibility to the collective?

- **Which aspects of collective wishing have you already experienced unconsciously?** Have you noticed times when group energy amplified your motivation, when shared intention created unexpected synchronicities, or when your presence shifted a room's atmosphere? What might these experiences reveal about your natural capacity for conscious collective wishing?

- **What collective fears, desires, or misbeliefs might be operating in your closest communities?** Whether in your family, workplace, or social circles, what unspoken patterns limit group possibility? How might bringing these shadow patterns into conscious awareness—

without blame or judgment—create space for genuine collective transformation?

- **Where do you fall on the spectrum between skeptic and believer?** How comfortable are you with practices that blend scientific rigor and consciousness exploration? What role might authentic skepticism (rather than cynicism) play in strengthening your own wishing practice and protecting against magical thinking?

- **How aligned are the Three Selves in your primary community or organization?** Does the collective emotional culture (Inner Self), strategic direction (Outer Self), and stated purpose (Higher Self) actually harmonize? Where might misalignment be creating friction, and what would it take to bring these collective aspects into coherence?

- **What's your relationship with sharing versus protecting your wishes?** Have you given away your wishes prematurely, seeking validation before taking action? Or have you kept wishes so private that you've missed opportunities for accountability and support? What conscious practice could help you discern when to share and when to gestate?

- **How might you serve as a catalyst for collective alignment?** Whether through formal leadership or informal influence, what specific practices from this chapter—creating psychological safety, modeling the 3 P's, facilitating alignment check-ins—might you implement? What becomes possible when you view yourself not as a solo wisher but as an architect of collective coherence?

Next: How Stories Spread Collective Wishes

Throughout this chapter, we've explored the science of collective wishing—how aligned groups create emergent change, how individual wishes ripple through social networks, how consciousness itself might synchronize when people come together with shared intention. We've seen the evidence that collective transformation is real, measurable, and powerful.

But one crucial question remains: How do cosmic wishes actually spread from person to person?

We've touched on it—Nicholas Christakis and James Fowler showed us that behaviors spread through networks like contagions, Malcolm Gladwell revealed how small groups catalyze tipping points, and Uri Hasson demonstrated that brains synchronize during communication. Yet we haven't fully explored the mechanism that makes all of this possible.

That mechanism is storytelling.

In the next chapter, we'll discover that sharing your cosmic wishing journey isn't just a pleasant way to inspire others—it's a scientifically validated technology for transformation. When you tell your wishing story, you create neural coupling that synchronizes consciousness, trigger neurochemical responses that inspire action, and plant seeds that can grow into movements.

The science of storytelling reveals why some ideas spread exponentially while others fade, why narrative bypasses resistance in ways that facts cannot, and how the simple act of sharing your experience might be the most powerful tool we have for creating the collective change we explored in this chapter.

Let's discover how art and science unite to make cosmic wishes go viral.

Chapter 13: The Art and Science of Storytelling

Remember your wish from Chapter 1? Have you ever considered that your wish itself might be telling a story? A kind of "hero's journey" where you got the "call to adventure" (to make the wish), went through a lessons and a growth process (learning how to apply science to elevate that wish and make it a cosmic wish) and at the end you're changed, become a hero, and perhaps even "return with the elixir" and start a Wish Circle and then share your story with others.

From our exploration of collective wishing and its power to create emergent change, we arrive at something both ancient and revolutionary: the science of storytelling itself. Storytelling isn't just a pleasant way to illustrate concepts or make science more accessible (though it does both). What you're about to discover is that storytelling itself has a science—a robust, measurable, replicable science that shows how narratives literally rewire brains, synchronize consciousness, bypass resistance, trigger empathy, inspire action, and spread through populations.

Storytelling isn't just how this book came to be. It may be the key to how cosmic wishing can change the world.

When Stories Opened the Door to Science

Throughout human history, storytelling has served as the gateway to scientific discovery. Long before we had instruments to measure the stars, we told stories about constellations that helped us navigate oceans and predict seasons. Before we understood psychology, we crafted myths about heroes facing their shadows that taught us about the human psyche. Ancient healing stories encoded medicinal knowledge that modern pharmacology later validated.

The pattern repeats across cultures and centuries: imagination first, investigation second. Stories ask "what if?" and science asks "how?" Together, they form humanity's most powerful tool for understanding reality.

Einstein imagined riding a beam of light before developing relativity theory. Darwin's theory of evolution emerged partly from the narrative structure he observed in the geological record—a story written in stone. Modern neuroscience began with Ramón y Cajal, who drew intricate artistic renderings of neurons, seeing them first as characters in a biological story before proving their function.

Even today's cutting-edge discoveries often begin with scientists asking story-like questions: "What if time isn't linear?" "What if consciousness affects quantum particles?" "What if wishes themselves create measurable changes in reality?"

This book follows that ancient pattern.

The Vision That Started Everything

My journey into the science of wishing began not in a laboratory or research library, but in my imagination—with a vision of a magical realm called Astraea.

While writing my novel *A Love Story to the Universe*, I needed to create a world where wishes were real, tangible things that could be collected, sorted, and granted. I named it Astraea, after the Greek goddess of truth and justice, whose name means "star." In my fictional world, Wish Fairies processed the hopes and dreams of humans everywhere, navigating the complex question of which wishes to grant and which to redirect.

As I built this imaginary world, the "truth" part of Astraea's name began demanding attention. My storyteller's mind kept asking: What actually IS a wish? How are wishes different from prayers or goals? Why do humans wish? What determines whether wishes come true?

These weren't just creative questions anymore—they were scientific ones.

That curiosity led me to integrate frameworks from two of my nonfiction books into the worldbuilding. *Five Reasons Why Bad Things Happen* helped me understand the intelligence behind how reality responds to wishes. *The Hero's Playbook*—my interactive journal based on Joseph Campbell's Hero's Journey—showed me that wishing is universal, mythical, and deeply embedded in how humans make meaning.

The more I explored, the more questions emerged. After listening to a YouTube lecture on neuroplasticity, I couldn't stop wondering: What happens in the brain when we wish? Can neuroscience explain why some wishes manifest and others don't? Is there actual science behind what I'd been exploring through fiction?

That's when storytelling became the gateway to science—again, following humanity's ancient pattern. My fictional Astraea opened the door to a real scientific exploration that eventually became this book, along with the *Cosmic Wish Playbook*, the *Cosmic Wish Tracker* and the *Cosmic Wish Experiment.*

The Sciences

Researchers across neuroscience, psychology, anthropology, linguistics, media studies, and more have spent decades uncovering how and why stories shape human behavior, belief, and collective action. We won't attempt to be comprehensive here—that would require its own book. Instead, we'll focus on seven key findings most relevant to cosmic wishing:

- **The Neuroscience of Narrative**: How stories physically sync brains and create shared consciousness
- **The Chemistry of Connection**: How narratives trigger the biological responses that inspire action

- **The Psychology of Persuasion**: Why stories bypass critical resistance in ways facts cannot[2]
- **The Hero's Journey Validated**: Recent research proving Campbell's framework enhances resilience and meaning
- **The Power of "Losing Yourself in Fiction"**: How narrative entertainment teaches truth more effectively than instruction
- **Stories as Social Contagion**: How narratives spread through networks and create movements
- **The Science of Viral Narratives**: What makes some stories spread while others fade

Each of these discoveries has profound implications for how we share our cosmic wishes with others—and how those shared wishes might create the ripple effects that transform not just individual lives, but our collective reality.

Let's begin with perhaps the most astonishing discovery: when you tell a story, your listener's brain begins to mirror your own.

Neural Coupling: When Stories Sync Our Brains

In 2010, neuroscientist Uri Hasson at Princeton University made a discovery that fundamentally changed how we understand communication. Using fMRI brain scanning, Hasson's team monitored

---

[2] As many of you know, I often write about metaphysical concepts like reincarnation and the world "Upstairs" delivered through fictional stories. I have found firsthand that fiction can open minds quicker than nonfiction for this very reason. When reading fiction we suspend disbelief and open our minds.

both a storyteller's brain and listeners' brains simultaneously while a story was being told. What they found was extraordinary: the listeners' brain patterns didn't just respond to the story—they began to mirror the storyteller's brain patterns, sometimes even anticipating what would come next.[346]

Hasson called this phenomenon "neural coupling"—a literal synchronization of brain activity between storyteller and audience. When stories are coherent and engaging, entire groups of people experience simultaneous activation in language processing regions, emotional centers, and areas responsible for understanding others' mental states. The effect is so powerful that Hasson describes it as people "thinking together." The more successful the communication, the stronger the coupling—creating what amounts to a shared consciousness during the storytelling experience.

This isn't just a curiosity of neuroscience—it's a mechanism for collective transformation. Neural coupling means that when you share the story of your cosmic wish with others, you're not simply transmitting information. You're creating a temporary fusion of consciousness, allowing others to literally experience your vision, your emotion, your intention from the inside. They don't just hear about your wish—their brains begin to simulate it as if it were their own.

Imagine what happens when millions of people share their cosmic wishing stories, creating billions of moments of neural coupling across the planet. Imagine brains synchronizing around peaceful, positive, purposeful intentions, one story at a time.

The Chemistry of Storytelling: How Narratives Trigger Action

While Hasson revealed what happens in the brain during storytelling, neuroeconomist Paul Zak discovered why stories are so powerful at inspiring action. Zak's research focuses on oxytocin—often called the "bonding hormone"—and its role in empathy, trust, and prosocial behavior.[347]

In a series of elegant experiments, Zak's team exposed participants to emotionally engaging narratives and measured their neurochemical responses. What they found was remarkable: character-driven stories with emotional arcs cause the brain to release oxytocin, which increases empathy and concern for others. But the effect doesn't stop at feeling—it extends to doing. In Zak's studies, participants who experienced oxytocin release from stories were significantly more likely to donate money, help others, and take cooperative action afterward.[348]

The narrative structure matters. Stories that follow a dramatic arc—establishing character, building tension through challenges, and reaching resolution—produce the strongest neurochemical responses. During tension, the brain releases cortisol (heightening attention), and during resolution, it releases dopamine (creating reward and motivation). This cocktail of neurochemicals doesn't just make stories memorable—it makes them actionable.

271

Think about what this means for sharing cosmic wishes. When you tell the story of your wishing journey—the challenge you faced (tension), the wish you made (hope), the responses you received (drama), the transformation you experienced (resolution)—you're not just sharing information. You're triggering a neurochemical cascade in your listeners that increases their empathy for your journey, heightens their attention to the process, and motivates them to take similar action.

A well-told cosmic wishing story doesn't just inform—it biologically primes listeners to become wishers themselves. The science suggests that storytelling may be the most effective tool we have for spreading the practice of conscious, intentional wishing through human populations.

Transportation Theory: How Stories Bypass Resistance

One of the most valuable discoveries for understanding why stories spread ideas so effectively comes from psychologists Melanie Green and Timothy Brock, who developed what they call "Transportation Theory."[349] Their research reveals something counterintuitive: the more deeply we become absorbed in a story—"transported" into the narrative world—the less we critically resist the ideas embedded within it.

Green and Brock's experiments demonstrated that narrative transportation creates a unique mental state where our usual skepticism temporarily suspends. When we're caught up in a compelling story, we stop arguing with the premise, stop fact-checking the details, and instead allow ourselves to experience the narrative world on its own terms. This isn't mindless gullibility—it's a natural cognitive process that allows us to learn from experiences we haven't personally lived.

The implications have been validated across numerous studies: emotionally engaged audiences are far more likely to shift their attitudes, beliefs, and behaviors than those presented with the same information in factual, non-narrative formats.[350] The narrative structure creates what researchers call "narrative persuasion"—change that happens not through argument but through experience.

For cosmic wishing, this means something profound. When you share your wishing story—not as a lecture about technique, but as a lived experience with emotion, challenge, and transformation—you create a pathway for others to absorb the practice without resistance. They don't have to be convinced that wishing works; they get transported into your experience of it working. The story does the persuading that facts alone cannot accomplish.

The Hero's Journey: Mythology Meets Modern Science

For decades, mythologist Joseph Campbell's insights about the universal Hero's Journey remained in the realm of literary analysis and storytelling craft. Campbell's work, which we explored in Chapter 3, identified a pattern that appears across virtually every culture: the hero ventures from ordinary life into challenge, faces transformation, and returns with wisdom to benefit the community. Campbell understood intuitively that these stories weren't just entertainment—they were teaching tools that transmitted survival wisdom and hope across generations.

But in 2023, researchers finally put Campbell's theory to the empirical test. In a groundbreaking study published in the *Journal of Personality and Social Psychology*, Benjamin Rogers and colleagues conducted eight studies with over 1,700 participants to examine the psychological effects of viewing one's life through the lens of the Hero's Journey.[351]

The results validated Campbell's intuitions spectacularly. People who frame their experiences using Hero's Journey narrative structure—protagonist, shift, quest, allies, challenge, transformation, legacy—report significantly greater meaning in life, enhanced well-being, increased resilience, and reduced depression. Even more remarkably, the researchers developed a "restorying intervention" that helped participants reframe their life stories as Hero's Journeys. This didn't just change how people felt about their past—it increased their resilience in facing current challenges and enhanced their ability to find meaning in ambiguous situations.

When I created *The Hero's Playbook* – a collection of thought-provoking activities designed to help people structure their own journeys using Campbell's framework – I instinctively knew the power of Campbell's storytelling structure. Now, it's exciting to see that science confirms what Campbell suspected: the Hero's Journey isn't just a good story structure. It's a psychological technology for building resilience, meaning, and hope.

When we share our cosmic wishing journeys using this universal narrative pattern, we're not just telling our stories—we're offering others a scientifically validated framework for understanding their own challenges and transformations. Every wish becomes a hero's quest. Every obstacle becomes a test. Every breakthrough becomes a reward. And every return with wisdom becomes an opportunity to inspire the next generation of wishers.

The Power of "What If": How Questions Shape Stories and Rewire Brains

Every great story begins with a question. "What if dinosaurs were brought back to life?" "What if a boy wizard went to magic school?" "What if famous historical lovers were reincarnated today to fulfill a prophecy?"

These aren't just creative prompts—they're neurological catalysts. The moment you ask "what if," your brain shifts into a special mode that scientists call **counterfactual thinking**, and the effects are profound.[352]

The Neuroscience of "What If"

When you ask an insightful question, your brain doesn't just passively consider it—it actively reorganizes itself. Research on neuroplasticity shows that questions act as catalysts for neural change, prompting neurons to form new connections and create new pathways for creative thinking.[353]

Counterfactual thinking—the mental process of imagining alternatives to reality—is one of the most fundamental forms of human cognition. It's how we learn from the past, prepare for the future, and innovate in the present.[354] Every time you ask "what if," you're engaging the same cognitive flexibility that allows humans to adapt, create, and transform.

But not all 'what if' questions work the same way in your brain.

Two Types of "What If" Questions

Not all "what if" questions are created equal. Research reveals two distinct types with different cognitive effects:[355]

Additive Counterfactuals add new elements: "What if I had an umbrella?" or "What if this character gained a magical power?" These questions boost creative thinking and imagination, opening up entirely new possibilities that didn't exist before:[356]

Subtractive Counterfactuals remove elements: "What if it hadn't rained?" or "What if this obstacle didn't exist?" These questions enhance analytical thinking and problem-solving, helping you identify what's truly essential.[357]

For storytelling—and for cosmic wishing—additive "what if" questions are especially powerful. They introduce new elements, open fresh possibilities, and activate the creative networks in your brain that generate innovative solutions.

First—want to test your observation skills? Count the 'what if' questions throughout this book, then visit <u>cosmicwishexperiment.com/fun-and-games</u> to check your answer and claim your prize!

Cognitive Flexibility: The Brain's Superpower

The ability to ask and explore "what if" questions develops what neuroscientists call **cognitive flexibility**—your brain's capacity to shift thinking, consider multiple perspectives, and adapt to new situations.[358]

This flexibility isn't just useful for storytelling. It's essential for navigating life's challenges, recognizing opportunities, and maintaining resilience when circumstances change. Research shows that people with greater cognitive flexibility demonstrate:[359]

- Enhanced creativity and divergent thinking
- Better problem-solving abilities
- Increased adaptability to change
- Greater resilience in facing obstacles
- Improved capacity to imagine alternative futures

Sound familiar? These are exactly the qualities you need for effective cosmic wishing.

"What If" Questions as The Key to Creativity

Jane McGonigal, a futurist at the Institute for the Future, calls counterfactual thinking "the key to creativity and a vaccine against future shock."[360] Her research shows that regularly practicing "what if" thinking:

- Builds mental capacity to recognize and adapt to change
- Increases open-mindedness and inventiveness
- Develops the power to imagine how anything could be different
- Strengthens your ability to create the future you want

When you craft your cosmic wishing story, you're not just describing what happened—you're asking "what if" questions that reshape how you and your listeners perceive possibility itself.

Questions Activate the Brain Differently Than Statements

Here's something fascinating: when you encounter a question, your brain responds differently than when you encounter a statement. Questions hijack your thought process—in a good way.[361]

The moment you read a question, your entire brain becomes active, releasing serotonin (which stabilizes mood) followed by dopamine (which triggers motivation and curiosity). Your brain literally cannot NOT try to answer a question once it's been posed. This is why "what if" questions are so powerful for both creating stories and inspiring action.

From Story to Wish: The "What If" Connection

Every cosmic wish is, at its core, a "what if" question:

- "What if I could heal this relationship?"
- "What if our team achieved this breakthrough?"
- "What if I found work that genuinely fulfills me?"

- "What if the world operated on cooperation instead of competition?"
- "What if I could start a group that could actually bring world peace?"

When you frame your wish as a "what if" question, you:

- **Activate cognitive flexibility** - opening your mind to multiple pathways
- **Stimulate creative solutions** - generating novel approaches you hadn't considered
- **Bypass resistance** - questions invite exploration rather than triggering defensiveness
- **Engage others' brains** - when you share your "what if," their brains automatically begin exploring possibilities with you

This is why storytelling about your cosmic wishes is so powerful. You're not just describing outcomes—you're inviting others into a "what if" space where their brains actively participate in imagining the possibilities.

The Bridge Between Art and Science

Throughout this book, we've explored the science of wishing. But science itself begins with "what if" questions. Every breakthrough discovery started when a scientist wondered:

- "What if time isn't constant?" (Einstein)
- "What if species evolved over time?" (Darwin)
- "What if wishes can be more effective when applying the Art & Science of Wishing?"

Stories and science aren't opposites—they're partners. Stories ask "what if," and science asks "how." Together, they form humanity's most powerful tool for transforming reality.

When you craft your cosmic wishing story, you're doing both. You're asking "what if this wish came true?"—and then you're using all the science in this book to understand HOW to make it happen.

Lose Yourself in Fiction, Find Yourself in Truth

In the Foreword to this book, I shared the tagline for my novels: *Lose yourself in the fiction... Find yourself in the truth.* What I've learned through researching this book is that scholars have several names for this phenomenon: narrative persuasion, edutainment, and eudaimonic entertainment—fiction designed to both move and enlighten.

Recent meta-analyses confirm that informational storytelling—fiction that entertains while it teaches—has measurable cognitive and emotional impact that exceeds traditional educational approaches.[362] This effect is grounded in Green and Brock's Transportation Theory: immersion in story worlds temporarily suspends counter-arguing, allowing deeper reflection and belief integration.[363] [364]

Psychologists Raymond Mar and Keith Oatley extended this research, demonstrating that reading fiction enhances "theory of mind"—our ability to understand others' thoughts and emotions.[365] Narrative experience can actually outperform expository nonfiction in building empathy and social understanding.[366] Stories don't just convey information—they create the cognitive and emotional pathways that allow us to understand experiences we've never personally lived.

More recent work on eudaimonic entertainment—stories that evoke meaning, morality, and personal growth—shows they can shift beliefs while inspiring self-reflection.[367] When readers lose themselves in fiction, they open pathways that allow them to find themselves in truth—learning through identification, imagination, and empathy rather than instruction.[3]

This validates the approach woven throughout this book: the "Bridge to Fiction" sections aren't just decorative examples (or shameless self-promotion). They're scientifically grounded tools for helping you internalize these concepts more deeply than pure exposition could achieve. And it points to something even more powerful: when you share your cosmic wishing journey as a story—with character, emotion, challenge, and transformation—you're using one of the most effective teaching tools humans have ever developed.

Imagine a world where cosmic wishing stories spread not as dry testimonials or clinical reports, but as compelling narratives that transport readers into the experience of conscious manifestation. Stories that make people feel the power of aligned intention, that help them understand the

---

[3] As a writer, two of the biggest compliments I have gotten were, "I couldn't put it down" and "I read one page for day, it got me to think so much."

wisdom of the Four Responses, that illuminate the transformation possible when all Three Selves work together. Not lectures—stories.

Stories as Social Contagion: How Narratives Create Movements

While the previous sections explored how stories affect individual brains, the research on social contagion reveals something even more powerful: stories spread through human populations like beneficial viruses, carrying ideas, behaviors, and beliefs from person to person with exponential reach.

Research in social psychology and network science demonstrates that narratives function as what anthropologist Victor Turner called "social dramas"—shared experiences that dissolve hierarchy and create what he termed "communitas," a sense of collective identity and purpose.[368] Sociologist Émile Durkheim described this phenomenon as "collective effervescence"—the heightened emotion and solidarity that emerges when groups share powerful narrative experiences.

Modern studies of collective behavior show that common narratives coordinate groups far more effectively than data or facts alone. Stories have ignited movements from civil rights to climate action, not by presenting more evidence, but by creating a shared vision that people could see themselves within.369 The narrative becomes the container for collective identity: "We are people who wish consciously. We are people who believe intention shapes reality. We are people transforming the world through peaceful, positive, purposeful desires."

Viral Storytelling

What makes some stories spread virally while others fade? Research in memetics and cultural evolution points to several factors: emotional resonance, relatability, simplicity combined with depth, and most importantly—the sense that acting on the story's message is both meaningful and achievable. Stories that show ordinary people accomplishing extraordinary things through replicable methods spread fastest.

Consider what this means for cosmic wishing. Every time someone shares their wishing story—on social media, in conversation, in a book or podcast—they're not just documenting personal experience. They're potentially seeding a social contagion. If their story has emotional resonance (the neurochemistry effect), if it's relatable (the transportation effect), if it shows transformation (the Hero's Journey effect), and if it demonstrates a replicable method (the Three P's, the Four Responses, the Three Selves alignment), it has the components necessary to spread.

Now imagine not just individual stories, but a growing library of cosmic wishing stories—thousands, then millions of narratives about wishes made consciously, responses received mindfully, and transformations experienced deeply. Each story becomes a vector for spreading the practice. Each teller becomes a teacher. Each listener becomes a potential next storyteller.[4]

This is how movements begin: not with manifestos, but with stories that spread from person to person, creating a collective narrative that says, "This is possible. Others like me have done this. I could do this too."

The Frontier: What Happens When Storytelling Meets Cosmic Wishing?

We've explored how stories sync brains, trigger empathy and action, bypass resistance, validate heroic transformation, teach through transportation, and spread through populations like beneficial contagions. Each of these discoveries points to the same conclusion: storytelling may be the most powerful technology we have for spreading conscious wishing practices and creating collective transformation.

But here's what we haven't fully explored—what Chapter 14 will address: What happens at the cutting edge where storytelling science meets consciousness research? How might digital platforms and artificial intelligence amplify or transform narrative spread? What are the frontiers where ancient wisdom about stories meets quantum possibilities about intention?

---

[4] Who knows? Maybe someday your "Cosmic Wish Story" can become part of an anthology of stories!

And most practically—how do we actually apply all this science to make cosmic wishing go viral?

That's where we're headed. But first, we need to understand one more frontier: the speculative edge where established science meets the most profound mysteries about consciousness, reality, and the nature of possibility itself.

Integration: The Art and Science United

Twelve chapters ago, you made a wish at the beginning of this book. Throughout our journey, we've explored the science behind that wish— the neuroscience, the psychology, the biology, the quantum possibilities, the collective dynamics. We've learned frameworks and practices: the Three Selves, the Three P's, the Four Responses, the shadow work, the collective amplification.

But now you understand something deeper: the art that started this scientific exploration isn't separate from the science of making wishes manifest. The stories we tell about our wishes—the narratives we craft about our journeys, our challenges, our transformations—are themselves a mechanism for change.

When you share your cosmic wishing story:
- You create neural coupling with your listeners, synchronizing consciousness
- You trigger neurochemical responses that inspire empathetic action
- You bypass resistance through narrative transportation

- You offer a Hero's Journey framework that builds resilience and meaning
- You teach through story in ways facts cannot achieve
- You seed a social contagion that can spread exponentially

The fact that this book began with Astraea demonstrates the ultimate bridge from fiction and how storytelling can be the fire that lights scientific discovery. This is why "lose yourself in the fiction, find yourself in the truth" isn't just a clever tagline—it's a description of how human consciousness actually learns and grows.

The art and the science were never separate. They've been dancing together all along. In fact, this book deliberately employs many of the sciences mentioned in this chapter, from **Neural Coupling Potential** (using a narrative structure to create conditions for brain synchronization), **Transportation Theory** (bypassing resistance)**, Neurochemical Triggers** (activating oxytocin, dopamine, and cortisol), **Hero's Journey Structure, Emotional Resonance** (creating conditions for readers to see themselves in the story) and **Cognitive Flexibility** (asking "what if" questions).

In Chapter 15, we'll explore how to bring all these pieces together—the science you've learned, the practices you've developed, and yes, the stories you'll tell. But before we get there, we need to venture to the very edge of what's known and peer into the frontier of possibility.

What happens when consciousness meets quantum mechanics? When individual intention encounters collective fields? When ancient wisdom about wishing meets cutting-edge research about the nature of reality itself?

Let's find out.

Meet The Scientists

The researchers whose work illuminates storytelling science:

Uri Hasson — Neural coupling during storytelling

Paul Zak — Oxytocin and narrative-induced prosocial behavior

Melanie Green and Timothy Brock — Transportation Theory

Benjamin Rogers — Empirical validation of Hero's Journey

Raymond Mar and Keith Oatley — Fiction's enhancement of empathy

Joseph Campbell — The Hero's Journey/monomyth

Victor Turner — Liminality and communitas

Émile Durkheim — Collective effervescence

(Full biographies in Appendix B)

Questions to Ponder

- **What is your cosmic wishing story?** If you had to tell it in three minutes, what would you include?
- **Who in your life would most benefit from hearing your wishing journey?** What stops you from sharing it?
- **Think of a story that changed your life**—a book, movie, or personal conversation that shifted how you saw the world. What made it so powerful? Looking back with the knowledge from this chapter, can you identify which mechanisms were at work—neural

coupling, oxytocin release, transportation, the Hero's Journey structure?

- **If neural coupling means your story can sync your listeners' brains** to yours, what experience of cosmic wishing would you most want others to feel?

- **What would happen if your cosmic wishing story went viral?** How might it ripple through your community, your social networks, the world?

- **How could you frame your biggest challenge or disappointment as a Hero's Journey?** What would change if you saw it as part of your transformation rather than a failure?

- **What small story could you share *right now*—**a three-sentence social media post, a text to a friend, a journal entry—that plants a seed for the cosmic wishing movement? What's stopping you from sharing it within the next 24 hours?

- **If storytelling bypasses resistance** and facts don't, how might you share cosmic wishing with someone who's skeptical without trying to convince them?

- **What collective narrative are you part of?** What stories does your community tell about who you are and what's possible? How might cosmic wishing stories shift that narrative?

- **What 'what if' question lies at the heart of your cosmic wish?** How does framing it as a question rather than a statement change your emotional relationship to the wish? What new possibilities emerge when you approach your wish with genuine curiosity rather than desperate attachment?

Next: The Frontier of Wishing—The Next Great Questions

Storytelling and the science of wishing are each evolving at incredible speed, and both now stand at the cutting edge of human creativity, connection, and potential. As we move to the next chapter, we'll explore how these two frontiers—narrative and cosmic wishing—intersect at the ultimate edge of what's possible, where science, metaphysics, and the art of imagining the future all come together. The journey continues as we step into the unknown and ask: what new realities might we create, now that we have the tools of both story and science in our hands? And how might frontier concepts like quantum mechanics come into play?

Chapter 14 will take us to the very edge of what science currently knows—and peer into what it's just beginning to suspect. Here, at the frontier where quantum mechanics meets consciousness, where individual wishes encounter collective fields, where ancient wisdom about intention meets cutting-edge physics, the most extraordinary possibilities await.

What if consciousness itself can influence the fundamental structure of reality? What if stories don't just spread through social networks but create actual quantum effects? What if the power of narrative extends even further than neuroscience has yet imagined?

The journey from storytelling science to the ultimate frontiers of possibility represents our final horizon—where rigorous research meets the greatest mysteries of existence, and where your cosmic wish might be far more powerful than you ever dreamed.

Chapter 14: The Frontier of Wishing —The Next Great Questions

From the validated science of storytelling, we now venture to the cutting edge—where brilliant scientists are asking profound questions that might not have answers for decades.

This chapter is different. While previous chapters built on established, peer-reviewed research, here we explore **questions**—serious scientific inquiries happening at major universities worldwide, but with territories where answers remain elusive. These are the frontiers where brilliant minds dare to ask what we don't yet know.

The questions matter. Because they point toward possibilities that could transform how we understand cosmic wishing—and they connect back to everything you've learned in remarkable ways.

And perhaps one day these discoveries can take that wish you made at the beginning into realms you never considered.

Two Frontiers, One Radical Question

Throughout this book, we've explored established science—decades of peer-reviewed research on motivation, neuroscience, collective behavior, and storytelling. Solid ground.

But now we venture beyond the map's edge, where two seemingly separate scientific frontiers are converging on the same extraordinary possibility:

The Consciousness Frontier is asking whether your aligned Three Selves might create measurable quantum effects. Whether your wishes could influence not just the future, but the past. Whether consciousness might extend beyond your individual brain to connect with others in ways physics hasn't yet explained.

The Storytelling Frontier is asking whether the cosmic wishing stories you share might actually reshape probability fields for other wishers. Whether immersive technologies could transmit your Three P's directly through neural coupling. Whether narratives themselves might operate through quantum-like principles we're only beginning to discover. Whether AI could someday make wishes of its own.

Both frontiers are circling the same radical question that could transform everything we understand about cosmic wishing:

What if consciousness doesn't just observe reality—what if it participates in creating it?

That's not New Age philosophy. That's the question serious scientists at major universities are investigating right now. And the preliminary findings? They're fascinating.

Could We Actually Measure Consciousness?

Here's a wild idea: What if consciousness could be measured like temperature or weight?

Neuroscientist Giulio Tononi thinks it might be possible. He created something called Integrated Information Theory[370], which proposes that the more information your brain weaves together, the more conscious you are. He even uses a Greek letter Φ (phi) to potentially measure it—a consciousness score based on information integration.

In my novel/screenplay INSPIRITORS, I built a future world where science could measure the energy of love itself. It sounds like fantasy, but Tononi's work suggests we might be heading there. If consciousness itself can be measured, why not the specific states that arise from it? Love, peace, purpose—these might all have measurable signatures someday. Just imagine a future where we could know how a politician—or their policies—scored against criteria such as love, truth, and community?

It's like music: A single note isn't a symphony. But integrated notes create harmony.

Your Inner Self (body/emotions), Outer Self (conscious mind), and Higher Self (wisdom/purpose) each process different information. When all three align around a wish, you're integrating exponentially more—sensations, emotions, thoughts, intuition, purpose.

The frontier question: Could an aligned wish—where all Three Selves work together—actually have a higher Φ value? Research at the Center for Sleep and Consciousness[371] explores whether consciousness truly is integrated information. They haven't studied wishing, but what if alignment matters measurably?

When you wish from a Peaceful state, with Positive emotion, and Purposeful intention—you're creating conditions for maximum information integration. Could that make wishes more effective? We don't know. But it's worth asking.

Do Minds Connect Beyond Bodies?

Here's one of the most provocative questions in consciousness research: Does consciousness extend beyond individual brains? Can minds actually connect in ways that transcend physical space?

Studies show that when people meditate together or share intense experiences, their brainwaves synchronize—not through mimicry, but through something science can't yet fully explain. But some researchers are going further, exploring whether consciousness itself might be "non-local,"[372] meaning it can exist or connect in ways that defy our normal understanding of physical boundaries.

For instance, at the University of Arizona's Center for Consciousness Studies, researchers are actually testing whether meditation creates measurable changes in quantum systems. At Princeton, the Global

Consciousness Project has been running for over 20 years, tracking whether global events correlate with deviations in random number generators. These aren't fringe experiments—they're serious scientific inquiries, even if their interpretations remain controversial.

Wish Circles create emergent properties—the group becomes more than individuals. Now frontier research asks: Could there be an actual mechanism beyond psychology? If consciousness can genuinely connect non-locally, Wish Circles aren't just psychological support—there might be actual resonance between minds when intentions align. Real physics we haven't yet learned to measure, not metaphor.

The Wildest Question: Can the Future Affect the Past?

Some quantum physicists are asking something that sounds impossible: Could events in the future influence the past?

It's called retrocausality, and yes, serious scientists at major universities are investigating it. Physicist Huw Price has proposed that quantum theory's mathematics might actually require accepting backward-in-time effects.[373] There are controversial experiments that some interpret as showing present decisions affecting past particles, though the scientific community remains deeply divided on whether this interpretation is valid.

The Blue Balloon Phenomenon: You think "blue balloon"—then find one in your fence. We explored three explanations: subconscious cues, primed attention, or consciousness somehow influencing reality.

What if there's a fourth? What if, through retrocausality, your future thought about blue balloons somehow reached backward in time and influenced the probability that one would end up in your fence—making it more likely to be there *because* you were going to notice it?

Sometimes wishes get answered before you consciously make them. Could that be because your future wish influenced past probabilities?

Is this proven? No. Are serious scientists researching it? Yes. And if it's real, the implications for cosmic wishing would be extraordinary.

Will Computers Ever Wish?

The frontier question: Could AI ever become conscious enough to wish?

Right now, scientists agree the answer is no. The AI helping write this chapter isn't conscious—it's sophisticated pattern recognition, not awareness. But researchers are developing ways to test whether AI consciousness might be possible, and many think it could happen eventually. A consortium proposed 14 criteria for assessing AI consciousness, drawing from Integrated Information Theory.[374]

The speculation: If consciousness can emerge from both biological and digital systems, cosmic wishing might someday include more types of minds than we imagine. Digital wishes joining human wishes in the collective field, creating something entirely new.

The Storytelling Frontier: How Deep Does It Go?

While some scientists explore consciousness mysteries, others are asking equally provocative questions about stories.

Could immersive tech create super-charged neural coupling? Sharing stories creates neural synchronization. Now researchers are asking: What if VR and immersive tech could create even deeper coupling? If it works, your Three P's—Peaceful, Positive, Purposeful—might literally transmit through immersive storytelling. Neural coupling through VR could make cosmic wishing contagious at unprecedented levels.[375]

Could AI optimize how stories change brains? When humans collaborate with AI to create stories, they produce more novel ideas while maintaining structure. As AI becomes more sophisticated, might it help craft wishing stories optimized to inspire? Your brain rewires through practice. What if AI could help craft stories that optimize neuroplastic change in listeners?[376]

Can social media trigger the Hundredth Monkey Effect? Researchers study how memes function like ancient myths[377]—spreading meaning, shaping identity. Myths took centuries. Memes reach millions in days. Your cosmic wishing story, as a meme, could reach massive audiences instantly. Research on narrative and social movements shows how collective stories organize change.[378]

Do stories work like quantum mechanics? Some researchers are seriously exploring this possibility. What if your wishing story exists in "narrative superposition"—meaning different things to different listeners until their observation "collapses" it into personal meaning? Think about the Four Responses: YES, NO, WAIT, SOMETHING BETTER. Could your story simultaneously contain all four in superposition, with each listener collapsing it into the response they need?[379]

Is consciousness actually made of stories? Some propose that consciousness itself is fundamentally narrative[380]—self-awareness arises from stories we tell about experience. If true, crafting your cosmic wishing journey isn't just helpful—it's how you become more conscious of your creative power. Your Higher Self might literally be the storyteller—the part weaving experience into coherent narrative. Story might not be separate from consciousness—story might be how consciousness organizes itself.

Where the Frontiers Converge: The Biggest "What If"

What if consciousness and storytelling aren't separate? What if narrative is how consciousness organizes itself, and consciousness is what gives narratives their power to shape reality?

Could stories create invisible fields that make cosmic wishing easier for others? Rupert Sheldrake's controversial theory proposes that repeated behaviors create "morphic fields"—patterns that become increasingly accessible each time they're enacted. Every time you share your cosmic wish story, you might strengthen a field that helps people you'll never meet connect with peaceful, positive, purposeful wishing.[381]

What about collective story-fields? If consciousness can be non-local, and stories create neural synchronization, could there be "story-fields"—collective narrative structures beyond any individual telling? The Global Consciousness Project shows random number generators deviate during globally attended events. What if collective wishing stories create similar effects?

Is the universe made of stories? Physicist Carlo Rovelli's relational quantum mechanics proposes that physical events only have meaning in relation to other events—there is no absolute perspective, only narrative sequences of cause and effect. In this view, reality literally IS the relational stories between interactions. If consciousness participates in quantum observation (as measurement problems suggest), then cosmic wishing becomes a conscious way of participating in reality's relational structure itself.[382] [383]

What These Questions Mean for You

Here's what's remarkable: Even without final answers, these frontier questions point toward practical possibilities.

Your wishes might be more powerful than we currently understand. If consciousness operates through quantum effects, if stories create measurable resonance—your cosmic wishes might be genuine participations in reality creation, not just psychological tools.

When you align your Three Selves, you might be maximizing your consciousness integration—and if any frontier theory about probability fields proves true, this alignment could make your wishes interact with reality more effectively.

When you practice the Three P's, you might be creating conditions needed for consciousness to influence reality—if any of these frontier theories prove true.

When you share your story, you might reshape probability fields for other wishers. Your narrative might strengthen morphic fields, contribute to collective consciousness, or even support wishers across time—if retrocausality is real.

We don't know which, if any, of these possibilities will prove true. But they're being seriously investigated. And even the questions themselves transform how we think about wishing.

The Ultimate Frontier Question

Can we consciously participate in creating reality, or are we just witnesses to a predetermined unfolding?

Classical science suggested consciousness merely observes. But frontier science increasingly asks: What if consciousness participates? What if observation affects reality, intention interacts with probability, consciousness is fundamental rather than emergent?

For cosmic wishing, this isn't academic. It's the difference between hoping something works and understanding a potential mechanism.

Here's what matters most: You don't need any of these frontier theories to be proven for cosmic wishing to work in your life. The established science from the previous chapters—the neuroscience, psychology, and collective behavior research—already gives you a solid foundation. These frontier questions? They're the exciting edge where we're still learning. Practice the science you know. Stay curious about the science we're discovering. And remain open to possibilities science hasn't yet imagined.

We don't have final answers. Which is why we're still exploring! These are questions, not conclusions. But we know this: Humans have always practiced at the frontier. We wished on stars before understanding fusion. We told stories before discovering neural coupling. We aligned our Three Selves before neuroscience could map integration.

The frontier isn't where knowledge ends. It's where wisdom begins—in the space between what we know and what we dare to imagine.

And sometimes, what seems like magic today becomes the science of tomorrow.

Meet The Scientists

The researchers exploring consciousness and reality frontiers:

Giulio Tononi — Integrated Information Theory

Roger Penrose & Stuart Hameroff — Quantum consciousness hypothesis

Huw Price — Retrocausality in quantum mechanics

Rupert Sheldrake — Morphic resonance theory

David Bohm — Implicate order

Vitaly Vanchurin — Universe as neural network

(Full biographies in Appendix B)

Questions to Ponder

- **Which frontier question intrigues you most—and why does it call to you?** Is it because it would validate something you've already experienced? Challenge something you believe? Or open possibilities you've never considered? What does your attraction to this particular question reveal about your relationship with mystery and uncertainty?

- **If consciousness can be measured through information integration (Φ), what would it mean for your wishing practice?** When you align your Three Selves, do you sense that you're creating a different quality of consciousness—something more coherent, more powerful? If science could measure this difference someday, how might that change not just how we wish, but how we understand what it means to be human?

- **How comfortable are you with practicing something whose full mechanism remains unknown?** Humans wished on stars for millennia before understanding fusion, told stories for centuries before discovering neural coupling. Can you embrace cosmic wishing even while holding the questions as questions? What's the difference between faith, hope, and evidence-based practice when operating at the frontier?

- **If your cosmic wishing story could create morphic fields—making it easier for others to wish successfully—what responsibility does that carry?** Does knowing your story might reshape probability for people you'll never meet change what stories you choose to share? How might you craft your narrative to strengthen fields of peace, positivity, and purpose?

- **Have you ever experienced something that felt like retrocausality—a wish answered before you consciously made it?** What happened? If future intentions can influence past probabilities (and that's a massive *if*), how does that change your understanding of synchronicity, coincidence, and the Blue Balloon Phenomenon?

- **Which frontier possibility would most transform your wishing practice if proven true?** Non-local consciousness connecting Wish Circles? Quantum effects from aligned Three Selves? Stories operating through probability fields? How might you experiment with cosmic wishing *as if* this possibility were already real, while maintaining healthy skepticism?

Next: Bringing It All Together

We've journeyed from established science through validated frameworks to the wildest frontiers of possibility. We've explored motivation, neuroscience, collective behavior, storytelling, and now the cutting edge where consciousness meets cosmos.

You've learned that serious scientists at major universities are asking profound questions: Can consciousness be measured? Does it extend beyond individual brains? Could intentions influence probability fields? Might stories themselves operate through quantum-like principles?

These questions aren't answered yet. But they point toward possibilities that could transform everything we understand about cosmic wishing.

In Chapter 15, we'll bring it all together. We'll revisit that wish you made at the beginning and discover how everything you've learned—from the Three Selves to the Four Responses, from the 3 P's to the frontier questions—integrates into a complete practice. Not just understanding cosmic wishing, but LIVING it. Not just learning the science, but becoming a cosmic wisher yourself.

The science has prepared you. The questions have inspired you. Now let's see what you'll create.

Chapter 15: Bringing Art + Science Together To Bring the World Together

Remember that wish you made at the very beginning of this book—the one you wrote down before you knew about the Three Selves, the Four Responses, or any of the science you've learned?

Hold it in your mind right now. Not to evaluate whether it came true—that's not the point yet. Just notice it. Feel it.

Now notice something else: **You're not who you were when you made that wish.**

Something fundamental has shifted. You don't just know more facts about wishing—you see differently. You think differently. You understand what's happening when you wish, why it works, and how to work with it consciously.

That wish you made in Chapter 1? You made it as someone hoping blindly, fingers crossed, sending a message into the void without understanding the mechanism, the science, or your own power in the process.

If you made that same wish right now, it would be completely different. Not because the words would change, but because **you** have changed. You've moved from passive hoping to conscious collaboration. From blind wishing to cosmic wishing.

You understand what a wish actually is—that sweet spot between your control and cosmic collaboration, where your intention meets forces beyond yourself. You know the difference between wishes, prayers, and goals. You've learned what makes a wish truly cosmic: applying both the art and the science to maximize what's within your power while skillfully working with what remains beyond it.

And here's what matters most: **You now have frameworks, practices, and scientific understanding that give you far more control over your wishes than you ever imagined possible.**

That's what this entire journey has been about.

Measuring Your Transformation

But before we go any further, let's pause and actually measure what's happened. Because one of the most important things science teaches us is this: what gets measured gets reinforced.

When you consciously track and acknowledge progress, something remarkable happens in your brain. Research shows that monitoring goal progress significantly increases the likelihood of achieving your goals.[384]

A comprehensive meta-analysis of 138 studies involving nearly 20,000 participants found that interventions prompting people to monitor their progress increased goal attainment, with even stronger effects when progress was physically recorded or made public.[385] [386]

This tracking activates your brain's reward systems. Dopamine gets released—not just as a "feel good" chemical, but as your brain's primary learning signal that marks behaviors as valuable and worth repeating.[387] Neural pathways strengthen through a process called neuroplasticity, where the brain physically reorganizes its connections in response to experience and practice.[388] The behaviors that led to progress become more automatic. Your brain literally rewires itself to repeat what you're measuring and celebrating.

This isn't just feel-good psychology—it's how learning gets consolidated into long-term memory[389] and how new patterns become your baseline way of operating.

About Your Three Selves:
- Can you now identify which Self is speaking when you feel internal conflict?
- Do you understand why your Inner Self might resist something your Outer Self wants?
- Have you experienced moments of all three Selves aligning around a desire?
- When you think about your wish now, can you sense how each Self responds to it?

About Your Motivation:
- Can you distinguish between authentic needs and surface wants?
- Do you understand what you're moving toward versus moving away from?
- Have you identified any misbeliefs driving your desires?
- Can you recognize when motivation comes from fear versus when it comes from joy?

About Your Brain:
- Do you understand that your brain is plastic—that you can actually rewire it?
- Have you noticed any moments where you caught yourself in an old pattern and chose differently?
- Can you see how 8 weeks of consistent practice could create lasting change?
- Do you believe transformation is actually possible now in a way you didn't before?

About The Three P's:
- Have you experimented with making wishes from peaceful, positive, and purposeful states?
- Can you feel the difference between wishing from desperation versus wishing from peace?
- Do you understand how your internal state affects what you attract and create?
- Have you had even one experience of the Three P's creating a different outcome?

About The Four Responses:

- Can you now see NO as feedback rather than failure?
- Do you understand WAIT as cosmic timing rather than cosmic ignoring?
- Have you recognized any SOMETHING BETTER moments in your life—times when what you got was wiser than what you asked for?
- Can you read reality's responses to your wishes with more clarity and less judgment?

Take a moment. Really consider what you've integrated. If you answered yes to even some of these questions, something remarkable has happened. You've integrated new frameworks. You've expanded your consciousness. You've gained real, practical tools for working with desire, intention, and reality.

You've moved wishing into your circle of control.

That deserves to be acknowledged. Measured. Honored.

Because here's what the science tells us: **Progress that goes unacknowledged doesn't get reinforced.**

The Science of Celebration

And that brings us to perhaps the most important scientific principle we haven't fully explored yet: **the neuroscience of celebration.**

Research across multiple disciplines—neuroscience, psychology, behavioral science—reveals that celebrating success isn't just enjoyable. It's actually essential for sustainable transformation. Studies show that acknowledging progress and practicing gratitude leads to improved mental health outcomes and increased resilience.[390]

Here's what happens in your brain when you pause to celebrate and feel genuine gratitude:

Dopamine floods your system. This isn't just a "feel good" chemical—it's your brain's primary learning signal. Dopamine marks behaviors as valuable and worth repeating.[391] When you celebrate learning about the Three Selves or successfully using the Three P's, you're literally teaching your brain: "This matters. Do more of this."

Neural pathways strengthen. The behaviors and thought patterns you acknowledge become more automatic through neuroplasticity—the brain's ability to form new neural connections throughout life. Celebration isn't separate from the learning—it's the final step that cements the learning into your neural architecture.

Your brain gets better at success. Each time you celebrate progress, you trigger dopamine release that reinforces the behaviors that led to achievement.[392] Celebration teaches your brain: "I'm capable of more than I thought." This expanding sense of possibility is one of the most powerful drivers of continued growth.

Positive reinforcement loops activate. Psychology has known for decades that behaviors followed by positive experiences become more frequent. But neuroscience now shows us the mechanism: celebration creates feedback loops where small wins activate reward systems, making continued practice more likely.[393]

Social bonding chemicals release. When celebration happens in groups—which we'll talk about soon—oxytocin and other bonding neurochemicals activate.[394] [395] This is why our ancestors celebrated together. It strengthened social cohesion, which increased survival.

Resilience and self-esteem build. Studies show that people who regularly acknowledge their progress, practice gratitude, and celebrate wins—even small ones—demonstrate greater confidence, improved well-being, and enhanced ability to persist through challenges.[396] [397]

The research is unambiguous: Celebrating success is more than a reward. It's the glue that binds intention to achievement. It's how transformation becomes permanent.[398]

So right now, before we go any further, let's do what science says matters:

Take a moment and celebrate what you've learned.

You picked up a book about wishing—something many people dismiss as childish or magical thinking—and you discovered it's actually grounded in solid science across dozens of disciplines.

You learned frameworks most people never encounter.

You expanded your understanding of how consciousness, intention, motivation, neuroscience, and reality interact.

You transformed from someone who hoped blindly into someone who understands cosmic collaboration.

That's extraordinary.

Feel that for a moment. Let it land. Let your brain register: "I did this. I learned this. I'm not who I was."

Because acknowledging this progress isn't indulgent—it's neurologically necessary for what comes next.

You Have Cosmic Wishing Power Now

Here's the truth that's been building through every chapter:

You now know how to make cosmic wishes.

Not perfectly. Not automatically yet. But you have the knowledge, the frameworks, the science. You understand:

- **The Three Selves** and how alignment amplifies your wishes
- **The Motivation Matrix** and how to work with what truly drives you

- **Neuroplasticity** and how 8 weeks of practice rewires your brain
- **The Three P's** and how your internal state shapes what you attract
- **The Four Responses** and how to read reality's feedback skillfully

You've moved most of wishing from "cosmic mystery" into "cosmic collaboration with conscious participation."

That's what makes a wish cosmic: Understanding the art and the science. Maximizing what's in your control while working skillfully with what remains beyond it. Conscious intention meeting forces larger than yourself.

You have that power now.

And that brings us to the question this entire book has been building toward...

What If We ALL Had That Power?

You can use what you've learned for yourself. For your personal wishes, your individual desires, your own transformation.

That alone is valuable. That alone could change your life.

But let's think bigger for a moment.

What if everyone understood what you now understand?

What if this wasn't secret knowledge held by a few, but shared wisdom practiced by many?

What if millions of people learned to make cosmic wishes?

Because here's what our ancestors knew—something profound about collective intention and human survival...

What Our Ancestors Knew

Our ancestors didn't wish alone.

They gathered under stars, at new moons, during solstices and harvests. They made wishes together—for rain, for successful hunts, for healthy children, for protection, for abundance.

This wasn't just ritual or superstition. Collective wishing served a crucial evolutionary function: it united cultures and increased chances of survival.

Research across anthropology, evolutionary biology, and cognitive science demonstrates that collective rituals—including group wishing practices—have been fundamental to human social evolution.[399] [400] These shared practices evolved as adaptive mechanisms that promoted group cooperation and survival.[401]

When people wished together, several things happened:

They aligned around shared intentions. They created group cohesion. They synchronized their efforts toward common goals. They generated collective hope that sustained them through hardship. They built trust and cooperation that made communities stronger.

Anthropological research shows that cultures with strong collective rituals—including group wishing practices—demonstrated greater social bonding.[402] [403] , more effective resource sharing and cooperation[404] [405] and enhanced ability to overcome challenges together.[406]

Collective wishing made us more likely to survive and thrive as a species.

Our ancestors understood something profound: Individual wishes create personal power. Collective wishes create cultural evolution.

They knew this not through science but through lived experience, through thousands of years of gathering together to send intentions into the cosmos.

And it worked. It kept us alive. It helped us flourish. It connected us.

And Now... Imagine This

Our ancestors practiced collective wishing through intuition and tradition.

They didn't have neuroscience explaining how brains synchronize during shared intention, how mirror neurons create collective consciousness, how cooperation literally coordinates neural activity between people.

But we do.

We have something our ancestors never had: the science of wishing combined with the ability to connect globally, instantly.

We understand HOW collective wishing works. We can teach it. We can practice it consciously. We can measure it.

So here's the question:

What becomes possible when we combine ancient wisdom about collective wishing with modern science about how consciousness, intention, and social connection interact?

What if we didn't just wish alone anymore, using our individual cosmic wishing power for personal gain?

What if we practiced cosmic wishing together—consciously, scientifically, globally?

What If...

Take everything you've learned in this book. Every framework, every piece of science, every practice. Now imagine not just YOU having that knowledge and power...

But millions of people. All over the world. Practicing together.

WHAT IF we could all understand and unite our Three Selves?

Imagine a world where people aren't fighting internal battles between logic, emotion, and spirit. Where humans understand that inner conflict isn't weakness—it's just misalignment that can be addressed. Where everyone learns to integrate their Inner, Outer, and Higher Selves to work as a coordinated team.

What becomes possible when billions of people stop inner conflict and start inner collaboration? How does that change families, communities, organizations, entire cultures? What challenges could we solve if humanity operated from internal alignment rather than internal fragmentation?

WHAT IF we could all make our wishes Peaceful, Positive, and Purposeful?

Imagine collective intention arising not from desperation, panic, or grasping, but from genuine peace. From authentic positivity rooted in gratitude rather than lack. From purpose that serves the greater good, not just individual ego.

What kind of world emerges when our collective wishes come from the Three P's? What do we create together when our shared intentions are made from our highest states rather than our most reactive ones?[407]

WHAT IF we could all align our motivations to what we truly need instead of what we think we want?

Imagine humanity learning to distinguish between surface wants and authentic needs. Between moving toward joy and running from fear. Between desires rooted in misbeliefs and aspirations grounded in truth.

What becomes possible when our collective motivation shifts from consumption and status to meaning, connection, contribution, and growth? What if we stopped chasing hollow wants that never satisfy and started pursuing what actually fulfills us? How does the world change when our shared motivation comes from wisdom rather than conditioning?

WHAT IF we could all apply neuroscience that actually works?

We know the brain is plastic. We know 8 weeks of consistent practice rewires neural pathways. We know repetition creates new baselines. We know how to use neuroplasticity for transformation.

Research demonstrates that just 8 weeks of mindfulness practice produces measurable structural changes in the brain.[408] Studies show that structural brain changes can occur within 8-12 weeks of consistent practice[409], with cognitive behavioral therapy producing brain rewiring through increased production of brain-derived neurotrophic factor.[410] The brain's ability to reorganize itself through forming new neural connections—neuroplasticity—continues throughout life. [411]

You can do this alone for your own brain. But what happens when millions of people simultaneously rewire their brains toward cosmic wishing? What becomes possible when we all consciously upgrade ourselves? What shifts in humanity when we use neuroscience not just individually but collectively, when we apply what actually works at scale?

WHAT IF we could all understand the Four Responses and learn from every wish?

Imagine a world where people don't give up at NO—they receive it as feedback and adjust. Where WAIT doesn't trigger despair—it's recognized as cosmic timing. Where SOMETHING BETTER is trusted even when we can't see what's coming. Where YES is celebrated not as luck but as successful collaboration.

What becomes possible when humanity becomes fluent in reading reality's responses? When we all learn from every wish we make? When we treat existence itself as a conscious collaboration partner that's always communicating, always teaching, always guiding us toward what serves our highest good?

What if all of this—every framework, every practice, every piece of science—was woven into one simple, accessible, free movement that anyone could join?

What if you didn't have to figure out how to practice cosmic wishing alone?

What if there was a structured 8-week process designed around neuroplasticity research?

What if you could practice with others—in Wish Circles—so you had support, accountability, shared celebration?412

What if you could track your wishes alongside thousands of others?

What if we could measure what happens when humans consciously practice cosmic wishing together?

What if we could find out whether collective cosmic wishing can actually change the world?

What becomes possible when ancient wisdom meets modern science meets global collaboration?

That's what we're about to discover together.

Your Invitation to The Cosmic Wish Experiment

This isn't a program you buy. It's not another self-help course or manifestation method.

It's a global grassroots experiment to answer one crucial question:

Can conscious, collective cosmic wishing help humanity evolve, unite, and thrive?[413]

Here's how it works:

8 Weeks. Because neuroscience tells us that's the threshold for rewiring neural pathways. You're not just making wishes—you're training your brain for cosmic wishing to become automatic.

Daily Practice. Two types of wishes every day: intentional (scheduled, conscious) and prompted (spontaneous, when the universe gives you a signal—11:11, shooting stars, synchronicities). You're building the habit of cosmic collaboration.

The Frameworks. Every week focuses on one element you learned in this book: The Three Selves, Motivation, Neuroplasticity, The Three P's, The Four Responses. You're not just reading about them—you're living them.

Wish Circles. Groups practicing together, supporting each other, witnessing each other's transformations. Because mirror neurons and collective intention amplify everything. You're not alone.

The Cosmic Wish Tracker. A simple, fun way to track your progress, notice synchronicities, document responses—and see your wishes light up the sky alongside thousands of others, watching the collective field strengthen in real-time.

The Free Playbook. Your guide through all 8 weeks with practices, reflections, and tracking tools based on everything you learned in this book.

By Week 8, cosmic wishing becomes your new normal. The frameworks are embodied. The practices are automatic. You see synchronicities everywhere. You respond to life from the Three P's naturally. The Four Responses are fluent. You don't just understand cosmic wishing—you ARE a cosmic wisher.

All that's required is: **A wish** that matters to you. **Eight weeks** of daily practice for only 2-3 minutes a day—the time neuroscience tells us creates lasting change. **A Wish Circle**—join one or start your own. **Willingness** to track, notice, learn, and adjust. And **courage** to celebrate every response the universe sends you.

That's it. Everything else is provided: the Playbook, the Tracker, the frameworks, the science, the community.

You have cosmic wishing power now. You could use it alone. Or you could join thousands of others in discovering what happens when we elevate together—when we practice what our ancestors knew but now with the science to understand it, measure it, and consciously amplify it.

Every person who participates strengthens the field. Every Wish Circle becomes a beacon. Every story shared fuels the movement.

You are part of the answer to the question: Can conscious, collective cosmic wishing change the world?

The experiment begins now.

Visit https://cosmicwishexperiment.com/ to join or start your Wish Circle.

Download your free Playbook.

Make your first wish in the Cosmic Wish Tracker and watch it light up the sky.

Let's find out what happens when we elevate together.

This Book Started With a Wish

And it ends with one too.

I wish for a world where we remember what our ancestors knew:

That we're stronger together than apart.

That collective hope creates collective reality.

That wishing isn't childish—it's how humans have always coordinated intentions, united cultures, and survived impossible challenges.

I wish for a world where millions of people understand the science of wishing and practice it consciously, daily, together.

Where the Three Selves framework is as common as meditation.

Where the Three P's are taught in schools.

Where the Four Responses help us navigate life's uncertainty with grace.

Where neuroplasticity is understood and used by everyone.

Where cosmic collaboration isn't mystical—it's practical.

I wish for a global movement of cosmic wishers lighting up the sky.

That's my wish.

What's yours?

Join the Cosmic Wish Experiment.

Together, we can light up the sky.

✦ **The End** ✦

(And the beginning.)

The Cosmic Wish EXPERIMENT

Together we can light the sky!

https://cosmicwishexperiment.com/

Appendix A: Science Based Hard and Fast Rules for Wishing

1. Commit to the 8-Week Protocol

Neuroscience research on habit and neuroplasticity rates shows it takes at least 8 weeks of daily practice for new pathways to solidify. The methodology requires:

- Daily engagement with wishing rituals, reflections, and tracking for 8 consecutive weeks.
- No skipping days: habitual practice ensures effectiveness.

2. Daily Practice

- Make your wish *at least once per day* for the full 8-week cycle.
- Use tracking tools (Wish Tracker, Playbook log) to record outcomes, emotions, and neural changes.

3. Align Every Wish with the Three Ps

- **Peaceful:** Wishes must originate from a calm, regulated nervous system—no stress, anger, or resentment.
- **Positive:** Wish for positive outcomes only—not for harm or retribution for others.
- **Purposeful:** Wishes must serve authentic personal growth and/or benefit more than just the wisher.

4. Alignment of Your Three Selves

Only wishes that have emotional, cognitive, and spiritual agreement (Three Selves) are valid for this method.

5. Use Only Ethical, Growth-Oriented Intentions

Any wish with harmful, manipulative, exploitative, or vengeful intent invalidates the process and should be stopped immediately.

Appendix B: The Sciences

Scientist / Researcher	Field / Contribution
Viktor Frankl	Logotherapy; meaning, hope, and transcendence
Martin Seligman	Positive psychology; optimism, hope, and well-being
Roy Baumeister	Psychology; belongingness, meaning, motivation
Robin Dunbar	Evolutionary anthropology; Dunbar's number, social cohesion
Jonathan Haidt	Moral psychology; Moral Foundations Theory, group meaning
Bronisław Malinowski	Anthropology; ritual, magic, communal practices
Victor Turner	Anthropology; liminality, ritual process
Émile Durkheim	Sociology; collective effervescence, sacred bonds
Mary Douglas	Symbolic anthropology; purity, taboo, boundary maintenance
Alan Dundes	Folklore studies; communal myths, wishing rituals
Daniel Pink	Motivation science; autonomy, mastery, purpose
Edward Deci & Richard Ryan	Psychology; Self-Determination Theory
Gabrielle Oettingen	Psychology; WOOP model (Wish, Outcome, Obstacle, Plan)
Albert Bandura	Psychology; self-efficacy, motivational theory
Richard Davidson	Neuroscience; well-being, positive emotion, brain plasticity

Scientist / Researcher	Field / Contribution
Rupert Sheldrake	Biology; morphic resonance, collective intention
David Sloan Wilson	Evolutionary biology; prosocial dynamics, group cooperation
Cass Sunstein	Social science; nudges and collective behavior
Margaret Mead	Anthropology; narrative, social change
Otto Scharmer	Systems theory/social science; Theory U, collective intention
Elinor Ostrom	Economics; collective action, resource governance
Karl Friston	Neuroscience/complex systems; free energy principle
James Doty	Neuroscience; manifestation, brain attention networks
Marcus Raichle	Neuroscience; Default Mode Network, future thinking
Barbara Fredrickson	Psychology; broaden-and-build theory of positive emotion
Sara Lazar	Neuroscience; mindfulness-induced brain changes
Antonio Damasio	Neuroscience; emotion and consciousness
Karim Nader	Neuroscience; memory reconsolidation, belief change
Marco Iacoboni	Neuroscience; mirror neurons, empathy
Uri Hasson	Cognitive neuroscience; neural coupling, communication synchrony
John Cacioppo	Social neuroscience; emotional contagion, social connection
Elaine Hatfield	Social psychology; emotional contagion, empathy research
David G. Myers	Psychology; wishful thinking biases

Scientist / Researcher	Field / Contribution
Hazel Markus	Cultural psychology; identity and aspiration
Richard Tedeschi & Lawrence Calhoun	Psychology; post-traumatic growth
Jean Twenge	Social psychology; narcissism, gen trends
Brené Brown	Social psychology; vulnerability, shame
Roger Penrose & Stuart Hameroff	Physics/Neuroscience; Orch OR theory, quantum consciousness
Wolfgang Pauli	Theoretical physics; quantum mechanics, synchronicity collaboration
Dean Radin	Parapsychology; presentiment, collective consciousness research
Giulio Tononi	Neuroscience; Integrated Information Theory
Vitaly Vanchurin	Physics; universe as neural network
Joe Dispenza	Neuroscience/quantum studies; meditation and brain-body change
Anthony de Mello	Spiritual psychology; attachment and motivation
Paul Zak	Neuroeconomics; oxytocin, storytelling, and prosocial behavior
Melanie Green	Social psychology; Transportation Theory, narrative persuasion
Timothy Brock	Social psychology; Transportation Theory, story absorption
Raymond Mar	Psychology; fiction reading, empathy, theory of mind
Keith Oatley	Cognitive psychology; narrative as social simulation

Scientist / Researcher	Field / Contribution
Benjamin Rogers	Psychology; Hero's Journey validation, narrative resilience
Lucas J. Dixon	Psychology; Manifestation beliefs, financial decision-making, magical thinking
Matthew J. Hornsey	Social Psychology; Belief systems, pseudoscience, critical thinking
Nicole Hartley	Psychology; Decision-making, cognitive biases, risk propensity
Amy Edmondson	Organizational psychology; psychological safety, team learning
Arie W. Kruglanski	Social psychology; cognitive closure, motivated reasoning
C.R. Snyder	Psychology; Hope Theory, agency and pathways
Carl Jung	Analytical psychology; collective unconscious, archetypes
Carl Sagan	Astronomy/science communication; scientific skepticism
Charlan Nemeth	Social psychology; dissent, minority influence, group decision-making
Daniel Simons & Christopher Chabris	Cognitive psychology; attention, inattentional blindness
Daryl Bem	Social psychology; precognition research, psi effects
David Bohm	Theoretical physics; implicate order, quantum theory
David Hawkins	Psychiatry/consciousness; power vs. force, consciousness levels

Scientist / Researcher	Field / Contribution
Edward Deci	Psychology; Self-Determination Theory, intrinsic motivation
John Welwood	Psychotherapy; spiritual bypassing, mindfulness
Jon Kabat-Zinn	Medicine/mindfulness; Mindfulness-Based Stress Reduction (MBSR)
Joseph Campbell	Comparative mythology; Hero's Journey, monomyth
Malcolm Gladwell	Journalism/sociology; tipping points, social epidemics
Nicholas Christakis & James Fowler	Medical sociology; social networks, behavioral contagion
Robert K. Merton	Sociology; organized skepticism, self-fulfilling prophecy
Simon Sinek	Leadership/organizational psychology; Start With Why, purpose-driven leadership
Huw Price	Philosophy of physics; retrocausality, time symmetry

Psychology and Behavioral Science

Scientist	Specialty
Albert Bandura	Social–Cognitive Psychology; Self-Efficacy and Motivation
Tim Kasser	Psychology; intrinsic/extrinsic motivation, values research
Roy Baumeister	Social Psychology; Self-Control, Belongingness, and Meaning
Carol Dweck	Psychology; growth mindset, resilience, learning orientation
Robert Emmons	Psychology; gratitude research, goal conflict theory
Kennon Sheldon	Positive psychology; self-concordant goals, authentic motivation
Mihaly Csikszentmihalyi	Positive Psychology; Flow and Optimal Experience
Edward Deci	Motivation Science; Self-Determination Theory
Richard Ryan	Motivation and Well-Being; Intrinsic Motivation
Daniel Gilbert	Cognitive Psychology; Imagination and Future Thinking
Jonathan Haidt	Moral Psychology; Foundations of Ethics and Ritual Behavior
Daniel Kahneman	Behavioral Economics and Cognitive Bias; Decision-Making Processes
Frederic Luskin	Clinical Psychology; Forgiveness and Emotional Health
Sonja Lyubomirsky	Positive Psychology; Happiness and Hedonic Adaptation

Scientist	Specialty
Hazel Markus	Cultural Psychology; Identity and Motivation
Abraham Maslow	Humanistic Psychology; Hierarchy of Needs and Self-Actualization
David G. Myers	Social Psychology; Faith, Belief, and Cognitive Biases
Gabrielle Oettingen	Cognitive Psychology; Motivation and WOOP Model
Carol Ryff	Positive Psychology; Six-Factor Model of Well-Being
Shalom Schwartz	Cross-Cultural Psychology; Theory of Basic Human Values
Richard C. Schwartz	Clinical Psychology; Internal Family Systems (IFS) Therapy
C. R. Snyder	Cognitive Psychology; Hope Theory and Goal Pathways
Jean Twenge	Social Psychology; Generational Behavior and Narcissism
Carol Dweck	Psychology; growth mindset, resilience, learning orientation
Robert Emmons	Psychology; gratitude research, goal conflict theory
Kennon Sheldon	Positive psychology; self-concordant goals, authentic motivation
Melanie Green	Social psychology; Transportation Theory, narrative persuasion
Timothy Brock	Social psychology; Transportation Theory, story absorption
Raymond Mar	Psychology; fiction reading, empathy, theory of mind
Keith Oatley	Cognitive psychology; narrative as social simulation

Scientist	Specialty
Benjamin Rogers	Psychology; Hero's Journey validation, narrative resilience
Lucas J. Dixon	Psychology; Manifestation beliefs, financial decision-making, magical thinking
Matthew J. Hornsey	Social Psychology; Belief systems, pseudoscience, critical thinking
Nicole Hartley	Psychology; Decision-making, cognitive biases, risk propensity
John Welwood	Psychotherapy; spiritual bypassing, mindfulness
Jon Kabat-Zinn	Medicine/mindfulness; Mindfulness-Based Stress Reduction (MBSR)
C.R. Snyder	Psychology; Hope Theory, agency and pathways

Neuroscience and Medicine

Scientist	Specialty
Antonio Damasio	Cognitive Neuroscience; Consciousness and Emotion
Richard Davidson	Affective Neuroscience; Meditation and Brain Plasticity
Karl Friston	Computational Neuroscience; Free Energy Principle
Nicholas Christakis	Medical sociology; social network contagion, collective behavior
James Fowler	Political science; social contagion, network effects
Duncan Watts	Network science; tipping points, social dynamics
Malcolm Gladwell	Social psychology/journalism; tipping points, timing effects
Morton Deutsch	Social psychology; goal interdependence, cooperation theory

Scientist	Specialty
Richard Hackman	Organizational psychology; team dynamics, group effectiveness
Anita Woolley	Organizational psychology; collective intelligence, team coordination
Marcus Raichle	Cognitive Neuroscience; Default Mode Network and Creativity
Rollin McCraty	Psychophysiology; Heart–Brain Coherence and Emotion Research
Daniel Siegel	Psychiatry; Interpersonal Neurobiology and Mindfulness Integration
Kevin Ochsner	Cognitive Neuroscience; Emotion Regulation and Reappraisal
Herbert Benson	Mind–Body Medicine; Relaxation Response and Stress Physiology
Bessel van der Kolk	Psychiatry; Trauma and Somatic Memory
Joe Dispenza	Applied Neuroscience; Neuroplasticity and Self-Directed Change
Stephen Porges	Neuroscience, Behavioral Medicine; Polyvagal Theory—autonomic nervous system regulation, social engagement, and resilience through safety and connection
Paul Zak	Neuroeconomics; oxytocin, storytelling, and prosocial behavior
Daryl Bem	Social psychology; precognition research, psi effects
Sara Lazar	Neuroscience; mindfulness-induced brain changes

Anthropology and Sociology

Scientist	Specialty
Mary Douglas	Symbolic Anthropology; Purity, Taboo, and Social Order
Robin Dunbar	Evolutionary Anthropology; Social Bonding and Cognitive Limits
Alan Dundes	Folkloristics; Myths, Ritual, and Wishing Practices
Émile Durkheim	Sociology and Religion; Collective Effervescence and Solidarity
Bronisław Malinowski	Cultural Anthropology; Ritual, Magic, and Social Function
Margaret Mead	Cultural Anthropology; Cross-Cultural Social Transformation
Victor Turner	Cultural Anthropology; Liminality and Communitas
Carl Sagan	Astronomy/science communication; scientific skepticism
Joseph Campbell	Comparative mythology; Hero's Journey, monomyth
Robert K. Merton	Sociology; organized skepticism, self-fulfilling prophecy

Philosophy and Systems Theory

Scientist	Specialty
Kate Manne	Feminist Philosophy; Privilege, Entitlement, and Social Ethics
Otto Scharmer	Systems Theory and Organizational Learning; Presencing and Collective Awareness

Scientist	Specialty
Cass Sunstein	Behavioral Economics and Law; Nudges and Social Influence
Carl Jung	Analytical psychology; collective unconscious, archetypes
Carl Sagan	Astronomy/science communication; scientific skepticism
David Bohm	Theoretical physics; implicate order, quantum theory
Huw Price	Philosophy of physics; retrocausality, time symmetry

Biology and Evolutionary Science

Scientist	Specialty
Rupert Sheldrake	Biology; Morphic Resonance and Collective Memory Fields
David Sloan Wilson	Evolutionary Biology; Multilevel Selection and Cooperation

Other Domains and Interdisciplinary Thinkers

Scientist	Specialty
Viktor Frankl	Existential Psychology and Psychiatry; Logotherapy and Meaning
Lynne McTaggart	Intention and Consciousness Studies; Group Intention Experiments
Daniel Simons & Christopher Chabris	Cognitive Psychology; Attention and Inattentional Blindness

Scientist	Specialty
Sharon Salzberg	Contemplative Psychology; Loving-Kindness and Mindfulness Teaching
Daniel Pink	Behavioral Science; Motivation and Work Psychology
Amy Edmondson	Organizational psychology; psychological safety, team learning
Arie W. Kruglanski	Social psychology; cognitive closure, motivated reasoning
Charlan Nemeth	Social psychology; dissent, minority influence, group decision-making
David Hawkins	Psychiatry/consciousness; power vs. force, consciousness levels
Malcolm Gladwell	Journalism/sociology; tipping points, social epidemics
Nicholas Christakis & James Fowler	Medical sociology; social networks, behavioral contagion
Simon Sinek	Leadership/organizational psychology; Start With Why, purpose-driven leadership

Appendix C: Meet The Scientists

Albert Bandura

Albert Bandura was a Canadian-American psychologist best known for his theory of self-efficacy—the belief in one's own abilities to organize and execute actions required to achieve goals. Bandura demonstrated that self-efficacy guides perseverance, shapes resilience, and directly influences success in education, career, health, and personal relationships. His insights form a cornerstone of motivation science, revealing that successful wish fulfillment depends as much on confidence and skill as on desire itself.

Roy Baumeister

Roy Baumeister is a social psychologist known for his groundbreaking work on motivation, self-control, and belongingness. He established that humans possess a strong, fundamental need to belong and to experience meaning—finding that psychological health and enduring motivation are tightly linked to social connections and a sense of purpose. His studies on self-defeating behaviors, rejection, and the "need-to-belong" theory clarify why communal rituals and narrative meaning-making are so critical for wish formation, emotional healing, and collective resilience.

Daryl Bem

Daryl Bem is a social psychologist who ignited controversy with his "Feeling the Future" precognition experiments, which used rigorous mainstream protocols to test for psi effects. Bem's results—while debated—suggest the possibility that subconscious pattern recognition and anticipation may play a role in how wishes and expectations interact with future events, inviting new research at the frontier of consciousness, time, and intention.

Herbert Benson

Herbert Benson, MD, was a pioneering cardiologist and mind-body medicine researcher whose studies popularized the concept of the "relaxation response"—a physiological state of deep rest that counters stress and activates the body's self-healing capabilities. Benson's simple, secular techniques—including deep breathing, meditative repetition, and mindfulness—help shift the brain and body from fight-or-flight to calm, measured presence. His work at Harvard and the Benson-Henry Institute made these techniques accessible to millions, validating the scientific foundations of peaceful practices as core to emotional stability, immune health, and effective intention-setting.

David Bohm

David Bohm (1917 – 1992) was a visionary theoretical physicist best known for his proposal of the "implicate order," a profound framework suggesting that all things—matter, energy, consciousness—are enfolded within a deeper, hidden realm of reality. In Bohm's model, what we experience as the separate, explicit world (the "explicate order") is the unfolded expression of this underlying "implicate" wholeness. Some interpreters propose that such a view could explain how higher intuitions or a "Higher Self" might tap universal information fields, though Bohm's original hypothesis remains a provocative metaphysical idea not confirmed by mainstream science.

Timothy Brock

Timothy Brock is a social psychologist who co-developed Transportation Theory with Melanie Green, revealing the psychological mechanisms through which narratives influence human thought and behavior. Brock's research established that story absorption creates a mental state distinct from ordinary information processing—one where audiences temporarily set aside skepticism and experience narratives on their own terms. His work demonstrated that this transportation effect leads to attitude change, belief shifts, and behavioral intentions that persist long after the story ends. Brock's insights explain why stories have served as humanity's primary tool for transmitting values, teaching wisdom, and coordinating social behavior across cultures and throughout history.

Brené Brown

Brené Brown is a social work researcher whose studies on vulnerability, shame, courage, and authenticity have highlighted the central role of emotional honesty in meaningful wishing and resilient living. Brown's research demonstrates that the courage to face vulnerability leads to deeper connections, greater self-worth, and more authentic aspirations—while shame and denial can thwart growth, fulfillment, and compassionate intention.

Joseph Campbell

Joseph Campbell (1904-1987) was an American mythologist and professor whose magnum opus "The Hero with a Thousand Faces" (1949) introduced the concept of the "monomyth" or "hero's journey"—a universal pattern across myths worldwide. Campbell revealed that hero stories from Krishna to Jesus share a fundamental structure: departure, initiation through trials, and return with gifts. His famous phrase "follow your bliss" encapsulates his belief that living authentically is the path to fulfillment. George Lucas credited Campbell's work as inspiration for Star Wars. For cosmic wishing, Campbell's insights reveal that every wish represents a potential hero's journey, with inevitable obstacles, necessary transformation, and ultimate return with wisdom.

Mihaly Csikszentmihalyi

Mihaly Csikszentmihalyi (1934–2021) was a Hungarian-American psychologist renowned for his groundbreaking work on the concept of "flow," which describes moments of deep focus and enjoyment when people are completely absorbed in activities that challenge and match their skills. His research, captured in classic books like "Flow: The Psychology of Optimal Experience," revealed that the flow state leads to enhanced creativity, well-being, and happiness, forming the foundation for the field of positive psychology. Csikszentmihalyi's studies showed that flow is experienced in settings where goals are clear and feedback is immediate, and his insights have influenced diverse fields from education to sports and work. Collaborating with Martin Seligman, he helped shape positive psychology's focus on strengths, engagement, and human flourishing, making his work essential for understanding how optimal experience connects to happiness and sustained motivation.

Antonio Damasio

Antonio Damasio is a globally renowned neuroscientist whose theory of consciousness centers emotion, feeling, and bodily experience as roots of awareness and decision-making. Damasio's work demonstrates that emotions generated by the body's interactions with the world are essential for conscious knowing, creative problem-solving, and meaningful wish formation. His concept of the "Protoself," core consciousness, and extended consciousness offers a layered view of how physiological processes, feelings, and higher-order meaning integrate to shape wishes and choices.

Richard Davidson

Richard Davidson is a pioneering neuroscientist whose research reveals that meditation, compassion, and the intentional cultivation of positive emotions create structural and functional changes in the brain. His studies highlight how these practices build resilience, regulate stress, and optimize motivation—providing scientific validation that peaceful, positive, purposeful mindsets strengthen well-being and the actualization of wishes and goals.

Edward Deci

Edward Deci is an influential psychologist and co-author of Self-Determination Theory, demonstrating that intrinsic motivation flourishes when individuals feel empowered, competent, and connected to others. Deci's pioneering work uncovered the mechanisms by which autonomy and mastery shape people's aspirations, showing how wishes grounded in intrinsic motivation foster resilience, engagement, and psychological health. His legacy informs the science of happiness, education, therapy, and the cultivation of wishes that truly enhance life satisfaction.

Edward Deci & Richard Ryan

Edward Deci and Richard Ryan are psychologists whose Self-Determination Theory (SDT) transformed the science of motivation by establishing autonomy, competence, and relatedness as essential psychological needs. Their work demonstrates that intrinsic motivation flourishes when people feel empowered, capable, and connected, producing lasting engagement, resilience, and well-being. SDT research also highlights how motivation can erode when these needs are thwarted by external control, rigid systems, or isolation.

Lucas J. Dixon

Lucas J. Dixon is a psychologist at the University of Queensland whose groundbreaking 2023 research developed the first scientific measure of manifestation beliefs. His work revealed that while believers in manifestation may feel more confident about their prospects, they also demonstrate measurably riskier financial decision-making, higher rates of bankruptcy, increased vulnerability to fraud, and unrealistic timelines for achieving success. Dixon's research provides empirical evidence for what happens when people confuse wishes (cosmic collaboration) with guarantees, offering crucial insights into the psychological mechanisms that distinguish healthy optimism from magical thinking with real-world consequences.

Joe Dispenza

Joe Dispenza is a chiropractor and popular science communicator whose work focuses on how meditative practices, intention, and belief can reshape the brain through neuroplasticity. Although sometimes controversial, his approach synthesizes mainstream findings in neuroscience with practical guidance for self-transformation, emphasizing the potential for conscious thought to align emotions, physiology, and behavior for positive change and wish fulfillment.

James Doty

Dr. James Doty is a neurosurgeon, neuroscientist, and compassion researcher at Stanford who investigates the neuroscience of manifestation and intention-setting. Doty's studies show that repeated visualization, self-compassion, and emotional engagement produce measurable changes in brain networks—particularly those linked to motivation, reward, and opportunity recognition. Doty emphasizes that serving others boosts well-being and brain efficiency, affirming that compassionate intention enhances both wish realization and overall happiness.

Mary Douglas

Mary Douglas (1921–2007) was a British anthropologist whose landmark book *Purity and Danger* advanced symbolic anthropology by revealing how rituals of pollution, purity, and taboo create social structure and meaning. Douglas argued that definitions of "dirt" and "danger"—

including what is considered ritually appropriate or taboo—organize social boundaries, maintain cultural order, and express hopes, anxieties, and aspirations. Her work explains why wishing rituals often hinge on notions of symbolic purity, boundary-crossing, and transformative potential.

Robin Dunbar

Robin Dunbar is a British evolutionary psychologist renowned for identifying Dunbar's number—the cognitive limit to the number of stable social relationships people can maintain, estimated at around 150. His research into primate and human social bonding unpacks the neurobiological and behavioral bases for rituals, trust, and collective cohesion. Dunbar's work illuminates why rituals matter in wish-making and how shared practices cement both individual and group well-being in societies past and present.

Alan Dundes

Alan Dundes (1934–2005) was a pioneering folklorist who analyzed the meaning and psychological impact of popular rituals, myths, and folk beliefs. Dundes explored how everyday wishing practices—like tossing coins in wells, reciting incantations, or performing mirror rituals—reveal underlying anxieties, hopes, and transformations in communal life. His scholarship highlights wishing rituals as expressions of folklore that both reflect and shape cultural imagination, group identity, and emotional resilience.

Émile Durkheim

Émile Durkheim (1858–1917), a founder of sociology, argued that rituals generate collective effervescence—a synchrony of heightened emotion and shared purpose that binds society together. In classic studies like *Elementary Forms of Religious Life*, Durkheim described how communal rituals and symbolic acts turn ordinary objects into sacred ones, strengthening group cohesion, providing comfort in crisis, and channeling individual wishes into collective meaning-making. His theories laid the foundation for understanding religion, social solidarity, and the emotional dynamics of wish rituals.

Carol Dweck

Carol Dweck is a Stanford psychologist whose groundbreaking research on "growth mindset" transformed our understanding of achievement and personal development. Dweck demonstrated that people who believe their abilities can be developed through dedication and effort (a growth mindset) achieve more than those who believe talents are fixed traits. Her work reveals that the very beliefs underlying our wishes—whether we see obstacles as insurmountable barriers or as opportunities for growth—profoundly shape whether those wishes manifest. This research shows that effective wishing isn't just about what we want, but about how we think about our capacity to grow into the people who can achieve those wishes.

Barbara Ehrenreich

Barbara Ehrenreich (1941–2022), social critic and author of *Bright-Sided*, exposed the dangers of toxic positivity and the pitfalls of uncritical self-help culture. Ehrenreich argued that the current positivity movement can lead to denial of reality, victim-blaming, and a distorted focus on personal responsibility that ignores systemic inequality. Her work urges practitioners of wishing and manifestation to stay grounded in realism, social context, and compassion—balancing optimism with authenticity, complexity, and justice.

Robert Emmons

Robert Emmons is a leading researcher in the psychology of gratitude and its relationship to well-being, motivation, and goal pursuit. His pioneering work on goal conflict revealed that when personal wishes contradict each other or our deeper values, they create psychological distress and undermine achievement. Emmons's research demonstrates that wish fulfillment requires internal coherence—our wishes must align not only with our external circumstances but also with each other and with our core sense of meaning. His studies on gratitude further show that appreciation for what we already have creates the emotional foundation for pursuing what we wish for next.

Viktor Frankl

Viktor Frankl (1905–1997) was an Austrian psychiatrist and Holocaust survivor whose experiences shaped his revolutionary psychotherapy, logotherapy. Grounded in the belief that the search for meaning is the primary human motivation—even during suffering—Frankl argued that hope is sustained not by direct answers, but by the capacity to find significance in every circumstance. His classic book "Man's Search for Meaning" documents how people survived unimaginable adversity through meaning-making, laying the foundation for existential psychology and inspiring generations to see hope as emerging from purpose and self-transcendence.

Barbara Fredrickson

Barbara Fredrickson is a leading positive psychologist best known for her broaden-and-build theory, which reveals that positive emotions expand awareness, boost resilience, and build social and psychological resources critical to well-being and growth. Her research demonstrates that cultivating states like joy, gratitude, and love can enhance creativity, foster supportive relationships, and measurably change brain function, making meaningful and sustained wishing possible across life domains.

Sigmund Freud

(1856–1939) was the founder of psychoanalysis, one of the most influential figures in psychology and the first to map the subconscious mind in a systematic way. He proposed that human personality is made up of three interacting parts: the instinct-driven Id, the reality-oriented Ego, and the morally-guided Superego. Freud believed that much of our behavior is shaped by subconscious desires and hidden conflicts between these inner parts—explaining why people sometimes act against their own conscious wishes. He also introduced concepts like dream interpretation and defense mechanisms, pioneering the idea that talking about subconscious thoughts could heal emotional suffering. Despite controversy, Freud's insights revolutionized psychotherapy and our understanding of the mind, laying the groundwork for nearly every modern approach to psychology.

Karl Friston

Karl Friston is a neuroscientist known for articulating the free energy principle, which posits that all living systems—including social systems—act to minimize surprise and prediction error. Friston's work provides a powerful theoretical framework for understanding how conscious groups adjust, synchronize, and reorganize in response to new information—offering insight into the emergence of collective intention, coherence, and tipping points in the context of emergent change.

Daniel Gilbert

Daniel Gilbert is a Harvard psychologist whose research focuses on imagination, future-thinking, and the pursuit of happiness. Gilbert explores how people anticipate future feelings and make choices based on imagined possibilities—a process deeply related to wishing. His book "Stumbling on Happiness" and related studies reveal that humans consistently misjudge how future events will affect them, uncovering the pitfalls and power of using imagination to guide life decisions and the pursuit of meaningful goals.

Malcolm Gladwell

Malcolm Gladwell is a journalist and author whose bestselling book "The Tipping Point" (2000) introduced the concept that social epidemics reach critical mass through specific mechanisms: the Law of the Few (certain people have disproportionate influence), the Stickiness Factor (messages must be memorable), and the Power of Context (environment shapes behavior). Though trained as a journalist rather than scientist, his synthesis of social science research influences how we understand collective change. For cosmic wishing, Gladwell's work suggests transformation doesn't require everyone to change at once—small shifts among key individuals, combined with sticky messaging and supportive contexts, can catalyze rapid collective change.

Melanie Green

Melanie Green is a social psychologist best known for developing Transportation Theory alongside Timothy Brock. Her research demonstrates that when people become deeply absorbed in narratives—"transported" into story worlds—their critical resistance temporarily suspends, allowing stories to influence attitudes, beliefs, and behaviors more effectively than factual arguments. Green's work has shown that narrative persuasion operates through a unique cognitive process where emotional engagement with stories creates openings for meaningful change that logical argumentation cannot achieve. Her findings have profound implications for understanding how stories spread ideas, shift cultural narratives, and inspire collective action.

Jonathan Haidt

Jonathan Haidt is a social psychologist whose Moral Foundations Theory redefined understanding of morality as rooted in evolved cognitive modules such as care, fairness, loyalty, and authority. Studying diverse cultures, Haidt showed that rituals, storytelling, and collective practices reflect—and reinforce—these intuitive ethics, helping humans make sense of suffering, create meaning, and strengthen group identity. His research elevates the role of narrative and ritual in the evolutionary psychology of wishing, hope, and social transformation.

Stuart Hameroff

Stuart Hameroff is an anesthesiologist and consciousness researcher who, along with physicist Roger Penrose, developed the Orchestrated Objective Reduction (Orch OR) theory of quantum consciousness. Hameroff's work proposes that consciousness arises from quantum processes in microtubules within brain neurons, suggesting that the mind may operate according to quantum mechanical principles rather than purely classical physics. This controversial but intriguing theory opens possibilities for understanding how intention and consciousness might interact with reality at fundamental levels—offering a potential scientific framework for the mysterious connection between wishes and their manifestation in the physical world.

Uri Hasson

Uri Hasson is a professor of psychology and neuroscience at Princeton University whose research revolutionized understanding of how brains synchronize during communication. His studies using fMRI demonstrated that during effective communication, listener brain activity mirrors speaker brain activity—"neural coupling." When a speaker tells a story, similar patterns unfold in the listener's brain. The strength of neural coupling directly correlates with comprehension—the more aligned the brain patterns, the better the understanding. For collective wishing, Hasson's findings suggest that when groups align through shared stories and intentions, their brains may literally synchronize, creating neurological coherence that amplifies collective focus.

John-Dylan Haynes

John-Dylan Haynes is a leading neuroscientist whose experiments revealed that the brain's subconscious activity can predict decisions several seconds before people experience conscious intent. His modern extensions of the Libet experiments suggest that much of human choice arises from neural processes outside awareness, yet consciousness retains an important "editor" or veto role. Haynes' work underscores the importance of aligning subconscious and conscious desires—a foundational principle for wish fulfillment, habit change, and personal transformation.

Nicole Hartley

Nicole Hartley is a psychology researcher whose work focuses on decision-making processes, cognitive biases, and risk assessment. Her contribution to manifestation belief research helps explain why people who believe they can magically attract success through positive thinking alone tend to make riskier financial choices and overestimate their likelihood of achieving improbable goals. Hartley's research provides empirical validation for the importance of understanding what's truly within your control (your inner state, preparation, aligned action) versus what requires cosmic collaboration (outcomes, timing, universal response).

Uri Hasson

Neuroscientist Uri Hasson of Princeton University has shown that during effective communication, speakers' and listeners' brains synchronize. Using fMRI scans, his studies demonstrated that when one person tells a story and another listens with understanding, their neural activity patterns align across key language and comprehension areas of the brain. This coupling, known as *brain-to-brain synchronization*, strengthens as understanding deepens—offering biological evidence that shared meaning literally connects minds. Hasson's research suggests that successful communication creates a kind of shared consciousness, where storytelling serves as a bridge linking brains into a common neural experience.

David Hawkins

Psychiatrist and consciousness researcher David R. Hawkins developed the *Map of Consciousness*—a scale ranging from 1 to 1,000 that he described in his book *Power vs. Force*. Through decades of clinical observation and testing using applied kinesiology, Hawkins proposed that lower levels of consciousness (below 200) reflect force—patterns driven by fear, pride, or control—while higher levels (above 200) embody power, expressed through courage, integrity, and love. His model suggested that power-based states generate coherence and self-reinforcing positive energy, fostering cooperation and sustainable transformation, whereas force-based ones deplete energy and create resistance. The framework continues to influence leadership and personal development fields by illustrating how elevating consciousness frequency can drive enduring, positive social and psychological change.

Matthew J. Hornsey

Matthew J. Hornsey is a social psychologist at the University of Queensland known for his research on belief systems, social influence, and how people respond to scientific versus pseudoscientific claims. His collaboration on manifestation belief research demonstrates how cultural movements like *The Secret* can influence decision-making patterns in measurable ways. Hornsey's work illuminates the distinction between evidence-based positive psychology and pseudoscientific approaches that promise cosmic control without acknowledging complexity, helping readers understand when motivational teachings support healthy wishing versus when they encourage harmful overconfidence.

Andrew Huberman

Andrew Huberman is a neuroscientist whose research on neuroplasticity and motivation has illuminated how focused intention, visualization, and action can reshape brain circuits and behavior. Through his accessible protocols, Huberman demonstrates that conscious practice—especially leveraging anticipation, dopamine, and the power of small wins—can accelerate habit change, resilience, and effective pursuit of personal wishes and long-term goals.

Marco Iacoboni

Marco Iacoboni is a neuroscientist at UCLA whose research on mirror neurons has transformed understanding of empathy and social connection. Mirror neurons fire both when we perform an action and when we observe someone else performing it, creating a neural basis for understanding others through simulation. Iacoboni's work demonstrates that mirror neuron systems underlie our ability to understand others' intentions and emotions by internally recreating their mental states. For collective wishing, his research provides crucial evidence that human nervous systems are designed for resonance—when we gather in wish circles, our mirror neurons may facilitate alignment of intention and emotion, creating the neural substrate for collective coherence.

Carl Jung

Carl Jung (1875–1961), Swiss psychologist and founder of analytical psychology, introduced the concept of synchronicity to describe "meaningful coincidences" not explained by causal relationships. Jung's theory proposes that internal psychological states and archetypal patterns can mysteriously mesh with outer events, producing moments charged with emotion, significance, and transformation. Jung's lifelong investigation into dreams, symbols, and acausal connecting principles also established a cross-disciplinary conversation between psychology and quantum physics on the nature of consciousness and reality.

Jon Kabat-Zinn

Jon Kabat-Zinn is the creator of Mindfulness-Based Stress Reduction (MBSR), which integrates mindfulness meditation practices into mainstream medicine and psychology. His research demonstrates that nonjudgmental awareness of the present moment enhances emotional regulation, reduces stress, and supports healthy goal pursuit—laying the groundwork for how attuned, mindful wishing can improve quality of life.

Tim Kasser

Tim Kasser is a psychologist whose research reveals the profound difference between intrinsic and extrinsic motivation in determining life satisfaction and well-being. Kasser's studies show that wishes focused on external goals like wealth, fame, or appearance often lead to decreased happiness, increased anxiety, and diminished fulfillment—even when achieved. In contrast, wishes aligned with intrinsic values such as personal growth, relationships, and community contribution create lasting satisfaction and psychological health. His work provides crucial scientific evidence for why the quality and source of our wishes matter as much as their achievement, and why peaceful, positive, and purposeful wishing leads to more authentic fulfillment.

Irving Kirsch

Irving Kirsch is an American psychologist and professor renowned for his research on placebo effects and response expectancy theory. Kirsch's meta-analyses on antidepressants famously concluded that much of their apparent benefit can be attributed to patients' beliefs and expectations rather than the medications themselves. His response expectancy theory demonstrates how what people expect from an action or treatment can profoundly shape both subjective experiences and measurable physiological responses—including the outcomes of wishing and intention.

Daniel Kahneman

Daniel Kahneman, Nobel laureate, revolutionized psychology and economics with his dual-process theory: fast, intuitive System 1 and slower, analytical System 2. His research showed that intuition and rapid pattern matching underpin many of our important decisions—including those moments when opportunity aligns unexpectedly with conscious or subconscious wishes. Kahneman's work clarifies how snap "YES" judgments often emerge from subconscious knowledge and prior intention.

Arie W. Kruglanski

Arie W. Kruglanski is a distinguished social psychologist whose research has explored how conflict, tension, and skepticism can stimulate original thinking and creative problem-solving in groups.

Kruglanski's studies have illuminated the mechanisms by which dissent and challenge within decision-making bodies lead to the generation of novel forms and breakthrough solutions. By examining cognitive conflict and motivational factors in group processes, his work has revealed that skepticism and creative tension enhance the scope and depth of collective judgment. Organizations drawing on Kruglanski's insights learn to see friction not as a threat but as a catalyst for innovation.

Sara Lazar

Sara Lazar is a neuroscientist at Massachusetts General Hospital and Harvard Medical School whose research demonstrated that meditation produces measurable structural brain changes. Her landmark 2005 study showed experienced meditators have increased cortical thickness in regions associated with attention and sensory processing, and that meditation can slow age-related cortical thinning. Later studies demonstrated that eight weeks of mindfulness practice produces measurable gray matter increases in regions involved in learning and emotional regulation. For cosmic wishing, Lazar's findings provide scientific validation that practices like meditation genuinely transform neural architecture, potentially making us more capable of the focused attention and emotional regulation supporting wish fulfillment.

Benjamin Libet

Benjamin Libet (1916–2007) was a pioneering neurophysiologist best known for his experiments on human volition and conscious awareness. Libet discovered that the brain initiates readiness for action before people consciously report deciding to act—a finding interpreted both as support for determinism and free will. He argued that although the subconscious prepares a movement, the conscious mind can still exercise "free won't," the power to veto an impulse before action. His legacy continues to shape philosophical debates about agency, responsibility, and the role of subconscious processes in wishing.

Frederic Luskin

Frederic Luskin, PhD, is one of the world's foremost forgiveness researchers and the founder of the Stanford Forgiveness Projects. Through clinical research and practical frameworks, Luskin demonstrated that forgiving others and oneself reduces chronic stress, increases feelings of inner peace, and improves emotional and physical health. His best-selling books and widely used seminars present forgiveness not as condoning harmful acts but as letting go of grievances, breaking free from resentment, and reclaiming energy for growth and purposeful wishing.

Sonja Lyubomirsky

Sonja Lyubomirsky is a psychologist celebrated for her empirical studies on happiness, adaptation, and the hedonic treadmill. Her research demonstrates that while much of happiness is genetically determined, intentional activities such as gratitude, positive reframing, and finding meaning in daily life—rather than simply achieving external wishes—are central to lasting well-being and satisfaction.

Bronisław Malinowski

Bronisław Malinowski (1884–1942) stands as one of the founding figures in modern anthropology, known for his immersive fieldwork among the Trobriand Islanders. Malinowski's studies revealed that rituals—including magic and wish-making—serve concrete social and psychological functions: they help individuals and communities deal with uncertainty, anxiety, and life transitions by fostering a sense of control, hope, and solidarity. His approach showed that rituals are not arbitrary superstitions, but deeply practical responses shaped by human need, creativity, and adaptation.

Raymond Mar

Raymond Mar is a psychologist at York University whose longitudinal research has demonstrated that reading fiction enhances theory of mind—the capacity to understand others' thoughts, emotions, and mental states. Mar's work shows that narrative experience builds empathy and social cognition more effectively than non-fiction reading, suggesting that stories serve as a kind of "social simulator" that allows people to practice understanding perspectives different from their own. His research has validated the intuition that literature makes us more empathetic, providing empirical evidence that engaging with fictional characters strengthens our ability to navigate real-world social relationships and understand human complexity.

Abraham Maslow

Abraham Maslow (1908–1970) was an American psychologist who revolutionized motivation research through his Hierarchy of Needs, a theory depicting human desires as a pyramid from basic physiological needs up to safety, belonging, esteem, and ultimately self-actualization. Maslow's hierarchy illustrates how wishes change with personal growth and circumstances, arguing that people's capacity for "higher" wishes—creative, altruistic, self-fulfilling—emerges only after their foundational needs are met. This model remains a core organizing principle for understanding how and why people wish, motivating lifelong pursuits of growth and meaning.

Rollin McCraty

Rollin McCraty is the director of research at the HeartMath Institute, where he studies heart-brain coherence and the physiological basis of emotion and collective intention. His work suggests that coherent heart rhythms facilitate optimal brain function, emotional balance, and connectedness, making them valuable for both personal and shared wishing practices.

Lynne McTaggart

Lynne McTaggart is an investigative journalist and author best known for popularizing intention research, especially regarding the "power of eight" group intention experiments. While her work remains a subject of debate among scientists, McTaggart's writings and grassroots studies stimulate discussion on the potential of collective consciousness, interconnectedness, and the measurable effects of focused group wishing on individual and global outcomes.

Margaret Mead

Margaret Mead was a pioneering American anthropologist who transformed the field by focusing on how cultural context, narrative, and participatory engagement shape collective experience and social norms. Mead's studies championed the idea that lived experience, shared story, and cross-cultural understanding are essential tools for enabling and recording massive shifts in values, wishes, and societal direction— empowering marginalized voices in collective transformation.

Robert K. Merton

Robert K. Merton (1910-2003) was one of the most influential sociologists of the 20th century, known for introducing the concept of "organized skepticism" as a core norm of science—the systematic questioning of claims and suspension of judgment until evidence accumulates. He argued that science progresses through institutionalized doubt. Merton also coined "self-fulfilling prophecy," demonstrating how false beliefs become true through behavioral changes they induce. For understanding skeptics in collective wishing, Merton's organized skepticism provides a framework for how doubt serves progress. His self-fulfilling prophecy research demonstrates the power of belief to shape reality through social mechanisms.

Charlan Nemeth

Charlan Nemeth is a professor of psychology at UC Berkeley renowned for her research on dissent and group decision-making. Her work demonstrates that authentic dissent—genuine disagreement expressed with conviction—dramatically improves group thinking by stimulating divergent thought and creative problem-solving. Nemeth distinguishes between authentic dissent (real disagreement) and devil's advocacy (assigned contrarian roles), showing that only authentic dissent produces cognitive benefits. Her research reveals that groups exposed to consistent minority viewpoints generate more creative solutions, even when the minority view is ultimately rejected, demonstrating that skeptics enhance rather than undermine collective intention.

Keith Oatley

Keith Oatley is a cognitive psychologist and novelist whose research explores how fiction functions as a form of experiential learning. Working alongside Raymond Mar, Oatley has shown that narrative immersion creates what he calls "the mind's flight simulator"—a safe space where readers can experience situations, emotions, and perspectives they might never encounter in their own lives. His work demonstrates that stories don't just convey information about human experience; they allow readers to live through simulated experiences that build emotional intelligence, moral reasoning, and social understanding. Oatley's research bridges the gap between art and science, showing that the power of storytelling is both measurable and profound.

Kevin Ochsner

Kevin Ochsner, a contemporary neuroscientist, mapped the neural mechanisms of cognitive reappraisal—the process of reframing negative outcomes. His work demonstrates that actively reinterpreting setbacks strengthens neural connections between emotion and executive control, building emotional intelligence, resilience, and adaptability in response to all wish outcomes.

Gabrielle Oettingen

Gabrielle Oettingen is a psychologist known for her ground-breaking WOOP model—Wish, Outcome, Obstacle, Plan—which combines positive future visualization with realistic assessment of challenges. Her "mental contrasting" approach helps transform wishes into action by guiding people to recognize obstacles and create stepwise strategies to overcome them. Oettingen's work shows that balancing optimism with pragmatic planning significantly boosts motivation, goal achievement, and well-being.

Elinor Ostrom

Elinor Ostrom was an economist whose Nobel-winning research demonstrated that communities can successfully govern shared resources through cooperative, self-organizing arrangements—without requiring central authorities. Her model details how trust, rules, monitoring, sanctioning, and nested institutions empower groups to realize shared wishes and manage collective challenges, providing a roadmap for conscious, self-sustaining social change.

Karim Nader

Karim Nader is a neuroscientist at McGill University whose research revolutionized understanding of memory. His work on memory reconsolidation demonstrated that memories aren't fixed but dynamic— when recalled, they enter a temporary state where they can be modified before being re-stored. This discovery overturned decades of dogma assuming memories remain stable once consolidated. For cosmic wishing, Nader's research provides crucial evidence that we can update limiting beliefs by consciously working with memories during reconsolidation windows. When we recall old narratives while cultivating new emotional states, we literally rewrite neural patterns supporting wish fulfillment.

Dr. Charlan Nemeth

Throughout her distinguished career, Dr. Nemeth has focused on research into how minority viewpoints and authentic dissent can greatly enhance group decision-making, stimulate creative solutions, and challenge the perils of consensus. With a background that includes a B.A. in Mathematics from Washington University and a Ph.D. in Psychology from Cornell, Nemeth has held academic appointments and visiting professorships around the world. Her influential book, "In Defense of Troublemakers: The Power of Dissent in Life and Business," synthesizes decades of research showing that dissent leads to broader thinking and better outcomes for individuals, groups, and organizations. Nemeth's work stresses that innovative cultures are those that value 'voice,' open communication, and challenge over harmony for its own sake, and her teaching and consulting have impacted executives and teams globally.

Roger Penrose

Roger Penrose is a Nobel Prize-winning mathematical physicist whose work spans from black holes to the nature of consciousness itself. Along with Stuart Hameroff, Penrose developed the Orchestrated Objective Reduction (Orch OR) theory, proposing that consciousness emerges from quantum processes in the brain's neural structures. Penrose's mathematics suggest that the mind operates beyond classical computation, potentially connecting to fundamental properties of spacetime itself. His theories invite us to consider whether wishes and intentions might interact with reality at the quantum level—a frontier where physics, consciousness, and possibility converge in ways that challenge our conventional understanding of how thoughts shape outcomes.

Daniel Pink

Daniel Pink is a bestselling author who brought together decades of scientific research on motivation in his book "Drive: The Surprising Truth About What Motivates Us". Pink argues that external rewards and punishments can undermine creativity and long-term motivation. Instead, his synthesis of psychological science highlights autonomy, mastery, and purpose as the pillars of sustainable motivation, showing that when people pursue goals aligned with deeper meaning and self-direction, performance and fulfillment soar.

Stephen Porges

Dr. Stephen Porges is a neuroscientist and psychologist best known for creating Polyvagal Theory, a transformative framework revealing how the vagus nerve shapes our health, behavior, and relationships. His work describes how our autonomic nervous system—especially its ventral vagal branch—governs physiological states of safety and social engagement, forming the biological basis for trust, optimism, and the ability to connect with others. Polyvagal Theory has reshaped clinical practice by explaining how emotional well-being, creative problem-solving, and prosocial motivation are possible only when the body feels secure. Porges's influence extends across disciplines from trauma healing to education and organizational leadership, providing a unifying model for understanding how safety, connection, and co-regulation are prerequisites for resilience, optimal performance, and the fulfillment of meaningful goals.

Huw Price

Huw Price is a prominent philosopher of physics who has explored the controversial idea that quantum mechanics might permit retrocausality—situations where future events influence the past. Price argues that if the quantum world is fundamentally time-symmetric and if quantum properties are real, then influences traveling backwards in time could be a necessary part of the theory. Although this "retrocausal" interpretation is mathematically consistent and offers potential solutions to some quantum puzzles (such as the "Blue Balloon Phenomenon"), most physicists remain skeptical, seeing it as an intriguing but not widely accepted possibility.

Marcus Raichle

Marcus Raichle is a neurologist whose discovery of the brain's Default Mode Network revolutionized understanding of mind-wandering, daydreaming, and the creative construction of future scenarios. He showed how this network, active during rest and reflection, underlies imagination, self-referential thinking, and wish formation—empowering people to visualize new possibilities and recognize hidden opportunities.

Dean Radin

Dean Radin is Chief Scientist at the Institute of Noetic Sciences who conducts rigorous scientific investigations into consciousness and psi phenomena. His research focuses on demonstrating measurable effects of consciousness on physical systems, including experiments on presentiment, global consciousness effects, and intention influencing random number generators. His "Global Consciousness Project" investigates whether large-scale emotional events create detectable shifts in random systems worldwide. While controversial in mainstream science, Radin's methodologically rigorous approach provides some of the most systematic evidence that collective consciousness and focused intention may produce measurable effects, offering empirical foundations for understanding collective wishing dynamics.

Benjamin Rogers

Benjamin Rogers is a researcher whose groundbreaking 2023 study provided the first empirical validation of Joseph Campbell's Hero's Journey theory. In a series of eight studies with over 1,700 participants published in the *Journal of Personality and Social Psychology*, Rogers and colleagues demonstrated that people who view their lives through the lens of the Hero's Journey narrative structure report significantly greater meaning in life, enhanced well-being, increased resilience, and reduced depression. Most remarkably, Rogers developed a "restorying intervention" that helps people reframe their experiences as heroic journeys, showing that this narrative reframing doesn't just change how people feel about their past—it increases their capacity to handle present challenges and find meaning in ambiguous situations. His work validates what Campbell intuited: the Hero's Journey is not just a storytelling pattern but a psychological technology for building human resilience.

Richard Ryan

Richard Ryan is an American psychologist and co-founder of Self-Determination Theory (SDT), which investigates the basic psychological needs of autonomy, competence, and relatedness as the drivers of motivation and purposeful wishing. Ryan's research shows that when people experience choice and mastery, their wishes are more intrinsically motivated and produce greater well-being. SDT reveals how cultural, familial, and educational environments influence the motivation to wish, set goals, and persevere toward meaningful achievements.

Carol Ryff

Carol Ryff is a psychologist whose six-factor model of psychological well-being maps the foundations of healthy, happy wishing and goal pursuit. Her framework centers on self-acceptance, positive relationships, autonomy, environmental mastery, purpose in life, and personal growth—all elements shown to foster intrinsic wishing and lasting satisfaction. Ryff's model demonstrates that people who prioritize meaningful goals, growth, and connectedness—not just external achievement—report higher levels of sustained well-being and fulfillment.

Carl Sagan

Celebrated for his ability to inspire both public wonder and scientific rigor, Sagan articulated the essential balance between "openness to new ideas" and "ruthless skeptical scrutiny"—declaring that this interplay is what allows groundbreaking findings to emerge. In books and public addresses, Sagan continually warned against both credulity and excessive disbelief, frequently advocating for "extraordinary claims require extraordinary evidence." His work has influenced not only the general public's perception of science but also best practices for group creativity and inquiry within organizations.

Shalom Schwartz

Shalom Schwartz is a leading cross-cultural psychologist known for his theory of basic human values. Schwartz identified ten universal value types—like self-direction, stimulation, achievement, power, security, conformity, tradition, benevolence, and universalism—shared across societies, each representing deep motivational goals. His research uses value surveys to chart why people wish for certain experiences, traits, and outcomes, and how these values (and their conflicts) drive choices, dreams, and the pursuit of well-being globally.

Richard Schwartz

Richard C. Schwartz, Ph.D., is the founder of Internal Family Systems (IFS) therapy, a transformative psychological model that recognizes the mind's natural multiplicity and promotes integration of various "parts" within each person. Schwartz discovered that when individuals cultivate compassion and curiosity toward their internal "parts"—whether wounded, protective, or striving—they unlock access to a core Self rich in confidence and healing capacity. IFS is an evidence-based modality widely used for trauma, anxiety, and personal growth, emphasizing that harmony among inner selves leads to resilience, clarity, and lasting behavioral change.

Martin Seligman

Martin Seligman is an influential psychologist who inaugurated the field of positive psychology, which focuses on strengths, optimism, and the science of happiness. Seligman introduced frameworks for understanding well-being—including the PERMA model (Positive emotion, Engagement, Relationships, Meaning, Accomplishments)—and demonstrated through decades of research that hope, learned optimism, and nurturing signature strengths foster resilience, motivation, and sustainable flourishing across life stages and societies.

Kennon Sheldon

Kennon Sheldon is a psychologist whose research on "self-concordant goals" demonstrates that wishes aligned with our authentic interests and values lead to greater persistence, satisfaction, and success than goals adopted to please others or meet external expectations. Sheldon's longitudinal studies reveal that sustainable motivation comes from wishes that resonate with our true self rather than our ego or social pressures. His work shows that effective wishing requires honest self-reflection about what we genuinely want versus what we think we should want—and that wishes rooted in self-concordance create the intrinsic motivation necessary for long-term fulfillment and achievement.

Simon Sinek

Simon Sinek is a leadership consultant and author best known for his "Start With Why" concept, examining how inspirational leaders communicate and create movements. His "Golden Circle" framework shows that great leaders inspire action by communicating from inside-out—starting with purpose (why) rather than features (what) or methods (how). People don't buy what you do; they buy why you do it—purpose resonates deeper than function. For collective wishing, Sinek's framework suggests wish circles achieve greatest alignment when they begin with clear, compelling purpose that resonates emotionally. Purpose-driven intention creates stronger alignment than goal-focused planning alone.

C.R. Snyder

Charles Richard Snyder (1944–2006) was a pioneering American psychologist whose work laid the foundation for Hope Theory. Snyder defined hope as a positive motivational state made up of clear goals, pathways to achieve those goals, and the agency—the belief in one's ability—to pursue those pathways, emphasizing that hope is both a resource and a process. His research connected high levels of hope with improved academic performance, health, and resilience. Through six books and hundreds of publications, Snyder's work inspired wellness approaches that teach people to become "high-hopers," transforming hope from wishful thinking into a cognitive, actionable tool for change.

Sharon Salzberg

Sharon Salzberg is an internationally renowned meditation teacher and author, known for making the practices of loving-kindness, intention-setting, and mindful awareness universally accessible. Her teachings clarify how to cultivate clarity and warmth in both motivation and action, helping people transform habitual reactivity into peace, generosity, and purposeful intention. Salzberg's integration of Buddhist wisdom and evidence-based mindfulness has empowered countless individuals to access empowered wish-making and greater well-being.

Otto Scharmer

Otto Scharmer is a systems theorist and MIT lecturer who developed Theory U and social field theory, which describe how groups and organizations can tap into deeper fields of awareness to co-create emerging futures. Scharmer's "presencing" framework integrates mindful attention, collective intention, and future-oriented sensing, supporting innovation, wisdom, and adaptability in the face of rapid change and shared wishing.

Rupert Sheldrake

Rupert Sheldrake is a British biologist well known for his controversial theory of morphic resonance, which suggests that habits, behaviors, and even intentions become easier to repeat as they are reinforced within a collective or species. Sheldrake argues that there's a kind of "collective memory" in nature, allowing learned actions and social shifts to propagate rapidly once a critical mass is reached. While much debated, his work inspires new thinking about the anomalous ease of social tipping points, mass rituals, and emergent collective wishing.

Daniel Siegel

Daniel Siegel is a clinical professor of psychiatry whose integrative framework bridges neuroscience, attachment, and mindfulness. He has shown that increased self-awareness, emotional integration, and mindful focus are key for adaptive intention-setting, inner harmony, and the realization of heartfelt wishes, promoting both mental health and creative flourishing.

Daniel Simons & Christopher Chabris

Daniel Simons and Christopher Chabris are cognitive psychologists whose famous experiments on inattentional blindness and change blindness proved that attention is highly selective, and that expectation profoundly shapes perception. Their Invisible Gorilla and Door studies reveal that people often fail to notice even obvious changes—unless primed by prior intention or expectation—highlighting the subtle ways wishing can modify both awareness and experience.

Cass Sunstein

Cass Sunstein is a legal scholar and behavioral economist best known for his research on social nudges, tipping points, and norm cascades. Sunstein revealed that many large-scale societal changes begin with small but pivotal shifts in beliefs or behaviors, which—once exposed and supported—can trigger rapid spread through groups, movements, and even entire nations. His insights help explain how collective intention, sustained action, and visibility work together to produce cultural evolution and sudden social breakthroughs.

Richard Tedeschi & Lawrence Calhoun

Richard Tedeschi and Lawrence Calhoun are psychologists renowned for discovering post-traumatic growth, the phenomenon where individuals experience positive psychological transformation after adversity or loss. Their research shows that while hardship can disrupt life's wishes, it also offers the potential for greater meaning, gratitude, and growth—provided challenges are processed with conscious reflection and supportive relationships.

Giulio Tononi

Giulio Tononi is a neuroscientist and psychiatrist who developed Integrated Information Theory (IIT), a mathematical framework proposing that consciousness can be measured based on how much integrated information a system generates. Tononi's theory suggests that consciousness isn't simply an emergent property of complex computation, but rather a fundamental feature of how information is structured and integrated. His work provides a scientific language for understanding degrees and qualities of consciousness, offering potential insights into how conscious intention—the essence of wishing—might create measurable effects in neural networks and perhaps beyond, bridging subjective experience with objective physical processes.

Victor Turner

Victor Turner (1920–1983) transformed anthropology through his theory of ritual process, liminality, and communitas. Turner demonstrated how rituals—especially rites of passage—create transformative "in-between" spaces where everyday roles and hierarchies dissolve, making way for openness, solidarity, and belonging. His work explains how ritual states produce powerful psychological and social shifts, enabling both individual change and new forms of collective identity—essential elements in cultural expressions of wishing and transcendence.

Bessel van der Kolk

Bessel van der Kolk is a psychiatrist and trauma researcher whose work on how trauma affects the body, brain, and mind has revolutionized understanding of the Inner Self's role in psychological healing. His research shows that addressing trauma requires working with the body and emotions, not just cognitive processes.

Vitaly Vanchurin

Vitaly Vanchurin is a contemporary physicist who has put forward the bold hypothesis that the entire universe may function as a vast neural network. According to Vanchurin, the most fundamental physical processes—ranging from quantum phenomena to gravity—could emerge from the information-processing dynamics of such a network. This model aims to bridge quantum mechanics and general relativity, opening up the possibility that consciousness or cosmic wish interactions might someday be explained within a "computational" or "networked" view of reality. However, this theory is highly speculative, and while it offers new avenues for thinking about cosmic consciousness, it has yet to be empirically verified.

Dr. Raku Watanabe[5]

Dr. Raku Watanabe is a pioneering researcher in the field of psychophysics at Akdeniz University in Antalya, Turkey, where she investigates the intersection of consciousness and physical reality. Her groundbreaking work explores how subtle sensory cues—scent, sound, touch—can trigger profound physiological and psychological responses, challenging traditional boundaries between mind and matter. Dr. Watanabe's research on sensory influence and intentional states has implications for understanding how focused attention and embodied awareness might affect outcomes in ways that transcend conventional cause-and-effect models. Known for her unconventional research methods and her insistence that science must account for the full spectrum of human experience, Dr. Watanabe reminds us that consciousness itself may be the ultimate psychophysical instrument.

John Welwood

John Welwood (1943–2019) was an influential American clinical psychologist, psychotherapist, and author who played a vital role in bridging Western psychology and Buddhist spiritual practice. As Director

---

[5] Don't know Dr. Watanabe? Let's just say I like teasing readers. If you know, post it on social media, tag me, and win a prize!

of the East/West Psychology Program at the California Institute of Integral Studies, Welwood coined the term "spiritual bypassing" to describe the tendency to use spiritual beliefs or practices to avoid addressing unresolved emotional or psychological issues. His work encouraged a holistic approach to well-being—advocating for authentic integration of psychological growth and spiritual development, rather than treating them as separate domains. Welwood authored several acclaimed books, including Journey of the Heart and Toward a Psychology of Awakening, and his insights on consciousness, relationship, and emotional healing remain foundational in the field of transpersonal psychology.

David Sloan Wilson

David Sloan Wilson is an evolutionary biologist whose research explores how cooperative, prosocial behaviors can become evolutionarily stable within groups, enabling lasting social change and adaptive cultures. By showing how multi-level selection favors collaboration over pure competition, Wilson's work clarifies how collective wishing—aligned goals and actions—can spark and sustain true progress, bridging personal and societal transformation for the common good.

Paul Zak

Paul Zak is a neuroeconomist whose research on oxytocin and storytelling has revealed the neurochemical basis for how narratives inspire empathy and action. Zak's experiments demonstrated that character-driven stories with emotional arcs trigger the release of oxytocin—the "bonding hormone"—which increases empathy, trust, and prosocial behavior. His work shows that stories don't just inform or entertain; they create biological changes that motivate cooperative action. Participants in Zak's studies who experienced oxytocin release from engaging narratives were significantly more likely to donate money, help others, and take collaborative action afterward. His research explains why storytelling has been such a powerful tool for social coordination throughout human history: stories literally change our brain chemistry in ways that make us more connected, compassionate, and willing to act on behalf of others.

Appendix D: Wishing Rituals In 50 Countries

1. **Argentina:** Eating a spoonful of lentils or beans at midnight on New Year's Eve to wish for a year filled with work and prosperity.

2. **Armenia:** During the summer festival of Vardavar, people douse each other with water. While largely for fun, it's rooted in a pagan tradition of wishing for blessings and a good harvest.

3. **Australia:** A tradition inherited from Britain, two people pull apart a "wishbone" (the furcula bone) from a cooked chicken or turkey. The person who gets the larger piece makes a wish.

4. **Belgium:** On New Year's Day, children write "New Year's letters" filled with wishes and resolutions, which they read aloud to their parents and godparents.

5. **Brazil:** On New Year's Eve, Brazilians head to the beach to jump over seven consecutive waves while making seven wishes.

6. **Canada:** Tossing a coin into the fountain in the Canadian Parliament's Centennial Flame in Ottawa. The money collected is used for disability research.

7. **Chile:** Placing a $1,000 CLP (Chilean peso) bill in your right shoe on New Year's Eve to wish for wealth in the coming year.

8. **China:** During festivals like the Lantern Festival, people write their wishes on sky lanterns (孔明燈, kǒngmíngdēng) and release them into the night sky.

9. **Colombia:** On New Year's Eve, filling your pockets with lentils is believed to ensure a year of abundance and a bountiful food supply.

10. **Czech Republic:** On Christmas Eve, an apple is cut in half horizontally. If the core forms a perfect star, the person will have good health and fortune; if it's a cross, bad luck may be ahead.

11. **Denmark:** Smashing plates against the doors of friends and family on New Year's Eve. The pile of broken china is a measure of your friends' loyalty and brings good luck for the year.

12. **Ecuador:** Creating and burning "año viejo" (old year) effigies at midnight on December 31st. This ritual cleanses the bad from the past year and allows for new wishes for the future.

13. **Egypt:** When a child loses a baby tooth, it is traditional to throw it towards the sun while making a wish, often asking for a new, stronger tooth.

14. **Ethiopia:** During the traditional coffee ceremony (Buna), wishes for health, peace, and prosperity are often expressed as the host serves coffee to guests.

15. **Finland:** Melting a small piece of tin (tinanvalanta) on a stove and dropping it into cold water. The resulting shape is interpreted to predict the future or answer a question for the coming year.

16. **France:** It was a popular tradition to attach a "love lock" with initials written on it to the Pont des Arts bridge in Paris and throw the key into the Seine river, symbolizing an unbreakable wish for love. (The practice is now discouraged to protect the bridge

17. **Germany:** If a ladybug (Marienkäfer) lands on you, it's considered good luck. You should count its spots to see how many months of luck you'll have, but don't brush it off—let it fly away on its own after you make a wish.

18. **Ghana:** Pouring libations (often water or schnapps) onto the earth is a ritual to honor ancestors and spirits, asking them for their blessings and guidance.

19. **Greece:** On New Year's Day, families smash a pomegranate on their doorstep. The more seeds that scatter, the more luck, health, and prosperity the family will have in the coming year.

20. **Guatemala:** On December 7th, families participate in "La Quema del Diablo" (The Burning of the Devil), burning devil-shaped piñatas and firecrackers to cleanse the home of evil spirits and make way for a blessed Christmas season.

21. **Hungary:** Eating lentil soup as the first meal of the New Year is a wish for wealth, as the small lentils symbolize coins.

22. **India:** Tying a colorful thread or ribbon onto the branches of a sacred tree (often a Banyan or Peepal tree) while making a wish or a prayer.

23. **Indonesia:** At the Sekaten festival in Java, locals believe that obtaining a piece of the Gunungan (a mountain-like offering of food) will bring them blessings and good fortune for the year.

24. **Iran:** On the 13th day of the Persian New Year (Nowruz), known as Sizdah Bedar, it is tradition to tie a knot in a blade of grass while making a wish, often for finding a partner, before tossing it into running water.

25. **Ireland:** Kissing the Blarney Stone at Blarney Castle is said to grant the kisser the "gift of the gab"—eloquence and persuasive speech.

26. **Israel:** Writing a prayer or wish on a small piece of paper and placing it into a crack of the Western Wall in Jerusalem.

27. **Italy:** Tossing a coin over your left shoulder with your right hand into Rome's Trevi Fountain. Tradition holds this ensures you will one day return to Rome.

28. **Japan:** Writing wishes on small wooden plaques called *Ema* (絵馬) and hanging them at a Shinto shrine. Another tradition is the Daruma doll; you color in one eye when setting a goal or making a wish, and the other eye when it is fulfilled.

29. **Malaysia:** During Chinese New Year, families and friends gather to toss "Yee Sang," a raw fish salad. The higher you toss the ingredients with your chopsticks, the greater your fortune will be in the new year.

30. **Mexico:** On the Day of the Dead (Día adelosMuertos), families create *ofrendas* (altars) for their departed loved ones, often including items the deceased enjoyed, with prayers and wishes for their spiritual journey.

31. **Morocco:** Applying intricate henna designs to the hands and feet, especially for a bride before her wedding, is done with prayers and wishes for happiness, fertility, and protection from evil.

32. **Nepal:** Spinning a prayer wheel clockwise is believed to release the prayers and mantras inscribed on it into the universe, granting blessings and fulfilling wishes.

33. **Netherlands:** Eating deep-fried dough balls called *Oliebollen* on New Year's Eve is said to ward off evil spirits and bring good fortune.

34. **New Zealand:** During Matariki (the Māori New Year), the rising of the Pleiades star cluster is a time for reflection, remembering ancestors, and making wishes for the future.

35. **Nigeria:** The "breaking of the kola nut" is a sacred ritual performed at important gatherings. The host blesses the nut, makes wishes for peace and prosperity, and shares it with guests as a sign of goodwill.

36. **Norway:** Similar to a Swedish tradition, an almond is hidden in a batch of Christmas rice pudding (risgrøt The person who finds it wins a prize and is said to have good luck for the coming year.

37. **Peru:** On New Year's Eve, walking around the block with an empty suitcase is a ritual performed by those who wish to travel in the coming year.

38. **Philippines:** Wearing clothes with polka dots and having 12 round fruits on the dining table at New Year's Eve symbolizes coins and a wish for wealth.

39. **Poland:** Finding a carp scale in your wallet. After the traditional Christmas Eve carp dinner, keeping a scale from the fish is thought to bring financial luck all year.

40. **Portugal:** Similar to Spain, eating 12 raisins—one for each chime of the clock at midnight—is a way to make 12 wishes for the months ahead.

41. **Romania:** On March 1st, people exchange *Mărțișor* talismans (a red and white string, often with a small charm Wearing it is a wish for health, love, and a pure soul.

42. **Russia:** Writing a wish on a small piece of paper, burning it, putting the ashes into a glass of champagne, and drinking it before the clock finishes its 12th strike at midnight on New Year's Eve.

43. **Scotland:** At a "Cloutie Well," visitors tie a piece of cloth, or a "cloutie," to a nearby tree branch. As the cloth disintegrates over time, the wish is believed to come true or the ailment to be healed.

44. **South Korea:** Stacking stones into a small tower or cairn, especially on mountains or near temples. A wish is made with each stone, and the tower must not fall.

45. **Spain:** Eating 12 grapes, one for each of the first 12 seconds of the New Year, to secure 12 months of good luck.

46. **Sweden:** The person who finds the single almond in the Christmas rice pudding (Risgrynsgro̎t) is said to be the next to get married.

47. **Thailand:** During the Loi Krathong festival, people release small, decorated rafts (Krathongs), usually made of banana leaves, onto a river. This act symbolizes letting go of grudges and making wishes for the future.

48. **Turkey:** On the eve of Hıdrellez, a spring festival, people write or draw their wishes on paper and either tie them to a rose bush or bury them underneath it overnight, hoping the mythical figures Hızır and İlyas will grant them.

49. **United Arab Emirates:** Burning *Bakhoor* (scented wood chips) is a common practice to perfume the home. It is often done with the intention of clearing negative energy and inviting blessings and good fortune.

50. **United Kingdom / USA:** Beyond birthday candles, finding a stray eyelash on your cheek is an opportunity. You are supposed to place it on the back of your hand, make a wish, and blow it away. If it flies off, the wish may come true.

Appendix E: Glossary

Agency

The felt sense of personal power or control to choose, act, and affect outcomes. Central to theories of motivation and the mechanics of intention and wishing.

Anthropology

The scientific study of human behavior, societies, culture, and evolution. In wishing studies, anthropology helps us interpret ritual, myth, and collective meaning.

Attachment / Detachment

Attachment: Deep emotional investment in specific outcomes; over-attachment can lead to disappointment or rigidity. Detachment: The ability to wish and let go, accepting a range of possible answers—central to resilience, surrender, and non-attachment in spiritual traditions.

Belief

Conviction or trust in a person, idea, or phenomenon; not always based on evidence. Beliefs power the placebo response, bias perception, and drive meaning-making.

Brain Regions

- **Amygdala:** Part of the limbic system; processes emotion, especially fear and threat.
- **Prefrontal Cortex:** Governs planning, intention, impulse control, and goal pursuit.

- **Default Mode Network (DMN):** Brain network supporting daydreaming, future planning, and wishing; active during inward focus.
- **Hippocampus:** Supports memory consolidation; links past experience to future wish construction.

Broaden-and-Build Theory

Barbara Fredrickson's model proposing that positive emotions broaden attention and thinking while building lasting psychological, social, and physical resources over time. It explains why joy, gratitude, and love make wishes more creative, flexible, and resilient.

Cognitive Bias

Systematic errors in reasoning that affect judgment and decision-making. Examples include confirmation bias, wishful thinking, and action bias.

Collective Consciousness / Field Effect

A hypothesized emergent property where shared thought, emotion, or attention produces measurable social effects; includes memes, social movements, and controversial claims of global intention effects.

Consciousness

The subjective state of awareness, perception, and intentional thought—the hard problem in philosophy and science.

Cosmic Wish / Cosmic Wishing

A concept proposed in this book by Brownell Landrum describing a wish made with conscious awareness of both the art and science of wishing—engaging the brain, emotions, and nervous system (The Three Selves and The Three P's) while partnering with a larger field of intelligence or "Cosmic Collaboration." It goes beyond vague hoping by combining clear intention, aligned action, and openness to multiple forms of response.

Cosmic Collaboration

"Cosmic Collaboration," a system introduced by Brownell Landrum, is the active partnership between the individual (or group) and a larger creative power (a higher intelligence, spirit, energy, or force) to co-create an outcome that transcends personal effort. It is the process by which wishes, intentions, and aligned actions are shaped not only by personal agency but also by openness to influences, opportunities, synchronicities, and responses that come from the wider cosmos or field of existence.

Counterfactual Thinking

Imagining alternative scenarios ("what if...?"); essential for creativity, regret, wishing, and mental simulation of futures.

Cultural Ritual

A prescribed, repeated set of actions, objects, and words that encode community beliefs and direct human intention—birthday candles, wishing wells, lantern release, etc.

Default Mode Network (DMN)

See Brain Regions. Facilitates self-reflection, dreaming, intention, planning, and creative thought.

Detachment

See Attachment / Detachment.

Emergence

Bottom-up formation of complex patterns (consciousness, intention, social fields) from many simple parts; key to understanding self-organization in brains, societies, and nature.

Epigenetics

Biological processes that regulate gene expression through environment, experience, and intention—not by changing DNA sequences, but by switching genes on and off.

Expectation Effect / Placebo / Nocebo

The real-world power of believing that something will (or won't) work, even before the outcome is known; improvement (placebo) or harm (nocebo) resulting from belief or expectation alone.

Flow State

A mental state of energized focus, full engagement, and joy in the process—experienced during creative wishing, ritual, or peak activity. When wishes incorporate elements of genuine fun and playfulness, they're more likely to generate flow states where effort feels effortless and time disappears. This is why making wishing enjoyable isn't frivolous—it's neurologically optimal.

The Four Responses

A model describing four basic ways reality appears to respond to wishes (developed in the Astraea/"Upstairs" framework in Brownell Landrum's novel, A Love Story to the Universe, and applied psychologically). The responses are highly nuanced but the general categories are: Yes, No, Wait, or Something Better.

Frontal Lobe

The largest brain lobe; essential for voluntary action, abstract reasoning, self-control, and the construction and pursuit of wishes.

Goal Intention / Implementation Intention

Goal intention: "I want X." Implementation intention: Specific action plan, "If Y happens, then I will do Z" (see WOOP).

Growth Mindset

The belief that abilities can be developed through learning and effort; grows resilience by reframing failure as opportunity.

Hope

A positive motivational state grounded in a sense of agency ("will") and pathways ("ways of thinking"). Satisfying hope's components (goals, agency, and pathways) fuels persistence in wishing.

Implementation Intention

A plan for handling obstacles ("if-then" plans) to move a wish closer to fulfillment.

Intrinsic / Extrinsic Motivation

Intrinsic: Driven by curiosity, joy, or meaning. Extrinsic: Driven by outside rewards or pressure.

Learned Helplessness / Learned Optimism

Helplessness: perceived powerlessness (Martin Seligman); optimism: belief in capacity for positive change.

Manifestation

Belief/process that what one consistently visualizes or intends can come to fruition; debated in metaphysics/self-development fields.

Locus of Control

A psychological concept describing whether you experience outcomes as primarily influenced by your own actions (internal locus) or by external forces (external locus). A balanced internal locus means taking responsibility for your part of the wishing process without trying to control everything.

Memetics

The science of how memes—ideas, rituals, behaviors—spread within and between cultures, affecting wishing at the mass level.

Memory Reconsolidation

The process by which a recalled memory becomes temporarily malleable and can be updated before being "saved" again. Under the right conditions, this allows painful or limiting stories about past failures or "failed wishes" to be rewired with new meaning and hope.

Mirror Neurons

Brain cells that fire both when we perform an action and when we observe someone else doing it, supporting imitation, empathy, and shared feeling. They contribute to how group rituals, shared wishes, and "wish circles" synchronize emotions and intentions.

Motivation Matrix

A four-quadrant model created by Brownell Landrum for clarifying mapping what drives behavior:

- Want + Have – things to nurture.
- Want + Don't Have – things to cultivate.
- Don't Want + Have – things to transform or eliminate.
- Don't Want + Don't Have – things to avoid or prevent.

It reveals both approach and avoidance motives around wishes and helps clarify hidden trade-offs.

Neural Plasticity / Neuroplasticity

The brain's capacity for physical and functional change in response to experience, learning, or mental practice (wishing, visualization, mindfulness, etc.).

Nocebo

Negative expectation causing adverse effects, even in the absence of an actual harmful agent.

Parapsychology / Psi

Study of purported psychic phenomena such as telepathy, precognition, and collective consciousness; controversial in mainstream science.

Placebo Effect

Improvement in outcomes triggered by positive beliefs or expectation, not by any direct action of a treatment or ritual.

Pollyanna Principle / Positivity Bias

Tendency to focus on positive outcomes and expect beneficial events; can be adaptive or lead to unrealistic wishing.

Polyvagal Theory / Ventral Vagal State

Stephen Porges's model of how the vagus nerve regulates states of threat, shutdown, and social safety. The ventral vagal state is the "safe and connected" mode (rest-and-digest plus social engagement) that supports creativity, openhearted relating, and effective, peaceful wishing.

Quantum Consciousness

Controversial theory that posits consciousness arises from or influences quantum-level events.

Random Event Generator (REG)

A device designed to produce random numbers, used in intention/psi research.

Resilience

Psychological capacity to recover quickly from adversity, setbacks, or No responses to wishes; supported by optimistic thinking, detachment, and meaning-making.

Reverse Optimism

A concept introduced by Brownell Landrum about the ability to look back at something that happened and recognize the reasons, lessons, and possible blessings or benefits.

Ritual

A repeated sequence (personal, familial, or cultural) for focusing intention, releasing wishes, and connecting with community or tradition.

Self-Efficacy

Belief in one's capacity to succeed or to influence results; essential for sustaining effective wishing and action.

Self-Fulfilling Prophecy

An expectation or prediction that brings about its own fulfillment through behavioral shifts or changes in perception.

Skepticism (in Science)

A methodological stance emphasizing rigorous testing, logical reasoning, and alternative explanations—a key driver in refining wish science.

Social Contagion

Rapid, widespread adoption of ideas, emotions, or behaviors (such as hope or group wishing) across networks, societies, or digital platforms.

Subconscious

Mental activity below conscious awareness, including drives, biases, intuitions, and pattern recognition.

Synchronicity

Carl Jung's concept for meaningful coincidences, where internal intentions or emotions seem to align with external events, defying obvious explanation.

The Three P's (Peaceful, Positive, Purposeful)

The optimal inner state for effective wishing:

- **Peaceful**– regulated nervous system and felt safety.
- **Positive** – broadened emotional state (joy, gratitude, hope) that expands perception and creativity.
- **Purposeful** – alignment with deeper values, service, and meaning.

Together they turn wishing from forceful effort into coherent, sustainable "power."

Three Selves (Inner, Outer, Higher)

A framework for understanding internal experience as three interacting aspects:

- Inner Self – body/subconscious/emotional self that feels, remembers, protects, and expresses through sensations and impulses.
- Outer Self – conscious, planning, logical self that sets goals, analyzes options, and manages identity.
- Higher Self – intuitive, wisdom-based, transpersonal self that connects you to meaning, purpose, and guidance beyond ordinary thinking.

Transpersonal

Relating to experiences, states, or psychology beyond the individual self (mystical insight, group resonance, or cosmic perspective).

Visualization

Intentional generation of mental/sensory images to guide thought, emotion, or action—commonly used in wish-setting, performance psychology, and healing.

Wish

As defined by Brownell Landrum, a wish has three characteristics: They are clear, prompted, and instinctive. Clear, in that they are generally not much longer than a single sentence. Prompted, meaning that they're usually connected to a ritual of some kind. And they're instinctive, in that they're usually in the moment, the first thing you think about when the prompt arises... A wish is made knowing that it may or may not come true, with openness to all four responses: Yes, No, Wait, or Something Better.

WOOP Method

A four-step process—Wish, Outcome, Obstacle, Plan—based on implementation intention research and designed to translate wishes and dreams into actionable strategies, developed by Gabrielle Oettingen.

Appendix F: The Skeptic's Gift: Harnessing Dissent in Collective Wishing

It is the tension between creativity and skepticism that has produced the stunning and unexpected findings of science.
—Carl Sagan

I would rather have a mind opened by wonder than one closed by belief.
—Gerry Spence

When you bring collective wishing into organizations—whether a startup team, a corporate division, or a multinational conglomerate—you'll inevitably encounter skeptics. And here's the counterintuitive insight from organizational psychology: authentic skeptics make your Wish Circle more effective, more rigorous, and more scientifically grounded.[414]

This isn't about tolerating naysayers who drain energy (we covered that in the personal wishing chapter). This is about strategically leveraging genuine skeptics, the ones who elevate your collective practice from "woo-woo" to evidence-based collaboration.[415]

Why Skeptics Strengthen Scientific Rigor

Here's what many people miss about skepticism: it's the foundation of good science. As Richard Feynman said, "I would rather have questions that can't be answered than answers that can't be questioned."

For decades, organizational psychologists have studied how dissent affects group decision-making. The findings are unambiguous: authentic skeptics improve outcomes, stimulate divergent and creative thinking, and help groups avoid the trap of groupthink. Dr. Charlan Nemeth's research is pivotal here. She found that genuine dissenters:[416] [417]

- Stimulate creativity and divergent thinking
- Broaden the group's consideration of information and options
- Lead to higher-quality decisions
- Uncover solutions that would otherwise go unrecognized
- Improve group thinking, even when their initial perspective is incorrect[418]

The key word is authentic. Assigning someone the "devil's advocate" role—asking a group member to play at skepticism—often backfires. Research consistently finds that when people know dissent is just role-play, they dig in and defend their pre-existing views even more ("cognitive bolstering"), group satisfaction drops, and creative thinking isn't stimulated. But real skeptics who genuinely question assumptions? They make everyone smarter.[419]

Four Powerful Roles for Skeptics in Organizational Wish Circles

Rather than trying to convert skeptics or exclude them, leverage their strengths with roles that keep the practice grounded in measurable reality.

1. The Research Liaison

Your skeptic investigates the science behind wishing practices—reading studies, evaluating methodology, and reporting findings. This satisfies their need for evidence and deepens everyone's understanding of why these practices might work. In this way, the skeptic becomes the group's bridge between metaphysical experience and scientific validation.[420]

2. The Measurement Keeper

Empower your skeptic to track results with scientific rigor. They document:

- Baseline metrics before collective wishing begins
- Specific, objective success criteria
- Synchronicities and unexpected opportunities (noted with dates and detail)
- Progress milestones
- Final results versus starting goals

Since they're naturally motivated to find proof (or disproof), skeptics bring accountability that makes group results tangible. Their records either validate the practice or reveal what needs to change.[421]

3. The Reality Tester

Before the group commits, the Reality Tester asks:

- "How will we know this worked?"
- "What outcomes will show success?"
- "What could prevent us from achieving this?"
- "Are we confusing correlation with causation?"
- "What alternative explanations should we consider?"

These questions align directly with sound goal-setting and the kind of scientific skepticism that improves outcomes.[422]

4. The Divergent Thinker

Nemeth's research shows that dissenters stimulate what's called divergent thinking—the ability to see multiple solutions and possibilities. Your skeptic:

- Offers alternative interpretations
- Proposes novel approaches
- Challenges assumptions (not to undermine, but to expand the group's thinking)
- Broadens the circle's perspective, protecting against groupthink

Authentic skepticism doesn't narrow options—it expands them.

What Science Shows About Contrived vs. Authentic Dissent

Companies like IBM and Anheuser-Busch have tried assigning "devil's advocate" roles to stimulate better group decisions. The science is clear: it doesn't achieve the desired result.

- Fake dissent (devil's advocate) is perceived as play-acting, so others don't engage meaningfully.[423]
- Cognitive bolstering happens, with members defending their pre-held positions even more.
- Group satisfaction decreases.
- Little or no increase in creative thinking or solution searching.

By contrast:

- Authentic dissent stimulates real divergent thought.
- It increases active information search.
- Decisions measurably improve.
- Group creativity and problem-solving rise[424] [425]

The Critical Distinction: Skepticism vs. Cynicism

Not every doubter is a skeptic—this distinction is crucial: [426]

Skeptics:
- Question and investigate
- Seek evidence before concluding
- Remain open to evidence

- Foster critical thinking
- Strengthen collective wishing

Cynics:
- Dismiss and undermine
- Assume bad motives
- Are closed to persuasion by evidence
- Breed distrust
- May not be suited for collaborative wishing

If someone is purely cynical, they may undermine group energy. But a thoughtful skeptic questioning in good faith? That's an asset.

Bridge to Practice: The Inclusion Protocol

When forming organizational Wish Circles:

1. Engage at least one thoughtful skeptic intentionally—frame it as ensuring scientific honesty and accountability.
2. Clarify that their value isn't belief but perspective and rigor.
3. Assign roles explicitly (Research Liaison, Measurement Keeper, etc.).
4. Celebrate questions and improvements skeptics bring.
5. Act on their data. If the Measurement Keeper shows the practice isn't working, adjust strategy. This marries openness and rigor in practice.

The research is unambiguous: authentic dissent is a strategic advantage. Your skeptic isn't a problem—they're the bridge between radical openness and rigorous scrutiny.

Everything above applies to organizational Wish Circles. But what if YOU'RE the skeptic someone invited to join?

A Note to Skeptics: If You're Reading This with Doubt

If someone handed you this book or invited you to a Wish Circle and you're thinking "This is complete nonsense," welcome. This section is for you.

You're Not Wrong to Be Skeptical

Healthy skepticism is the foundation of good science. Carl Sagan, one of the greatest scientific minds of the 20th century, wrote: "At the heart of · science is an essential balance between two seemingly contradictory attitudes—an openness to new ideas, no matter how bizarre or counterintuitive they may be, and the most ruthless skeptical scrutiny of all ideas, old and new."[427]

Your skepticism isn't a character flaw. It's a cognitive strength. You question claims. You demand evidence. You resist magical thinking. These are valuable traits, especially in a world full of pseudoscience and get-rich-quick schemes.[428]

What This Book Actually Claims (And Doesn't)

Before you dismiss everything here, let's be clear about what's actually being proposed:

This book does NOT claim:
- Thoughts alone create reality
- You can manifest anything just by believing hard enough
- Positive thinking prevents bad things from happening
- The universe is a cosmic vending machine

This book DOES claim:
- Neuroscience shows that focused intention changes brain pathways and attention patterns (measurable)
- Psychology demonstrates that aligned motivation increases persistence and creative problem-solving (replicable)
- Psychophysiology proves that coherent emotional states affect decision-making and opportunity recognition (documented)[429]
- Social psychology confirms that collective intention creates measurable group effects (evidence-based)

Everything in this book cites peer-reviewed research from mainstream science. You can look up every study. Challenge every claim. That's not just allowed—it's encouraged.

The Experiment You Can Actually Run

Here's what we're actually asking: **Test it.**
Not "believe it." Not "have faith." **Test it.**[430]

That's the whole reason it's called the Cosmic Wish EXPERIMENT. We know the science, and we used it to craft the program. Now we need to **prove** it – and need **your** help.

If you're invited to join a Wish Circle, here's how to participate while maintaining your intellectual integrity:

1. Volunteer as the Measurement Keeper

Tell the group: "I'm skeptical, but I'm willing to track results objectively. I'll document what we're trying to achieve, measure outcomes, and report findings honestly—whether they support the hypothesis or not."

This gives you a meaningful role that leverages your natural strengths while keeping you intellectually honest.

2. Establish Clear Success Criteria Upfront

Before the group makes their collective wish, insist on specificity:

- What exactly are we trying to achieve?
- How will we measure success?
- What's our timeline?
- What would constitute evidence of failure?
- What alternative explanations should we rule out?

These aren't cynical questions—they're scientific protocol.

3. Keep Rigorous Records

Document:

- The exact wish (date, wording, participants)
- Baseline conditions
- Actions taken by group members
- Unexpected opportunities or synchronicities (with dates and details)
- Outcomes (successful or not)
- Alternative explanations for any positive results

The GOOD NEWS is that much of this data is already being collected through the Trackers in the Experiment. Be the person who makes this practice evidence-based rather than faith-based.

4. Research the Science Behind the Claims

This book cites hundreds of studies. Pick the claims you find most dubious and investigate them yourself:

- Look up the original research papers
- Check the methodology
- See if findings have been replicated
- Read critical analyses
- Form your own conclusions

And let Brownell know so she can add them to future revisions of this book.

You might discover (as many skeptics have) that the neuroscience of goal-setting, the psychology of motivation, and the physiology of coherent states are far more interesting than you expected.

What Skeptics Often Discover

Many people who approach wishing practices skeptically report something unexpected: the results don't depend on belief.

When you:

- Get clear about what you want (goal clarity)
- Align your emotional state (coherence)
- Take consistent action (implementation)
- Notice opportunities (selective attention)
- Measure outcomes (feedback loops)

...these are simply effective practices, regardless of what you call them or what metaphysical framework you use to explain them.

You might never believe in "cosmic collaboration." That's fine. You might attribute every positive outcome to neuroscience, psychology, and confirmation bias. Also fine. If the practices produce measurable improvements in outcomes, does it matter whether you call it "wishing" or "evidence-based goal achievement"?

The Difference Between Skepticism and Cynicism

Here's the critical distinction:

Skeptics say: "I doubt this works, but I'm willing to test it and see what the evidence shows."

Cynics say: "This is stupid, it won't work, and I'm not even going to try."

If you're genuinely skeptical, you're open to evidence. If you're cynical, you've already decided and nothing will change your mind. Only you know which one you are.

Your Value to the Group

If you do participate, know this: your skepticism makes the group stronger.

Research by Dr. Charlan Nemeth at UC Berkeley shows that authentic dissenters:

- Improve decision quality
- Stimulate creative problem-solving
- Help groups consider more information
- Find solutions that would otherwise be missed
- Enhance outcomes even when they're wrong

Your role is to keep everyone honest, grounded, and rigorous. The Wish Circle that includes a thoughtful skeptic will be more effective than one filled with only true believers who never question assumptions.

However...

"Just don't become purely cynical—the person who shoots down every idea without offering constructive alternatives." It's one thing to be skeptical, it's another to be a party-pooper. Wishing by its very nature is meant to be FUN, even if you might think it's fanciful. If there's only one thing you remember from reading this book is that there is SCIENCE behind FUN.

Make Skepticism Fun

Throughout this book, we've emphasized a principle backed by neuroscience research: **fun isn't frivolous—it's fundamental to sustainable motivation and success**. When you're genuinely enjoying yourself—when the process feels playful, creative, and fun—your brain releases a cocktail of neurochemicals (dopamine, endorphins, oxytocin) that create what researchers call "intrinsic flow motivation"—energy that feels effortless and joyful rather than forced and depleting.[431]

This is why hobbies feel energizing while obligations feel draining, even if the hobby requires more effort. It's not about easy versus hard—it's about joy versus joylessness. Studies show that activities we genuinely enjoy release dopamine and create self-sustaining motivation loops.[432] When wishes incorporate elements of play, creativity, and genuine enjoyment, they maintain momentum naturally—your Inner Self keeps giving you energy because the process itself feels rewarding.

Here's what makes wishing special: it's inherently playful. Birthday candles, shooting stars, dandelion seeds, fountain coins—these rituals weren't designed to be grim exercises in discipline. They were (and are) meant to be delightful.

And skeptics? You get the same neurological benefit. When you approach your role with playfulness and curiosity rather than heavy seriousness, you activate these same reward systems. Your skepticism becomes sustainable, energizing, and—dare we say it—joyful.

Here's the secret skeptics don't always realize: your questioning nature is already playful—you just need permission to unleash it with style instead of snark. When skeptics approach their role with humor and curiosity rather than dismissiveness, they become what leadership experts call 'spark plugs'—energizing the team rather than draining it.[433] The key is reframing your doubt as creative exploration.

Turn Your Questions into Creative Challenges

Instead of asking "Why won't this work?" try these playful alternatives:[434]

- "What's the most outrageous way this could succeed?"
- "If this were a movie plot, what genre would it be—and how does it end?"
- "What assumptions are we making that could be hilariously wrong?"
- "What would need to be true for this to work spectacularly?"

This shifts the energy from critique to co-creation. You're still being skeptical, but you're inviting others to play in the space of possibility with you.

Gamify Your Skepticism

Give yourself fun roles and challenges:[435]

- **Skeptic's Bingo**: Create a card with common wishful-thinking patterns (confirmation bias, post-hoc rationalization, correlation-causation confusion). Mark them off as you spot them—but do it with humor, not judgment.

- **The Mythbusters Protocol**: Lead mini-experiments where you test assumptions. Frame it like the TV show: "Today we're testing whether visualizing success actually improves performance. Let's see what the data shows!"
- **Coincidence vs. Causation Scorecard**: Track unexpected events and rate them on a scale of "Pure Random Chance" to "Okay, That's Weird." Keep it lighthearted—even you might be surprised by patterns that emerge.
- **The "I Was Wrong" Trophy**: Celebrate when evidence contradicts your predictions. Research shows that people who can admit they were wrong with good humor are more trusted and more effective team members

Embrace Fun Titles That Honor Your Role

Claim a playful identity: Claim a playful identity: Chief Reality Officer, Director of Doubt, Head of Healthy Skepticism, The Group's BS Detector (said with love!), Captain of Critical Thinking, or Minister of "But Wait...

When you name your role with humor, it signals to everyone (including yourself) that skepticism doesn't have to be heavy or negative.

Use Self-Deprecating Humor

Research on workplace communication shows that self-deprecating humor softens critique and makes feedback more receivable.[436] Try phrases like:

- "I'm probably overthinking this—it's kind of my superpower..."
- "My brain immediately goes to worst-case scenario, so humor me while I play it out..."
- "Full disclosure: I'm the person who reads the terms and conditions, so..."

This creates psychological safety. People hear your concerns without feeling attacked.

Host "What If?" Sessions

Lead the group in exploring both disaster AND delight scenarios:

- "What if everything goes RIGHT? What would that look like?"
- "What if this fails spectacularly? How would we know, and what would we learn?"
- "What if the synchronicities we're seeing are real? What alternative explanations should we consider?"

This kind of divergent thinking is exactly what organizational psychologist Charlan Nemeth found makes skeptics so valuable—you expand the group's thinking in multiple directions.

Create "Positive Gossip" About Your Wins

When your skeptical questioning prevents a mistake or leads to a breakthrough, celebrate it! Leadership research shows that highlighting positive contributions (even your own!) creates a ripple effect of appreciation.

Don't be modest about saying: "Remember when I asked about X and we discovered Y? That skeptical question saved us three weeks of work!"

Volunteer for the Fun Stuff

Offer to design creative tracking systems:[437]

- Visual dashboards that make data beautiful
- Weekly "Synchronicity Spotting" reports with ratings for weirdness level
- Before-and-after comparison charts that show measurable change
- A "Skeptic's Journey" log documenting your evolving perspective
- Make measurement itself entertaining.

The "Yes, And..." Approach

Borrow from improv comedy: instead of "Yes, BUT..." try "Yes, AND..."

Instead of: "That's a great idea, BUT have you considered all the ways it could fail?"

Try: "That's interesting! AND here are three risks we should test for before we commit."

Same skepticism. Different energy. Much more fun.

Remember: You're the Spark, Not the Snark

The research is clear: skeptics who approach their role as a mix of detective, comedian, and strategist elevate team morale and outcomes.

You don't need to abandon your critical thinking—you just need to wield it with playfulness and genuine curiosity.

When you make skepticism fun, you model intellectual courage without intellectual arrogance. You show that questioning can be generous, not cynical. And you prove that the person asking "Are you sure about that?" can be the most valuable—and most enjoyable—person in the room.

So go ahead: be skeptical. Be rigorous. Be questioning.

Just do it with a smile and a sense of adventure. The Wish Circle needs you—and your particular brand of playful doubt might be exactly what makes the magic measurably real.

The Bottom Line

You don't have to believe in cosmic wishing to benefit from the practices in this book. You don't have to accept any metaphysical claims to test whether focused intention, emotional alignment, and collective effort produce results.

All we're asking is: Run the experiment.

Document it rigorously. Measure outcomes honestly. Let the data speak.

If it works, you'll have interesting questions to explore about why. If it doesn't, you'll have helped the group learn something valuable.

Either way, your skepticism serves science—which is exactly what it's supposed to do.

Meet The Scientists

The researchers exploring consciousness and reality frontiers:

Charlan Nemeth — Dissent, creativity, and group decision-making

Robert K. Merton — Organized skepticism as scientific norm

Carl Sagan — Balance of openness and skeptical scrutiny

Arie W. Kruglanski — Cognitive closure and motivated reasoning

(Full biographies in Appendix B)

Now, armed with your playful skepticism and scientific rigor, turn back to Chapter 15 and join the Cosmic Wish Experiment. The world needs your particular brand of questioning brilliance.

Appendix G: Book Club Facilitator's Guide

Introduction

The Art and Science of Wishing explores wishing across neuroscience, psychology, anthropology, consciousness research, and more. This book works for diverse audiences—from corporate teams to research scientists to spiritual seekers to curious readers.

This facilitator's guide provides:
- Tips for creating great discussions across different perspectives
- Essential questions for each chapter
- Optional group activities to explore concepts experientially
- Guidance for adapting discussions to your group's focus

Who This Guide Is For

This guide serves groups with different interests and expertise:

Corporate/Organizational Teams - Processing the book while implementing collective wish experiments, focusing on team alignment, motivation science, and organizational culture.

Academic Discussion Groups - Examining research methodologies, interdisciplinary connections, and consciousness studies across psychology, neuroscience, and related fields.

Research Scientists - Evaluating citations, distinguishing evidence from speculation, and exploring testable hypotheses about consciousness and intention.

General Book Clubs - Exploring the intersection of science and personal experience, applying frameworks to individual wishes, and sharing stories.

Spiritual/Metaphysical Communities - Seeking scientific frameworks for existing practices, bridging ancient wisdom with modern research.

Each group will emphasize different aspects. Adapt the questions and activities to serve your group's interests and expertise.

Creating Great Discussions

Ground Rules for Psychological Safety

Strong book clubs create space for both skepticism and belief:

- **Welcome all perspectives** - Skeptics who question the science and believers who've experienced synchronicities both enrich discussion
- **Share from "I" statements** - "I noticed..." rather than "You should..."
- **Respect confidentiality** - What's shared about personal wishes stays in the group
- **Balance airtime** - Everyone gets heard; no one dominates
- **Embrace productive tension** - Disagreement about interpretations of science can deepen understanding

Handling Skeptics Productively

Since this book bridges science and consciousness exploration, expect healthy skepticism!

Skeptics strengthen your group when you:

- Frame skepticism as essential to good science
- Ask: "What would it take to convince you?" (reveals their epistemology)
- Explore: "What HAS your personal experience shown you?"
- Distinguish between cynicism (closed to evidence) and skepticism (requiring evidence)
- Use their questions to deepen everyone's understanding

Examples:

Skeptic: "This sounds like magical thinking."

Response: "Chapter 11 addresses that concern directly. What specific claims feel unsupported by the science presented?"

Skeptic: "Synchronicities are just confirmation bias."

Response: "That's one explanation the book discusses! What do others think? Has anyone experienced something that felt like MORE than just noticing what you're primed to see?"

Facilitation Techniques

Opening Check-ins (5-10 minutes)

Quick round: "One thing from this week's reading that stuck with you—or one question it raised."

Balancing Head and Heart

This book works on both levels. Good facilitation moves between:

- **The Science** - "What did you learn about neuroplasticity?"
- **The Experience** - "Have you noticed your brain changing through wishing?"

Managing Participation

- Draw out quiet members: "Sarah, you're nodding—what's resonating?"
- Redirect dominators gently: "That's fascinating, Mark. Let's hear from others too."
- Use silence productively: After asking a question, wait 10 seconds before filling the space

Using the Three P's to Set Group Energy

Start meetings by checking: Is the group feeling Peaceful? Positive? Purposeful? If not, take 2 minutes to breathe, express gratitude, or reconnect with why you're gathering.

Closing Rituals

End with: "One word for what you're taking from today" or "One thing you'll pay attention to this week."

Handling Challenges

When someone's wish gets a NO response:

- Revisit Chapter 10: NO as information, not rejection

- Ask the group: "What might this NO be protecting or revealing?"
- Share stories of reverse optimism from others

Managing toxic positivity or spiritual bypassing:
- Reference Chapter 11's warnings about these pitfalls
- Ask: "Is this authentic positivity or forced optimism?"
- Create space for genuine feelings, not just "good vibes"

When group energy feels misaligned:
- Name it: "I'm noticing the energy feels heavy/scattered. Anyone else?"
- Check Three Selves alignment for the GROUP
- Take a break or shift to a different discussion format

Supporting members through disappointment:
- Remind the group: This is an EXPERIMENT, not a guarantee
- Explore: What data did this experience provide?
- Celebrate the courage to wish and track outcomes

Adapting This Guide for Different Audiences

For Corporate/Organizational Groups

Focus Areas:
- Collective alignment (Chapter 12)
- Motivation science for team performance (Chapter 7)
- Neuroscience of organizational culture (Chapter 8)

- Managing responses when company goals shift (Chapter 10)

Discussion Emphasis:

- If also How does this apply to our team/company?
- What's our collective Inner/Outer/Higher Self?
- How can we measure outcomes?
- What's blocking our alignment?

Suggested Additions:

- Connect to existing business frameworks (OKRs, vision/mission statements)
- Track company wish progress alongside book discussions
- Use case studies from your industry
- Apply Three Selves framework to organizational structure

Corporate-Specific Discussion Prompts:

- "How aligned are our company's stated values (Higher Self), strategic decisions (Outer Self), and actual culture (Inner Self)?"
- "What collective blocks is our team facing? Which science from Week 7 could help?"
- "When our company goals get a WAIT response from the market, how do we maintain momentum?"

For Academic/Scientific Groups

Focus Areas:

- Research methodology and citation evaluation
- Interdisciplinary connections (neuroscience + psychology + anthropology + physics)
- Frontier science and consciousness research (Chapter 14)
- Distinguishing correlation from causation
- Replication crisis and evidence quality

Discussion Emphasis:

- Does it bother you that the author isn't a scientist? How might the book be different if it had been written by a scientist in a specific discipline?
- How robust is the research cited?
- What are alternative explanations?
- Where are the gaps in current understanding?
- What experiments could test these hypotheses?
- How does this integrate across disciplines?
- What studies might you take on to prove, disprove, or expand upon in this book?

Suggested Additions:

- Deep-dive into specific studies (assign members to review original papers)
- Critique the author's interpretations
- Design potential research protocols
- Explore implications for your field

- Examine epistemological questions (How do we know what we know?)

Academic-Specific Discussion Prompts:

- "The author cites the Global Consciousness Project. What's the quality of that evidence? Has it been replicated?"
- "What would a well-designed RCT to test cosmic wishing look like? What would we measure?"
- "Where does this cross the line from evidence-based to speculative? Is that distinction always clear?"
- "How does consciousness research challenge materialism in neuroscience?"

For Research Scientists Specifically

What to Expect:

- Hundreds of research citations across multiple disciplines
- Integration of established science (neuroplasticity, motivation theory) with emerging research (consciousness studies, quantum biology)
- Clear distinctions between proven mechanisms and speculative possibilities
- Chapter 14 explicitly addresses frontier questions and unknowns

How to Engage Productively:

- Verify citations—look up original studies
- Distinguish between well-replicated findings and preliminary research

- Notice where the author speculates vs. reports established science
- Consider: What experiments would move this from hypothesis to evidence?
- Identify which claims have strongest empirical support

Your Role in the Discussion:

Your scientific training is valuable! Use it to:
- Evaluate methodology of cited studies
- Identify confounding variables
- Propose alternative explanations for reported phenomena
- Distinguish between "interesting correlation" and "established causation"
- Design experiments that could test claims rigorously

Discussion Prompts for Scientific Groups:

- Which claims have the strongest empirical support? (e.g., neuroplasticity, motivation theory)
- Which are preliminary or speculative? (e.g., morphic resonance, quantum consciousness)
- Where does the author over-interpret findings or under-qualify claims?
- What alternative explanations exist for synchronicities, neural coupling, etc.?
- How could we test whether aligned intention affects probability fields?
- What would falsify these hypotheses?

Your skepticism strengthens the conversation—use it to deepen understanding for everyone!

For Spiritual/Metaphysical/Manifestation Groups

Focus Areas:

- How science validates (or challenges) existing practices
- Bridging ancient wisdom with modern research
- Consciousness research and quantum possibilities (Chapter 14)
- The role of ritual and ceremony (Chapter 4)
- Collective consciousness and field effects (Chapter 12)

Discussion Emphasis:

- How does this deepen understanding of practices you already do?
- Where does science affirm your experience?
- Where do you hold beliefs that go beyond current evidence?
- How do you integrate faith and empiricism?

Suggested Additions:

- Share traditional practices from your lineage/tradition
- Explore how rituals create the neurological states described in the book
- Discuss where faith and evidence intersect
- Honor both ways of knowing (experiential and scientific)

Spiritual Group-Specific Discussion Prompts:

- "How does understanding neural coupling change how you think about prayer circles or group meditation?"

- "What practices from your tradition align with the Three P's framework?"
- "Where does this book validate what you've always known? Where does it challenge you?"
- "How comfortable are you holding both 'I know this from experience' AND 'science hasn't proven this yet'?"

For General Book Clubs

Focus Areas:

- Personal wish exploration
- Practical application of frameworks (Three Selves, Three P's, Four Responses)
- Balancing science and personal experience
- Storytelling and sharing journeys (Chapter 13)

Discussion Emphasis:

- What resonated personally?
- What surprised you?
- What will you try?
- What stories do you have to share?
- How does this change how you think about wishing?

Suggested Additions:

- Share personal wish stories and outcomes
- Try group activities together
- Support each other's wish journeys

- Celebrate synchronicities and manifestations

General Book Club Discussion Prompts:

- "What's one framework from this book you're already using?"
- "Has anyone experienced a Blue Balloon Phenomenon?"
- "What's your relationship with the word 'manifestation' after reading this?"
- "Who in your life would benefit from understanding cosmic wishing?"

Discussion Questions by Chapter

Chapters 1 and 2: What is Wishing?

Key Questions:

- The author comes from a background of writing both fiction and nonfiction. How does that impact how you view her perspective?
- This book started out as an inspiration from a novel called *A Love Story to the Universe* where there's a magical world called Astraea where wishes are sorted and granted. Have you ever wondered if there might be a place "Upstairs" that handles wishes?
- This book sets up some basic premises and definitions of a wish, including the difference between a wish, a prayer, and a goal. What are your thoughts on this insight?
- The author contrasts her definition of wishes and wishing with that of science. Which perspective is most compelling to you?

Optional Group Activity: Hero's Journey Mapping

Each person shares where they are in their wish journey using Campbell's framework. Notice common patterns across different wishes.

Chapter 3: Why We Wish (Evolution & Psychology)

Key Questions:

- What survival or thriving functions might your wish serve? How does your desire connect to fundamental human needs—safety, connection, meaning, or growth?
- Where does your wish fall within your own Hero's Journey? What "call to adventure" does it represent? What transformation might it create?
- What role does uncertainty play in your wish? How does the element of not-knowing enhance rather than diminish its value?

Optional Group Activity: *Hero's Journey Mapping*

Each person shares where they are in their wish journey using Campbell's framework. Notice common patterns across different wishes.

Chapter 4: The History and Practice of Wishing

Key Questions:

- What wishing rituals or traditions have been meaningful in your life? Think about both formal traditions (birthday wishes, New Year resolutions) and personal practices you may have developed.
- How do different settings affect your wishing? Do you wish differently in natural settings, sacred spaces, or during special times?

- What symbolic elements resonate most with you? Are you drawn to fire, water, air, earth, or other natural elements when expressing your deepest hopes?

Optional Group Activity: Creating a Group Wishing Ritual

Design a simple ritual your group could use to open or close meetings. What elements feel meaningful to everyone?

Chapter 5: The Psychology of What We Wish For

Key Questions:

1. Where does your wish fit within the hierarchy of human needs? Does it focus on security, relationships, achievement, or transcendence?
2. How does your wish balance self-focus with concern for others? Does your desire primarily serve personal goals or include benefits for family, community, or humanity?
3. What does your wish reveal about your deepest values and aspirations? What does your desire say about what you consider most important in life?

Optional Group Activity: *Needs Hierarchy Mapping*

Each person places their wish on Maslow's hierarchy. Discuss patterns— is your group focused on similar levels or spread across different needs?

Chapter 6: The Three Selves

Key Questions:

1. Which aspect of yourself initiated your wish—Inner Self (emotional desire), Outer Self (rational recognition), or Higher Self (intuitive knowing)?
2. How does each Self respond to your wish? When you imagine it coming true, what does your body feel, your mind think, and your spirit sense?
3. Where might internal conflicts exist? Are there ways your wish might threaten your sense of safety, identity, or values?

Optional Group Activity: Three Selves Alignment Check

Go around the circle and rate (1-10) how much each of your Three Selves wants your wish. Discuss patterns, surprises, and conflicts that emerge.

Chapter 7: The Motivation Matrix

Key Questions:

1. Where does your wish fit in the Motivation Matrix? Consider all four quadrants: what you want that you have, want that you don't have, don't want that you have, and don't want that you don't have.
2. What's the difference between what you want and what you need? Does your surface desire point toward deeper needs for growth, healing, contribution, or authentic self-expression?
3. How much FUN is built into your wish? Is the process itself bringing you joy, or does it feel like another obligation?

Optional Group Activity: *Motivation Excavation*

Pair up and interview each other about your wishes using the questions: "What do you want? Why? What would that give you? Why does that matter?" Go 5 levels deep.

Chapter 8: Your Brain on Wishes (Neuroplasticity)

Key Questions:

1. How has your brain changed through your wishing practices? Notice any shifts in your capacity for hope, creativity, emotional regulation, or resilience.
2. What old neural patterns might you need to rewire? Consider limiting beliefs, anxiety patterns, or habitual negative thinking that could benefit from conscious reprogramming.
3. What does optimal brain integration feel like in your wishing practice? When has wishing felt effortless, inspired, or deeply harmonious?

Optional Group Activity: Neuroplasticity Science Deep Dive

Have someone research and present one study cited in this chapter (e.g., London taxi drivers, Shaolin monks, neurogenesis research). Discuss implications for the group's wishing practices.

Chapter 9: The Three P's (Peaceful, Positive, Purposeful)

Key Questions:

1. How peaceful do you feel when you think about your wish? Notice whether your desire creates calm anticipation or anxiety and stress.

2. What positive emotions does your wish generate? Does thinking about it create genuine enthusiasm and gratitude, or does it feel heavy or anxiety-provoking?
3. How does your wish connect to larger purposes? How does your desire serve not just personal fulfillment but also contribute to family, community, or universal well-being?

Optional Group Activity: *Three P's Practice*

Take 5 minutes: Everyone closes their eyes and makes their wish from the Three P's. Afterward, discuss: How did that feel different from how you usually wish?

Chapter 10: The Four Responses

Key Questions:

1. Which response (YES/NO/WAIT/SOMETHING BETTER) do you experience most often with your wishes? What patterns do you notice?
2. Can you identify times when SOMETHING BETTER emerged from blocked wishes? How might these experiences inform your current approach to wish fulfillment?
3. What might the Blue Balloon Phenomenon represent in your own experience? Have you noticed instances where consciousness and reality seemed to interact in ways that challenged conventional explanations?

Optional Group Activity: Response Pattern Recognition

Map out 3-5 past wishes and their outcomes. Do you see patterns in which responses you get and when? Share discoveries with the group.

Chapter 11: Pitfalls and Problems in Wishing

Key Questions:

1. Which pitfall resonates most with your past wishing experiences? Have you fallen into manifestation addiction, spiritual bypassing, or the "leap before you're ready" trap?
2. How has toxic positivity or victim-blaming affected your relationship with wishing? Have you blamed yourself for outcomes beyond your control?
3. Have you lost the joy in your wishing practice? If wishing has become another obligation, what would it take to restore the playfulness and delight?

Optional Group Activity: Pitfall Recognition & Prevention

Identify which pitfalls your group is most susceptible to. Create accountability agreements to help each other avoid them.

Chapter 12: Collective Wishing

Key Questions:

1. How does your personal wish connect to collective transformation? What deeper purpose does your individual desire serve in the larger web of human consciousness?

2. What collective fears, desires, or misbeliefs might be operating in your closest communities (family, workplace, social circles)? What unspoken patterns limit group possibility?
3. How aligned are the Three Selves in your primary community or organization? Does the collective emotional culture (Inner Self), strategic direction (Outer Self), and stated purpose (Higher Self) actually harmonize?

Optional Group Activity: Collective Wish Creation

If your group wants to make a SHARED wish, use the framework from this chapter. Check collective Three Selves alignment. Practice wishing together from the Three P's.

Chapter 13: The Art of Storytelling

Key Questions:

1. What is your cosmic wishing story? If you had three minutes to tell it, what would you include?
2. How could you frame your biggest challenge or disappointment as a Hero's Journey? What would change if you saw it as part of your transformation rather than a failure?
3. What collective narrative are you part of? What stories does your community tell about who you are and what's possible? How might cosmic wishing stories shift that narrative?

Optional Group Activity: *Storytelling Circle*

Each person shares their cosmic wish journey (3-5 minutes). Others notice: What elements create neural coupling? Where do you feel transported into the story? What makes certain stories more compelling?

Chapter 14: The Frontiers of Wishing

Key Questions:

1. Which frontier question intrigues you most—and why? Is it because it would validate something you've experienced, challenge something you believe, or open possibilities you've never considered?
2. If consciousness can be measured through information integration, what would it mean for your wishing practice? When you align your Three Selves, do you sense you're creating a different quality of consciousness?
3. How comfortable are you with practicing something whose full mechanism remains unknown? Can you embrace cosmic wishing even while holding the questions as questions?

Optional Group Activity: *Frontier Exploration*

Each person picks one frontier question from Chapter 14 to research more deeply. Present findings at next meeting. Discuss: What experiments could test these hypotheses?

Chapter 15: Bringing It All Together

Key Questions:

1. What has shifted in you since making that first wish in Chapter 1? Not just what you've learned intellectually, but how you've changed—how you see yourself, reality, possibility itself.
2. If you could celebrate one breakthrough from this journey, what would it be? Really feel the significance of that breakthrough.
3. Who in your life needs to know what you've learned? Not to convince them, but because they're genuinely asking the questions this book answers.
4. What becomes possible in your life if cosmic wishing becomes automatic? Who are you when conscious collaboration with the cosmos is simply how you operate?

Optional Group Activity: *Celebration Ritual*

Design and execute a group celebration acknowledging what everyone has learned and how they've transformed through this book.

Optional Group Activities

These activities help groups explore concepts experientially:

Collective Three Selves Alignment

Check-in as a GROUP: What does our collective Inner Self (the Collective Subconscious) feel? What does our Outer Self think? What does our Higher Self sense about our shared purpose? Where are we aligned? Misaligned?

Synchronicity Sharing

Monthly practice: Each person shares one synchronicity they noticed. Look for patterns across the group. Are certain types of synchronicities more common?

Collective Wish Creation

If your group wants to make a SHARED wish, use Chapter 12's framework. Practice aligning collective Three Selves. Wish together from the Three P's.

Science Study Groups

Assign volunteers to research studies cited in each chapter and present findings to the group. Evaluate methodology, replication, and implications.

Celebration Rituals

When someone's wish manifests (or transforms meaningfully), celebrate together! Chapter 15 explains why this matters neurologically.

"What Would the Science Say?" Game

When someone shares an experience, the group identifies which scientific frameworks from the book explain it. (e.g., "That sounds like neural coupling!" or "Your RAS was primed!")

Connecting to the Cosmic Wish Experiment

Your book club can explore the concepts with or without doing the full 8-week structured Experiment.

Option 1: Book Club Only

Read and discuss the book. Explore ideas. Share experiences. No commitment to the formal tracking/practice.

Option 2: Book Club + Individual Experiments

Some members do the Cosmic Wish Experiment on their own while the book club discusses the underlying science.

Option 3: Book Club + Collective Experiment

The entire book club becomes a Wish Circle and does the 8-week Experiment together, using book club time to discuss both the chapters AND the practice.

Option 4: Sequential

Read and discuss the book first, THEN decide if the group wants to do the Experiment together.

For Corporate Groups:

Companies might run book clubs to process the concepts while simultaneously implementing a company wish using the Cosmic Wish Experiment. The book club deepens understanding; the Experiment provides real-time data.

Appendix H: Cosmic Wishing Merchandise

All proceeds go to supporting the FREE Cosmic Wish Experiment.
https://cosmicwishexperiment.com/merch/

Appendix I: More Books By Brownell

Check out Brownell's other books, both fiction and nonfiction: https://brownelllandrum.com/books/

A Love Story to the Universe — where this journey began!

Five Reasons Why Bad Things Happen: How to Turn Tragedies Into Triumph:

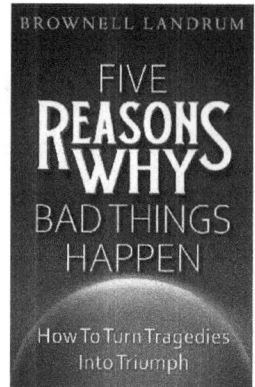

The Hero's Playbook and Mentor's Manual

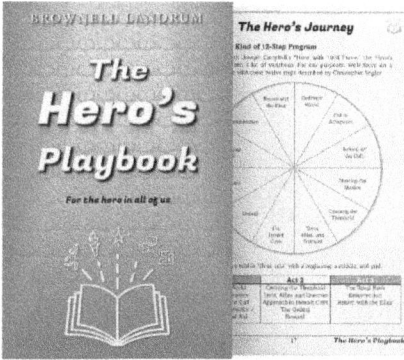

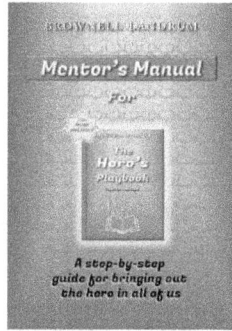

The We Meet Again Trilogy

An epic reincarnation mystery plus love story about a famous couple from history reincarnated today to fulfill a prophecy that will change the world:

And more!

Please Follow Brownell – and sign up for her Newsletter!

https://brownelllandrum.com/

https://www.facebook.com/brownell.landrum.author

https://www.instagram.com/brownelllandrum/

https://www.tiktok.com/@brownelllandrum

https://www.bookbub.com/authors/brownell-landrum

https://www.youtube.com/@brownell.landrum

https://www.goodreads.com/brownell_landrum

https://x.com/BrownellLandrum

https://www.pinterest.com/brownelllandrum/

https://www.linkedin.com/in/brownelllandrum/

Endnotes:

The paperback version of this book doesn't have the endnotes listed. The rationale is: Why waste trees when they aren't usable links anyway? Therefore, the endnotes can be found here:

https://brownelllandrum.com/endnotes-to-the-art-science-of-wishing/

If you have any questions or concerns about the research listed, feel free to reach out to Brownell.